OUT OF THE SHADOWS

Canada in the Second World War

W.A.B. DOUGLAS
and
BRERETON GREENHOUS

Toronto Oxford New York
OXFORD UNIVERSITY PRESS
1977

Canadian Cataloguing in Publication Data

Douglas, William A.B., 1929-
    Out of the shadows

Bibliography: p.
Includes index.
ISBN 0-19-540257-X

1. World War, 1939-1945 - Canada. 2. Canada -
Armed forces. 3. World War, 1939-1945 - Campaigns.
I. Greenhous, Brereton, 1929-   II. Title.

D768.15.D69   940.53'71   C77-001503-4

The maps are by William Constable

Publication of this book was assisted by the Canada Council
Oxford University Press (Canada) 1977
ISBN 0-19-540257-X
1 2 3 4 - 10 9 8 7
Printed in Canada by The Hunter Rose Company Limited

CONTENTS

PREFACE

This book is an attempt to give a popular overview of the events that comprised Canada's part in the Second World War. We were aware when we began that no adequate account of this subject had yet appeared, but the amount of historical research that still needs to be done is even greater than we had imagined. Although there is a very full official account of the Canadian army's activities, there are no adequate operational histories of the navy and air force. And although much has been written about politics and personalities, the social and intellectual history of this period is a void waiting to be filled. We have tried to compensate for some of the larger gaps in the record of armed-forces activities by going beyond secondary sources to a selection of documents in the archives, and have consulted the whole range of published works available on other aspects of the war. Inevitably there are still areas to be explored. Not nearly enough is known about the details of Canadian sea and air operations. Public opinion and wartime propaganda demand systematic analysis. The impact of the war on industry and society is still only partly understood. Scholars are now working in these fields and when they publish their findings it will be possible to prepare a much more comprehensive synthesis.

The reader should bear in mind that any honest book about Canada at war is not going to be limited to a list of gallant deeds and glorious achievements. Many such events there were, but war places men and societies under greater strain than any other human activity, and its conduct is full of errors because it is full of improvisations. Many Canadian mistakes are recounted in this book, not because Canadians necessarily made more mistakes than others but simply because this is a book about Canadians at war. The Americans, British, French, Germans, Japanese, and Russians also made mistakes, but the recitation and study of their blunders is a matter primarily for their own historians. We have concerned ourselves with those errors only when they directly affected Canadians.

The illustrations have been selected with the intention of evoking the atmosphere of the time. The immediacy of events was best portrayed by black-and-white photographs (colour photographs were rare and of poor quality); with these we have tried to illustrate the undertones and overtones of war. The best collections were found in the Department of National Defence and the Public Archives of Canada, supplemented by those at the Imperial War Museum in England and the Vancouver Public Library. Canadian newspaper photographs for the Second World War are particularly difficult to find, which makes the Montreal *Gazette* collection at the Public Archives especially important. By far the most useful source in the Archives for activities across Canada, however, was the extensive National Film Board collection, together with photographs from a number of industrial firms and those preserved among the papers of W.L. Mackenzie King.

The more than a million Canadians in uniform during the Second World War constituted a powerful element in the country's national growth because they spread abroad the tangible evidence that Canada believed not in profiting from war but in pulling its full weight in the struggle to overthrow forces that threatened the existence of basic human values. All the men and women who took part in the events we describe gave Canada unprecedented strength, significant diplomatic influence, and high prestige in the years immediately following the war. It is to those people that our book is dedicated.

ACKNOWLEDGEMENTS

1

We have many people to thank, especially General J.A. Dextraze, CBE, CMM, DSO, CD, Chief of the Defence Staff, who encouraged us in this project at its inception. Critical comment and valuable information from our colleagues in the Directorate of History, National Defence Headquarters, is gratefully acknowledged, especially on the part of Norman Hillmer, Fred Hatch, and William McAndrew. Previous official historians, notably C.P. Stacey and G.W.L. Nicholson, have paved the way for all scholars in this field. S.F. Wise gave us moral support, which we both appreciated. J.L. Granatstein, who also was an official historian at one time, is one of the most prolific scholars now working on this period and we have frequently consulted his writings; we are further in his debt because he read the entire manuscript, making invaluable suggestions. Peter Robertson of the Public Archives of Canada gave particular help in selecting photographs. Jacquie Stevens of the Vancouver Public Library, John Chown of the Canadian War Museum, and Robert Crawford and his staff at the Imperial War Museum also provided useful assistance in this task. Richard Teleky and Martha Dzioba of Oxford University Press (Canada) gave valuable editorial help. We owe more than we can say to William Toye, the indefatigable Editorial Director, who among other things kept us, as specialists in military history, mindful of the layman's point of view while we worked on our typescript.

WABD & BG

Humphrey Carver, *Compassionate Landscape* (University of Toronto Press). Lucien Dumais, *Un Canadien français à Dieppe* (Editions France-Empire). Alan Easton, *50 North: An Atlantic Battleground* (McGraw-Hill Ryerson Limited). Martha Gellhorn, *The Face of War* (Sphere Books Ltd). ©1936, 1937, 1938, 1939, 1940, 1941, 1942, 1943, 1944, 1945, 1959, 1967 by Martha Gellhorn. By permission of Elaine Greene Ltd, Literary Agency. Richard Gentil, *Trained to Intrude* (Bachman & Turner Publishers). J.E. Johnson, *Wing Leader* (Chatto & Windus Ltd and Ballantine Books, a Division of Random House, Inc.). Alexander McKee, *Caen: Anvil of Victory* (Souvenir Press Ltd). Daphne Marlatt, *Steveston Recollected* (Aural History, Provincial Archives, Victoria, B.C.). Jerrold Morris, *Canadian Artists and Airmen 1940-45*. By permission of the author. Donald Pearce, *Journal of a War* (The Macmillan Company of Canada Limited). L.B. Pearson, *Mike: The Memoirs of the Rt. Hon. Lester B. Pearson*, Vol. I: *1897-1948* (University of Toronto Press). Charles Ritchie, *The Siren Years: A Canadian Diplomat Abroad 1937-1945* (The Macmillan Company of Canada Limited). Gabrielle Roy, *The Tin Flute* translated by Hannah Josephson (The Canadian Publishers, McClelland and Stewart Limited, Toronto). Hans Rumpf, *The Bombing of Germany* (White Lion Publishers). Warren Tute, *D-Day* (Sidgwick & Jackson Ltd). John Windsor (ed.), *Blind Date* (Gray's Publishing Ltd). John Winton (ed.), *The War at Sea 1939-1945* (A.D. Peters & Co. Ltd, London).

ILLUSTRATION CREDITS
Atomic Energy of Canada: 131. Department of National Defence: 2, 11, 12, 13, 14, 16, 17, 23, 29, 30, 31, 32, 33, 34, 35, 36, 37, 38, 39, 40, 41, 42, 43, 44, 45, 46, 47, 48, 49, 50, 52, 53, 54, 55, 56, 57, 59, 60, 61, 62, 63, 64, 65, 66, 67, 68, 69, 70, 71, 72, 73, 74, 75, 76, 77, 79, 80, 81, 82, 83, 84, 85, 86, 87, 88, 89, 91, 92, 93, 94, 95, 96, 97, 98, 100, 101, 102, 103, 104, 106, 108, 109, 110, 111, 112, 114, 115, 116, 118, 119, 120, 121, 122, 123, 124, 125, 126, 127, 128, 129, 133, 135, 146, 147, 148, 149, 150. *Herbie*, Bing Coughlin (Thomas Nelson & Sons Limited): 78. Imperial War Museum: 90, 99. Metropolitan Toronto Library Board: 24, 28, 58, 140, 141, 142, 144. *Normandy and On* by Lieut. Les Callan (Longmans, Green and Co.): 113, 117. The Public Archives of Canada (National Photography Collection): 1, 4, 5, 6, 18, 19, 20, 21, 22, 25, 26, 27, 51, 130, 132, 136, 137, 138, 139, 151. The Public Archives of Canada (Montreal *Gazette*): 7, 9, 10, 134, 145. The Public Archives of Canada (Historical Photo): 15. Copyright©*Toronto Sun*: 143. Ullstein Bilderdienst, Berlin: 105, 107. Vancouver Public Library: 3, 8.

1 Young Canadians
awaiting the appearance
of the King and Queen,
June 1939.

1

'CANADA WILL RESPOND'
The Nation on the Eve of War

Under a clear blue sky the Canadian Pacific liner *Empress of Australia* sailed beneath the ramparts of the Citadel of Quebec on Wednesday morning, May 17, 1939, watched by thousands of people in a holiday mood. George VI and Queen Elizabeth had come to Canada, and the excitement surrounding the Royal Visit had reached a high pitch. It was the first visit to Canada by a reigning sovereign and the first time a British monarch had left Europe. Union jacks and tricolours flew from the buildings in Quebec's Lower Town; girl guides, boy scouts, and Papal Zouaves lined the streets; and twenty-five thousand children gathered on the Plains of Abraham waiting to sing 'God Save the King' in French.

W.L. Mackenzie King, Liberal Prime Minister of Canada, waited with the official party at Wolfe's Cove. The Royal Tour was something of a *coup* for him, planned while he visited London for the Coronation and the Imperial Conference in 1937. Besides certain political advantages (it would prove that loyalty to the Crown in Canada was not confined to the Tories), there were good diplomatic reasons for the visit. After the virtual collapse of the League of Nations, Europe seemed to be drifting to war and it was desirable to strengthen the emotional ties of Canadians to Britain and the Commonwealth in an unstable world. At the Imperial Conference of 1937 King successfully campaigned against those who would entangle him in an imperial foreign and defence policy; he gave his support, however, to a policy of economic and political appeasement to prevent conflict. His personal response to the threats to world peace that Hitler portended was a somewhat quixotic one: he resolved to try to bring Britain and Germany together himself. After the conference was over he visited the German dictator, with whom King felt he shared a sympathetic concern for the workingman, and endeavoured to explain the peaceful intent of the British Empire. As he told a later High Commissioner to Canada, Malcolm MacDonald, he warned Hitler 'that if Germany should ever turn her mind from constructive to destructive efforts against the United Kingdom all the Dominions would come to her aid and that there would be great numbers of Canadians anxious to swim the Atlantic!'[1] He came out of his interview, as so many had done before him, just as blissfully unaware of the real Hitler as when

2 Adolf Hitler: 'To His Excellency the Canadian Prime Minister Dr W.L. Mackenzie King as a friendly reminder of his visit on 29 June 1937.'

he went in. On his return, King told a Canadian radio audience that the Führer's charm had persuaded him of his host's 'great sincerity'.

The European situation worsened. In 1938—'Hitler's Year', in the words of one historian—came the Nazi takeover of Austria and Hitler's demand to incorporate the Sudeten Germans of Czechoslovakia into the Third Reich. At Munich in September he persuaded Prime Minister Chamberlain of England and Premier Daladier of France to accept his promise that he would ask for no more and was allowed to occupy Sudetenland. But in March 1939 he invaded the rest of Czechoslovakia.

Although King still hoped for appeasement, he came to believe that war was inevitable and envisaged 'bombers raining death on London'. The British Cabinet nearly advised George VI to cancel his Canadian visit. The monarch was in a difficult position. He wanted to be in Great Britain if war broke out, yet he believed his presence in Canada would strengthen its ties to the mother country at a crucial moment in history. In addition to this, he was most anxious to strengthen Anglo-American relations by means of personal diplomacy in the United States, a desire that President Roosevelt shared.

The enthusiastic and harmonious reception that greeted George VI in Quebec City belied a complex set of feelings in Canada. As a member of the British Empire—or the British Commonwealth of Nations, as it was later called—the country had taken part in the Great War (1914-18), sharing the common belief that future world peace depended upon the defeat of Britain's enemies. Canada was deeply affected by that war. Its slaughter had been so great that 'never again' became a frequent isolationist cry in the twenties and thirties. Readily identifiable segments of the population rejected the idea of becoming involved in any more European quarrels. Even when Hitler seized power in Germany in 1933, and peace again became a fragile thing, their isolationism prevailed. However, the Great War had reinforced a sentimental attachment to the imperial connection in a politically significant cross-section of the country whose views were made known in the press and, early in 1939, through political activists led by C.G. McCullagh, publisher of the Toronto *Globe and Mail* and organizer of the short-lived but nationally influential Leadership League. The European crisis that developed with Hitler's ascendancy brought out their deep-seated conviction that Britain must be supported in a war. The well-known editor of the *Winnipeg Free Press*, John W. Dafoe, had written in 1937 that in the case of a crisis 'the people of Canada will begin to get on one side or another of a line which will run through every province, every township and through a good many homes as well.'[2]

It was not simply the European crisis that created divisions in Canada. The economic depression that Canada and the United States had suffered for nearly ten years brought about hardships and privations that produced strong feelings of resentment towards government—federal, provincial, and municipal. These in turn spawned active political discontent—especially on the Prairies, which had undergone unusually severe droughts and dust storms. Their disastrous economic situation reinforced a chronic suspicion of Ottawa's policies and a complete distrust of eastern-Canadian interests. The thirties were a time of new political parties. The Co-operative Commonwealth Federation (CCF), a democratic socialist party, was formed by farm and labour groups in Calgary in 1932, and the Social Credit party took power in Alberta in 1935 under Premier William Aberhart, who preached an 'easy money' doctrine that would bring production and consumption into balance to overcome the paradox of plentiful goods and scarce money. Like some other provincial premiers, Aberhart also opposed the assumption of powers by the federal government. Widespread unemployment was epitomized by

3 Depression malaise: RCMP and Vancouver police clear out the post office after the sit-down strike by Relief Camp workers in June 1938.

the On-to-Ottawa Trek in June 1935, when 1,000 unemployed men headed east from Vancouver to protest their situation. When they entered Regina a week later, their numbers had increased to 2,000. The trek ended in abortive meetings and a riot, with no solution to the workers' problems. Strikes continued across Canada. A peaceful sit-down strike by Relief Camp workers in the Vancouver Post Office and other public buildings was broken up by the Royal Canadian Mounted Police on Bloody Sunday (June 19, 1938) and thirty-five people were injured. The Liberal premier of British Columbia, T. Dufferin Pattullo, responded to the protest by deporting unemployed non-residents of British Columbia back to their homes on the Prairies.

The difficulties in Canada worried the British, and Sir Maurice Hankey, the British secretary of the Committee of Imperial Defence, was asked in 1934 to assess the attitudes of Canada towards imperial defence, especially in case of a European war. Finding that the Depression had intensified an isolationist spirit in Canada, he observed that French Canadians were 'bitterly hostile to cooperation in Imperial Defence', along with 'great blocks of unabsorbed aliens' (Ukrainians, Russians, Poles, etc.), and that 'a number of people on the prairies and the west of British or American origin, who have fallen on hard times are in a bitter, resentful frame of mind.'

> To these adverse forces, which count for much in an election year must be added the 'highbrows' who meet in places like the Institute of International Affairs, and judged by what I heard, and read of their proceedings, talk a lot of dreadful 'slop'. The kind of idea they ventilate is that Canadian territory is secured by the Monro [sic] doctrine; that Canada ought to remain neutral in an Empire war; that Japan and Germany are so well aware of this sentiment, that they would be careful to avoid any action against Canada; but that it would be preferable to put up with insult and aggression, the sinking of Canadian ships and cargoes, and the loss of most of her overseas trade, rather than to fight![3]

In his report to the Committee, Hankey made the point that Britain would be drawn into a European war only through extreme provocation. Under those circumstances, he felt, Canadians would come to Britain's aid. He believed, correctly, that pressures from British leaders in 'the old country' were not sufficient to win Canadian support. It was essential for Canadian leaders to educate the public about British motives. There was none of the fervid imperialism he had found in Australia and New Zealand. Hankey did perceive, however, that in the event of Britain's becoming involved in a war against Germany, 'Canada would respond', as it had done in 1914. (With this statement he echoed the words of Mackenzie King at the time of the Imperial Conference of 1923 when, in a similar context, the Prime Minister avowed: 'Canada will respond.'[4]) Nevertheless, Hankey found in the Canada of 1934, and especially in Ottawa—which had gained autonomy over the nation's foreign policy with the Statute of Westminster of 1931—a 'calculating aloofness' that made assumptions about Canadian attitudes difficult.[5]

Yet assumptions became necessary. Remembering that Canada had made a significant industrial contribution to the First World War, the British Cabinet asked in 1935 for information on the potential of Canadian industry for the production of munitions. Responding to this initiative, the Canadian Army, Navy, and Air Supply Committee embarked on a continuing survey of industrial firms. By the end of 1938 reports on 1,227 enterprises indicated that Ontario was the largest single source, with 673; Quebec followed with 219. Both provinces exported large quantities of natural resources to the United States, particularly hydro-electric power and non-ferrous materials. Their potential contribution to the war effort was followed by that of British Columbia, which had managed to preserve a strong industrial base in spite of the Depression. The industrial contribution of the Maritimes would be insignificant. By their geographic position they were deprived of much of the trade going to central Canada, which moved through Montreal rather than through Atlantic ports. As a result, the hinterlands of Halifax and Saint John had not developed widespread industry.

Limited Canadian rearmament began in 1935—the year Mackenzie King became prime minister for the third time—but it did not reflect a sudden change of heart. Rather it represented the concern of the Cabinet, which had been warned by the Canadian service chiefs of unprepared armed forces, and it was pushed by a vocal and influential section of the populace that considered any dereliction in Canada's contribution to imperial defence tantamount to pulling out of the Commonwealth. Rationalizing his decision to rearm, Mackenzie King observed: 'Meighen [the Conservative ex-Prime Minister] would do so much more—at least so he says—and Woodsworth [leader of the CCF] would do nothing at all. The safe policy is the middle course between these two views—the safe policy is a rational policy of domestic defence.'[6] King was an experienced politician who had been at the forefront of Canadian politics for more than fifteen years by 1937, and he was probably right.

But in the spring of 1939, thoughts of war were far from the minds of those who thronged to see the King and Queen. Enthusiasm for the imperial connection seemed to be everywhere, even in Quebec City.

The old French-Canadian capital had been a critical choice for the start of the tour. The conscription crisis of 1917, which had polarized the conflicting attitudes of French and English Canadians towards overseas wars, had had a divisive effect on the nation. Quebec isolationists and nationalists, such as Henri Bourassa, had attacked British policies, arguing that Britain was an imperialist power engaged in a war for territory. Similar arguments reappeared in the thirties and could be expected to arouse strong feelings against participation once more. Yet the King and Queen arrived in Quebec to find a scene of apparent harmony and content. Loyal sentiments in the province had been stirred up by politicians, veterans' organizations, and church leaders. There were other ingredients of loyalty in the province that were of particular significance in the shadow of war. They were well represented by the Royal 22e Régiment du Canada (the Van Doos), whose colonel-in-chief was the King himself. The 22nd (French-Canadian) battalion of the Canadian Expeditionary Force—whose battle honours the Van Doos preserved—had been one of the most effective units in the Canadian Corps during the First World War, accumulating no less than 2 Victoria Crosses, 6 Distinguished Service Orders, and 10 Distinguished Service Medals, as well as many casualties. The proud military tradition with which the Van Doos were associated contributed to the festive and loyal mood.

Ernest Lapointe, Mackenzie King's Quebec lieutenant and the Minister of Justice, was an extremely powerful figure in Quebec and one Québécois who knew that Canada would have to participate in a major British war. Thus he was anxious to secure an enthusiastic reception for the King and Queen in French Canada. On his advice, presumably, Senator Raoul Dandurand was selected to greet the

4 The King and Queen sign the visitors' book at the Montreal City Hall, with Mayor Camillien Houde in attendance and Prime Minister Mackenzie King seated in the background. May 18, 1939.

royal couple, a choice that seemed to acknowledge the existence of isolationist feelings in the province, for it was Dandurand who had coined the famous isolationist phrase, 'We live in a fireproof house far from inflammable materials', in a speech to the League of Nations in Geneva in 1924. Dandurand still opposed commitments to imperial and European defence and he was inclined to blame Britain, the United States, Italy, and Germany, all more or less equally, for the threatening demise of the League and the impending approach of war. Above all, he was a patriot, a 'Canadien tout court', and in many ways he represented the outlook of French Canada. His demonstrated attachment to the Crown must have carried much weight in the province. When George VI responded to Dandurand's welcome in French, the onlookers were delighted; Queen Elizabeth's easy use of the language also made a favourable impression.

As the tour proceeded through Quebec, the King and Queen scored more political points. Mayor Camillien Houde of Montreal was allowed the place of honour in the royal procession through the city, taking precedence over the Prime Minister and all other dignitaries. When one hundred thousand people massed outside the Windsor Hotel in Montreal on May 18 to see the royal couple, Houde revelled in the reflected glory. A wily politician, he was happy to demonstrate friendship with such a popular monarch.

By the time the King and Queen reached Ontario—they arrived in Ottawa on May 19—they had caught the imagination of hundreds of thousands of Canadians. Wherever crowds gathered, allegiance to the monarchy was underscored by the presence of war veterans. Ten thousand gathered at the unveiling of the War Memorial in Ottawa and the King and Queen walked among them. Wherever they went, political leaders hastened to go too. Mackenzie King became the royal couple's constant shadow, eager to implant the idea that he was closely associated with the British Crown, and in the presence of the sovereign the inherent political disunity of the country tended to be forgotten.

Toronto, the provincial capital, was a traditional cradle of loyalism. Yet even there, isolationist sentiment was strong. Frank Underhill, the distinguished historian, was perhaps most outspoken about this feeling. He had written in the *Canadian Forum*: 'All these European troubles are not worth the bones of a Toronto grenadier.' His views, of course, were by no means universal in the Queen City. As Bruce Hutchison observed of Toronto in *The Unknown Country* (1942), it was there that 'the Colonial Mind, that vestigial organ which no longer functions but often can ache, still manages to exist without nourishment.' By the time the royal couple left on May 23, there was no question of the city's overwhelming loyalty.

When the King and Queen proceeded westward to the prairie provinces, the Royal Visit faced a major test. Here were to be found 'the great blocks of unabsorbed aliens' reported by Hankey in 1934, and here was the worst depression-induced poverty in the land. Here also were political leaders who showed ambivalent feelings towards the British connection. William Aberhart, for instance—later the opponent of the strong Anglo-American ties in the Atlantic Charter—would also proclaim in his popular daily religious broadcasts that the British Commonwealth and the United States were

'God's battle axe'. George VI seemed to confirm this belief in the Commonwealth as a force for good while speaking in Winnipeg on May 24: 'Hold fast to all that is just and of good report in the heritage which your fathers have left you . . . . ' The message would have fallen on deaf ears if Hankey's assessment of 1934 had been entirely correct. Yet again and again the King and Queen found the same welcome from war veterans and the same enthusiasm they had encountered in the two central provinces. Although Manitoba, Saskatchewan, and Alberta were unable to match Ontario and Quebec in population or industry, their reception of the monarch was no less fervent.

The response of British Columbia to the Royal Visit did not quite follow the pattern of the other provinces. According to Margaret Ormsby, the historian of British Columbia, cheers for the royal couple 'were less spontaneous' than those for the Prince of Wales (later Duke of Windsor) in the twenties. When the King and Queen appeared, accompanied both by the Prime Minister and the Premier of British Columbia, T.D. Pattullo, the crowds must have found it difficult to put out of their minds their smouldering resentment towards the Premier for his handling of the Vancouver Post Office riots a year before. They were not only still bitter about Pattullo's harsh treatment of unemployed Canadians, but compared it unfavourably with his disregard of so-called 'subversive elements' and 'fifth-columnists' in the province—spectres in the public imagination that had been created by war scares in both Asia and Europe. The substance of loyalty was undoubtedly there—the response to the Great War by British Columbians, many of whom were English-born, had been exemplary—but the appearance was somewhat muted.

After making a return journey across Canada, which brought a succession of enthusiastic demonstrations, the King and Queen visited the United States from June 7 to 10. They visited Washington and attended the World's Fair in New York—the city's mayor, Fiorello La Guardia, claimed that their visit 'did more good than the sending of a dozen ambassadors or the interchange of fifty diplomatic notes'—on their way to the Roosevelt home at Hyde Park, N.Y., where Eleanor Roosevelt gave her famous hot-dogs-and-beer picnic. The royal couple re-entered Canada from Vermont. Again they encountered an extraordinary French-Canadian enthusiasm.

They continued east to the Maritimes. Although New Brunswick, Prince Edward Island, and Nova Scotia had Liberal governments, their ties with Ottawa were weak. Anti-confederation feeling inherited from a past generation still ran strong, while suspicion of 'Upper Canada' was greater there than in any other region of the Dominion. But in the Maritimes generally, and particularly in Nova Scotia, there had always been a strong Empire sentiment. There could be no doubt of the affection for Britain, nor of the military tradition established by men from the Maritimes in the First World War. This spirit was reinforced by the military and naval presence in the old garrison town of Halifax, the port from which the King and Queen sailed on June 16 and the port from which, three months later to the day, the first wartime convoy would sail for England.

Not even the Prime Minister had expected the Royal Visit to be so successful. In his diary King paraphrased his farewell words to Their Majesties:

> I hoped they would go away feeling that they had helped to unite Canada and different parts of the Empire and to consolidate a continent in friendly feelings. That I honestly believed that they had done a service to the world at a time of the world's greatest need, and in a manner which only they could possibly have performed that service. The Queen said how extremely kind of you to say that. The King also said something similar.[7]

One provincial premier had told the King's private secretary: 'You can go home and tell the old country that any talk they may hear about Canada being isolationist after today is just nonsense.'[8] That was exaggerated, but isolationist feeling had indeed been dulled. Other causes of disagreement and even discontent remained, however. Canada still lacked cohesion. Provincial governments still contended against federal authority. There was still massive unemployment. The youth of the land resented their lack of opportunity. The government, in its response to the Depression, had shown extreme caution—'standpatism' had substituted for social reform. But it is probably true to say that the Royal Visit diverted attention from these problems and did so at an opportune moment.

When Hitler marched into Poland on September 1, 1939, and Europe prepared for war, Canada responded—but without the wave of enthusiasm that had characterized 1914. Instead the Cabinet laid its contingency plans rather timidly, preparing not for a total war but for a war of limited liability—one in which Canada's stake was not that of a principal power. The Prime Minister recognized that there had been some change in national sentiment as a result of the Tour, but he—and, he believed, the country—had no desire to plunge heavily into military commitments. Georges Héon, a Tory MP from Quebec, urged 'co-operation but was against the sending of an expeditionary force and against conscription', an attitude that vast numbers of French Canadians shared. O.D. Skelton, the Under-Secretary of State for External Affairs and King's most trusted adviser, counselled his chief to concentrate on air rather than land commitments so that military activity overseas and manpower problems at home would be kept to the minimum. And more important than any military effort, Skelton stressed, was the provision of munitions, raw materials, and foodstuffs. That would help Britain and help beat the Depression too.

6   The departure of the King and Queen from Halifax in the *Empress of Canada*, June 17, 1939. The sea and air escorts represented virtually all Canada's naval and air forces on the Atlantic coast.

At the end of August, shortly after Hitler had stunned the world by successfully concluding a pact with the Soviet Union, the Cabinet by Order in Council declared a state of apprehended war, thus enabling the armed forces to go onto a war footing. On September 3, Britain and France declared war. But Canada did not immediately follow suit. Mackenzie King had always maintained that 'Parliament will decide', and he meant what he had said. An emergency session was summoned to meet on September 7, and while the MPs began to converge on Ottawa, the government maintained its posture of apparent non-involvement.

In the quarter century since 1914, when Canada had gone to war without any say of its own people, the Statute of Westminster had given Canada autonomy, if not independence, in foreign policy. Now the Canadian people, through their elected representatives in Ottawa, would decide whether or not to go to war.

2

AN UNMILITARY PEOPLE

German tanks crossed the Polish border on the first day of September and Luftwaffe *Stukas* began their relentless dive-bombing attacks that became identified with the blitzkrieg, terrorizing all of Europe. Britain, honouring defence agreements with Poland, declared war on Germany two days later. France immediately followed suit. Though Canada preserved the appearance of neutrality by waiting for the authority of Parliament to declare war, the Cabinet went ahead with creating the machinery for wartime government. On August 30 the Emergency Council—consisting of the Prime Minister, the Ministers of Defence, Fisheries, Finance, Mines and Resources, and the Senate Government Leader—had come into being. It set in motion the mobilization of the armed forces on September 1.

On that day Mackenzie King also cabled Neville Chamberlain for advice about Britain's expectations of Canada. Anthony Eden, the newly appointed Dominions Secretary, responded on September 6. 'It is hoped that Canada would exert her full national effort as in the last war,' he wrote, 'even to the extent of the eventual dispatch of an expeditionary force.' The British Admiralty wanted operational control of Royal Canadian Navy ships; recruits were needed for the Royal Naval Reserve and the Volunteer Reserve; and the Air Ministry asked the Royal Canadian Air Force to recruit for the Royal Air Force, promising a 'Royal Canadian Air Force Contingent' when sufficient men had been found. The mother country looked to the Canadian army for support as well, although the British government realized that 'no statement of policy on these lines is likely to be possible for the moment.'[1]

King was still opposed to embarking on military adventures abroad and was surprised to discover that his chiefs of staff were thinking in terms of sending the army overseas. There was now a sound strategic basis for dispatching a British Expeditionary Force to the continent, something that had not seemed likely only a year before. To exclude a Canadian component from such a force was unthinkable to military planners and the pro-British segments of the population. But King, who was not well versed in the strategic and tactical implications of war, did not believe that this was the real reason for the proposal to send troops overseas. He looked upon it as a deliberate conspiracy to undermine his determination to restrict demands on manpower and to avoid conscription. By the time the

7 The British declaration of war attracted far more attention than the Canadian declaration a week later. This photograph from the Montreal *Gazette* was taken on September 3, 1939. The *Gazette* has preserved no such photograph for September 10.

Cabinet met on September 6 the war situation in Poland seemed grim, yet King was surprised to find that some of his ministers were showing more support for an expeditionary force than he had imagined they would. He was even more taken aback when he detected pro-conscription sympathies among some members. He sided with Ernest Lapointe and opposed conscription for overseas service, though he did not rule out the possibility of calling up men to defend Canada.

Parliament met in an emergency session on September 7. Though J.S. Woodsworth, the CCF leader, opposed the decision to go to war on pacifist grounds, and Liguori Lacombe, a Quebec Liberal member, opposed it in isolationist terms, there were few other voices of protest. The Conservative opposition not only supported the Liberal government but in March had adopted an identical attitude towards conscription. Not all Conservatives agreed, but Dr R.J. Manion, the party's leader, committed himself to the position that Canadian youth should not be conscripted to fight outside Canada's borders.

There is ample evidence to show that this emergency session in fact reflected a lukewarm response of the nation. Canadians generally supported the government with various reservations. Major-General W.A. Griesbach, a Conservative senator and veteran of two wars, represented the opinion of thousands with similar backgrounds who believed the country should participate but were worried that the youth of the nation—discontented as they were with their lot—would not react favourably. O.D. Skelton, like others of his essentially nationalistic and liberal persuasion, accepted the war partly as a blow dealt by fate, partly as a result of British bungling. In French Canada only André Laurendeau's *Le Devoir* showed any overt opposition to King's policy; the other newspapers in the province gave it their cautious support. Throughout the country the strong pacifist beliefs of many clergy held sway, but these were countered by a differing view of 'the church militant' held by many others. Perhaps the decisive factor was a realization that staying neutral would create unacceptable anomalies in relations with Britain and the rest of the Commonwealth.[2] Neutrality might tend to destroy the indivisibility of the British Crown with the Dominion of Canada—a principle successfully brought home by the Royal Visit only a few months before.[3]

Even overt opposition to Canada's participation in the war seemed to be half-hearted. As Bourassa's disciple, André Laurendeau, admitted later, 'I was a militant anti-participationist, but there was little evidence that I was followed by the majority of my compatriots.'[4] On the face of the evidence it is possible to argue, and indeed it has been argued, that most Canadians believed this was to be a war of 'limited liability' in which the principal contribution would be economic rather than military.

So on September 9 the Canadian Parliament approved the policy

8   The Militia in June 1937. Reflecting a grandiose paper organization of 11 divisions and 4 cavalry divisions, this small unit on church parade in Vancouver was called the 11th Divisional Signals.

of declaring war against Germany. The following day Canada cabled the text of a declaration of war to Vincent Massey, the Canadian High Commissioner, who would relay it to George VI for signature. It was a momentous occasion—the first time Canada had declared war on its own behalf—and proper form had to be observed. Lester Pearson, who was a member of Canada's diplomatic corps in London, later wrote in his memoirs:

> We had no experience in declaring war ... [I] wrote out the proper words on a plain sheet of paper. Then I telephoned my friend, Tommy Lascelles, at the palace, to ask whether I could show him the draft document for approval or amendment. He told me to come along, and in a few minutes I was in his office. ... since the king was in the office next door, he would 'pop in' and get royal confirmation. He returned in a few minutes to say that His Majesty had not only approved the text but had indicated this by signing it. This was satisfactory, but somewhat startling as it was only a draft for consideration....The written, formal submission which was to follow the cabled one did not arrive for some weeks. This was indeed reprehensible delay because the earlier informal document, a cabled message, obviously could not have on it the Prime Minister's written signature. A legal purist could claim, indeed, that without such a written signature the submission had no legal effect and that Canada was not, technically, at war until the formal submission signed in his own handwriting by the Prime Minister was received and approved by His Majesty. Therefore, on 24 October Mr. Massey had to telegraph Ottawa: 'Buckingham Palace enquiring when they may expect formal submission in writing.'[5]

A formal submission—signed by Mackenzie King and ante-dated September 10—finally reached the King for signature on November 27, eleven weeks after Canada had declared war.

The Prime Minister took much satisfaction in the way he brought the country into the conflict, 'with a quietude and peace almost comparable to that of a vessel sailing over a smooth and sunlit lake; ... we had kept down all passion and faction, and now were a united country.'[6]

Political consensus for a declaration of war was one thing; the military and industrial capability to back it up was another. Much effort was necessary before Canada would be able to make more than a token contribution. It would be an understatement to say that the country was not prepared for the scale of conflict about to be experienced. The pre-war army—the service most noticeably affected by mobilization—was based on a permanent force of only 4,000 men, buttressed by a militia that included 51,418 partly trained men at the beginning of 1939. According to the war plans of 'Defence Scheme Number Three', first drafted in 1930 with amendments as late as July 10, 1939, the army would form a Mobile Force for the direct defence of Canada. Some 10,000 men had been called out as a preparatory

9 The somewhat remote aspect of the war in this Montreal *Gazette* photograph of September 12, 1939, is reflected by the 18-pounder gun, a relic of the Great War; by the uniforms of similar vintage; and by the self-conscious pose of the recruiters.

measure on August 25, two days after the Russo-German non-aggression pact was signed. A flood of men arrived when mobilization began on September 1—so many that the chiefs of staff received orders by September 5 not to stimulate recruiting, 'as it is probable that more men are now available than can be conveniently handled'.

The militia had been so badly neglected that mobilization often took on the appearance of comic opera. As an example of peacetime penury, in June 1939 forty pairs of boots were issued (for the first time) to every hundred men of the Loyal Edmonton Regiment. Not until October 23 did 500 recruits who had joined in early September receive their rifles. The Royal Regiment had to delay medical examinations for lack of medical forms and the men, wearing armbands instead of uniforms, lived in the International Pavilion of the Canadian National Exhibition in Toronto with no heat, no cleaning utensils, and inadequate toilet and washing facilities. The West Nova Scotia Regiment in Bridgewater moved into the main building of the Lunenburg County Exhibition, using the cattle and poultry sheds for cook houses and mess halls. Thomas Raddall wrote in the regimental history: 'It was common to see a burly lumberjack wearing a flat-topped army hat, a mackinaw shirt, a khaki web belt, a pair of bulls-wool trousers (cut off at the calf, woods fashion and showing a length of gray woollen stocking) and shod in anything from a pair of battered shoe-packs to a pair of patent leather shoes lately purchased in a local shop.'[7] This sort of thing was repeated across the country, forcing soldiers to improvise in all kinds of situations.

Most problems had their origin in pre-war budget cuts. In December 1938 the government had slashed $8 million from a $28-million budget proposed for the army in order to meet expenses for air force and naval expansion. Partly because of this, many Canadian soldiers carried Ross rifles the following year—the same rifles that had been the subject of a public scandal when they proved totally unsuitable on the Western Front in 1916. There were equally severe shortages of armour (only 16 light tanks) and rapid-fire small arms (23 Bren guns and the obsolete Lewis gun, veteran of the 1914-18 war). The army had only 23 anti-tank rifles, 4 two-pounder anti-tank guns, and 4 modern anti-aircraft guns, making defence against armour and aircraft virtually non-existent. The militia was not fit to go to war—nor would it be for many months.

On the other hand, the permanent force had a well-trained nucleus to build upon. Between the wars the professional army preserved a distinctive military tradition. Though inter-war apathy towards the armed forces did not further efficiency, the Canadian professional soldiers of 1939—who included many with experience of combat in the Great War—had learned their business on exchange with the British army and with permanent militia units between the wars. Since 1918, for example, the Princess Patricia's Canadian Light Infantry had devoted most of its energies to the training of the Non-Permanent Active Militia. (As the regimental historian observes, 'Canadian governments are partial to cumbersome euphemisms to describe their military forces.') The greatest problems lay in restricted regimental strength and lack of equipment—this made it difficult to experiment and to develop military thought, so important to a peacetime army. There was another detriment in peace: restrictions on military advancement. Captain J.N. Edgar, who had commanded A Company, PPCLI, with great distinction in the Battle of Tilloy in 1918, was still in command of the same company seventeen years later.

The greater number of general and senior officers were products of the Royal Military College of Canada, which combined the educational objectives of West Point Military Academy in the United States with military doctrines of the British army. Graduates had proven their worth in the First World War, and they provided the core of general officers in the Second. Major-General T.V. Anderson, Chief of the General Staff, was a fair representative of this small élite. A graduate of RMC in 1900 who joined the permanent military in 1905, he had a distinguished career in the army, losing an arm in the First World War and receiving the DSO. Major-General A.G.L. McNaughton ('Andy' to the troops he would command overseas) was another representative of the army tradition. One of the few regular officers who was not a graduate of RMC, he had been a brilliant artillery and staff officer with the Canadian Corps in the First World War, had risen to be chief of the General Staff in 1929, and then had gone to the National Research Council, of which he became president in 1935. McNaughton's scientific accomplishments (he was joint inventor of the cathode-ray direction finder in 1926) extended his horizons far beyond his military career, but when war came he was

10 September 17, 1939: the Black Watch (Royal Highland Regiment) of Canada on its first wartime church parade. The men are more or less in step, with quite respectable bearing, but are wearing a curious miscellany of clothing.

considered by Mackenzie King the best choice to command Canadian troops in the field.

Canadian public opinion seemed to focus on the army where matters relating to the armed forces were concerned. The record of the Canadian Corps in the First World War was well known, and it is a fact that much less was known about the other two services. So the public, when thinking of a Canadian contribution to the war, probably thought more in terms of ground troops than of ships or aircraft. Cabinet decisions in September 1939 certainly seemed to recognize such a feeling, especially in the acceptance of General Anderson's statement on September 28 that army programs must not be cut back, even to satisfy the needs of the air force expansion that then appeared to be in the wind.

Anderson and the professionals on his staff had little difficulty convincing the government that an expeditionary force should be dispatched overseas. Asked to make recommendations on the best response to Eden's cable of September 6, they advised sending the

Mobile Force overseas. Anderson suggested that Canada should offer to send and maintain one division—about 23,000 men, including support personnel—as well as some technical units the British government had requested. He thought the country should aim at having nothing less than a corps of two or more divisions in the field. On September 19 the government announced its decision to dispatch one division 'to be available as an expeditionary force, if and when desired'. British reaction was prompt. 'The reputation Canadians earned in the last war has not been forgotten,' reported Colonel G.P. Loggie, the Canadian officer who, together with Lieutenant-Colonel E.L.M. Burns, had discussed the offer with the Imperial General Staff. 'Except for regulars and one or two territorial divisions, there are no troops whom the C. in C. would rather have with him.'[8] So the die was cast, and on October 17 McNaughton assumed command of the first Canadian Division.

The army had a tradition based on the oustanding performance of the Canadian Expeditionary Force in the First World War. But the navy had no such tradition. There is some truth in the popular view that in 1939 the Royal Canadian Navy, which barely survived as an independent service between 1924 and 1925, was little more than a small offshoot of the Royal Navy. Pre-war personnel derived not only their ships and weapons but also their British customs and professional standards from the RN. It would be wrong, however, to judge the RCN on its derivative characteristics. Although the oceans exert an impersonal sway over men who follow a life at sea and national idiosyncracies fade in the face of such relentless impartiality, nationality remains a powerful factor in motivating all armed forces. In 1939 the tightly knit ships' companies of the RCN were highly competitive groups determined to show that they were as good as Britain's best. A strong rivalry had grown up between east- and west-coast ships and British vessels of the North America and West Indies squadrons.

Though the RCN had been formed by authority of the Naval Service Act of 1910, it was not until 1934 that one of its own, Percy Nelles, became the third director of the Naval Service. (His predecessors, Rear-Admiral C.E. Kingsmill and Commodore Walter Hose, came to Canada from the Royal Navy.) The officers serving in 1939 had a variety of backgrounds. Between the wars some regular officers had gone to RMC for two years and then completed their training in the Royal Navy or the British Merchant Marine. Nelles began his training in the Canadian government ship *Canada* in 1908, even before the passing of the Naval Service Act. During the First World War he served on Royal Navy cruisers and afterwards became flag lieutenant to Rear-Admiral Kingsmill. Between the wars Nelles served mostly on British ships, but in 1931 he became first commander of HMCS *Saguenay*. Following a period with the Imperial Defence College, he was promoted to captain; shortly after he was

11 The navy goes to war. HMCS *Fraser* in the Panama Canal en route to Halifax from Esquimalt, September 1939. She would be the first ship lost by the RCN, June 25, 1940, when she was cut in half by the cruiser HMS *Calcutta* off the coast of France.

made commodore and was later appointed the first chief of the Naval Staff. He was promoted to rear-admiral in 1938. The pattern of his career was similar to that of other regular officers. All of them spent much too little time on Canadian ships, but there was not much that could be done about this because of the small size of the fleet.

In 1939 decisions concerning the navy did not have the political implications that manpower problems created for the army. With only six destroyers, Canada could not form an independent naval force, and there probably would not be a need for heavy reinforcements. There was no intention of satisfying the British Admiralty's request to recruit Canadians for the Royal Navy, and the only question at issue was whether Admiralty control of Canadian ships would be acceptable. The answer, predictably enough, was that the Cabinet would hear of no such thing. Eventually a compromise permitted Canadian ships to co-operate with the British naval forces 'to the fullest extent'. By this it was meant that British and Canadian naval forces would act as one and that the senior officer present from either service would take command of sea operations. It also meant that ultimate control of Canadian ships was exercised by Naval Service Headquarters in Ottawa. For the moment the chief concern was to expand the naval forces sufficiently to meet the requirements of controlling and defending seaborne trade in Canadian waters.

In March 1939 the combined strength of the permanent and reserve naval forces included 3,276 personnel. Not all of these men were immediately available—by the end of September less than 3,000 had been mobilized. Yet the moment the RCN was placed on active service, wartime sea duties began on HMCS *Saguenay* and

Skeena—the first warships to be built expressly for Canada—and on two minesweepers from their base at Halifax. *Fraser* and *St. Laurent* 'C'-class destroyers acquired from the Royal Navy in 1937, sailed for the east coast from Vancouver on August 31; they arrived at Halifax five days after Canada declared war. Their sister ships, *Ottawa* and *Restigouche*, remained on the west coast with three minesweepers based at Esquimalt.

On August 21 the Admiralty assumed control of British merchant shipping, and officers, both British and Canadian, earmarked as Naval Control Service Officers (NCSOs), received notice to take up their posts. Some were volunteer reserve personnel, some retired naval officers. On August 26 the Canadian government authorized the RCN to take control of Canadian registered ships and other merchant ships in Canadian waters, and by September 10 the Canadian NCSOs at Halifax, Sydney, Saint John, and Montreal were in full operation. They reported to the North American intelligence centre for the Admiralty, which was established in Ottawa.

Some warships lacked Asdic, the submarine detection device now known as sonar, and it had to be fitted as soon as the vessels arrived

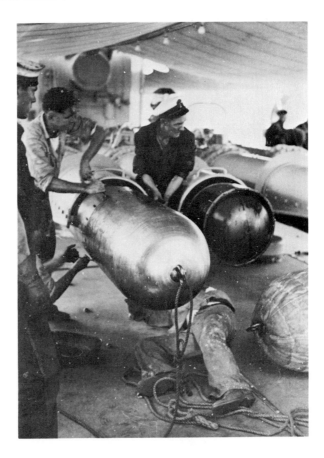

12 Mobilization. Fitting torpedo warheads in HMCS *Ottawa*, September 1, 1939—the first step in preparing for war.

from the west coast. Furthermore, boom defences—the system of nets and controlled entrances or 'gates' that were necessary to keep enemy submarines out of Halifax and Esquimalt harbours—were not ready. Until they could be made available, these ports (especially Halifax) would not have the security expected of a naval base in time of war. With some improvisation and ingenuity a system of port defence for Halifax was devised in the last days of peace: the construction and salvage firm, Foundation Maritime, received a contract on September 6 to lay an anti-submarine net, and two old minesweepers were named as gate vessels. By the end of the month preparations for constructing the defences were in full swing, but some material was still only on order. Esquimalt, on the west coast, was rather more advanced than Halifax.

The war brought an influx of reserve naval personnel from a wide cross-section of the community. The reserves were now about to become a major influence on the RCN. The Royal Canadian Naval Volunteer Reserve brought in large numbers of men with little maritime experience—some had never even seen the ocean; amateur sailors and retired naval personnel were also found in the organization. The Royal Canadian Naval Reserve was formed from the Merchant Service, which brought valuable professional experience into the wartime navy. Finally, there was a Fishermen's Reserve on the west coast that manned ten patrol vessels by the end of September 1939.

The Royal Canadian Air Force was the smallest of the three services in 1939. Founded in 1924, it functioned as a subordinate arm of the militia until 1938. Since 1935 considerable efforts had gone into expansion and rearmament, but the results were pathetic. The Permanent Active Air Force (as it was called after 1938) had increased from 569 to 1,031 personnel, which was totally inadequate for the needs of war. There was a desperate shortage of equipment. At the time of the Munich crisis in September 1938, the government authorized an expenditure of over $6 million for aircraft and equipment from the United States; on October 7, when the crisis was apparently over, the government rescinded its authorization. In August 1939, much too late, it approved the purchase of 20 bombers and 15 training aircraft in the United States. The order was never filled because of American neutrality laws. Apart from 19 Hawker Hurricanes, 10 Fairey Battles, 8 Supermarine Stranraers, and some training aircraft, all available military aircraft were obsolete. Even the Battles and Stranraers were obsolescent.

In spite of these shortcomings, Ian Mackenzie, Minister of National Defence, argued in June 1939 that the air force had a 'tremendous advantage over the other two services'. Canada was a 'natural flying country'—an allusion to the dependence on aviation to cover its vast distances. An aircraft industry had been established and the growth of civil aviation had created a reserve of experienced pilots. Aviation had taken firm root in Canada between 1915 and

13 RCAF recruits drill-
ing. Ottawa, September
1939.

1918 and a number of the experienced pilots available were Canadian veterans of the First World War in the British flying services—the Royal Naval Air Service, Royal Flying Corps, and Royal Air Force.

The senior officers of the RCAF often had markedly different backgrounds from those in the army and navy. Air Vice-Marshal G.M. Croil, for instance, Chief of the Air Staff since December 1939, had moved to Scotland with his family before the First World War, became a civil engineer, and later managed a tea and rubber plantation in Ceylon. In 1915 he returned to Britain as a captain in the Gordon Highlanders, joined the Royal Flying Corps in 1916, and served the remainder of the war in the Middle Eastern theatre, where he sometimes acted as pilot for Lawrence of Arabia. Croil returned to Canada in 1920 as a squadron leader to join the newly formed Canadian Air Board. He transferred to the RCAF on its formation in 1924 and became senior air officer in 1934. This was not a typical career, but there could be no such thing among the senior ranks of a force whose origins were so recent. Before 1935 there was little professional military training for air force officers. Some attended staff courses given by the Royal Air Force, some served as attachés in Britain. There were in Canada a few desultory courses and exercises in army co-operation, and some emphasis was given to precision flying in two aerobatic teams formed between the wars. RCAF personnel were used primarily to foster civil aviation, to engage in air surveying, or to co-operate with the RCMP in contraband patrols. As a result the RCAF was manned with highly professional airmen who lacked experience in modern air warfare.

Like the navy, the air force offered a means of contributing to the war effort without having to find excessive numbers of men as reinforcements. The RCAF claimed to need fighter squadrons to defend important places—especially Halifax and Esquimalt—from aerial bombing attack. Bombing and reconnaissance squadrons also had to patrol and protect the sea approaches to Canada; army co-operation squadrons would provide air observation for coastal defence. Overseas requirements would be minimal. On September 12, 1939, the Prime Minister offered Canadian squadrons for loan to the RAF, to be equipped by Britain at Canadian expense. Earlier in 1939 Canada had also offered Britain some training facilities, although in 1936 and 1938 the Prime Minister, supported by his advisers and the Cabinet, had turned down suggestions to train RAF pilots in Canada. It had been argued that the RCAF was planning its own schools and wanted no competition for facilities, equipment, or personnel, but the real fear was that the nation would give up some of its autonomy if British training took place in Canada, and that Britain intended to recruit Canadian manpower for the RAF.[9] The Conservative opposition got hold of the issue and eventually forced King to alter his policy of catering only to Canada's needs: in April 1939 the agreement had therefore been made to train 50 RAF as well as 75 RCAF pilots in Canada every year.

Mobilization revealed the inadequacy of pre-war preparations. At the outbreak of war there were seven RCAF bomber and reconnaissance squadrons available for service on the east and west coasts. Two squadrons were on the west coast; two fighter, one army co-operation, and two bomber and reconnaissance squadrons were either on, or assigned to, the east coast. On August 25 all leave was cancelled in the Permanent Active Air Force and two days later designated squadrons—only one of which was equipped with any completely up-to-date aircraft (two Hurricane fighters)—began to move to their war stations. An example of the condition of these units is given by 3 Squadron as it began to stage through a series of airports with its seven Wapitis on August 26. These aging machines gave no end of trouble as the squadron literally staggered across the country. Two came down with engine trouble at Millinocket, Maine, and nearly found themselves interned in the United States because the weather closed in. They finally were able to take off the day after Britain declared war and arrived at their destination two days later, after another delay caused by weather at Blissville, N.B.

On September 3 the three wing headquarters and eleven of the twelve squadrons of the Auxiliary Active Air Force went on full-time duty. In the following two weeks authority was given to call out reserve personnel and a Special Reserve came into being for wartime recruits.

14 Soldiers entraining for overseas. One man has a suitcase and is carrying a civilian raincoat; another has his bayonet—still in its scabbard—fixed to his rifle; many are wearing Great War ammunition pouches on their web equipment.

In spite of these modest beginnings the role played by the air force in the Second World War eventually transcended anything the Canadian government had foreseen. Although King had first rebuffed RAF requests for training facilities in Canada, and eventually made the agreement of April 1939 with the greatest reluctance, forces beyond his control were at work.

As in the First World War—when a British air-training scheme was established in Canada—the British Air Ministry knew that it would need training facilities beyond those available in the British Isles. Canada was by far the most suitable location. Not only were the flying conditions ideal, but Canada already had a great deal of the expertise and the facilities necessary to mount a large training program. The British training programs of the First World War had produced thousands of Canadian pilots for the British flying services, many of whom were still active airmen and important supporters of aviation in Canada. Encouraged by the RCAF and supported by the government's civil aviation department, numbers of them were running private flying clubs scattered across the country; these clubs were intended to provide elementary training for the RCAF in time of war. In addition, some of the airfields and buildings built in 1917 were still in use, and more fields had been constructed by Relief Camp workers in the thirties. Once more Britain looked to Canada for air-training assistance, even though there were other training areas in the British Commonwealth—Australia and Southern Africa, for instance. Canada was the closest training area to Britain, connected by the one lifeline that had to be kept open at all costs if Britain was to survive a European war: the North Atlantic. Responding to a British initiative, after consultation with the Royal Air Force, the Chief of Air Staff proposed on September 15 to train 12,000 men a year, including 8,000 ground staff, for the RAF. This would require a training force of 600 officers and 6,500 other ranks. Following the Emergency Council meeting of September 28, the Prime Minister accepted this proposal in principle. It came to be called the British Commonwealth Air Training Plan. As C.P. Stacey observes, the idea of a vital war contribution that demanded the retention of large numbers of men at home 'must have seemed the answer to any Canadian politician's prayer'.[10]

By the end of September the government had brought Canada into the war with little fanfare. The war potential of the nation had hardly been scratched, but it was already clear that intentions to defend only Canadian territory (the principle that had previously guided planning) had been replaced by involvement in all military aspects of the war. These developments had profound implications for Canadians. The event that had greatest impact was probably the formation of the 1st Canadian Division for service overseas.

Men of the 1st Division were later known by men of the 2nd Division as 'breadliners' because the war had offered countless unemployed men the chance to join the army. Put another way, unemployment was a form of conscription. However, more than half the men of the 1st Division were answering a call to duty as members of the permanent or non-permanent active militia. The unemployed themselves acknowledged that they were by no means the only volunteers. Thirty-five years later, one soldier recalled joining up:

> There was every type. There was us, out of the jungles. Lice on us, every one. . .There were men in business suits and college kids, I guess, and kids who looked like they should have been in school behind their books. There was old guys just itching to get in, guys from the last war. . .
>
> I wasn't patriotic. None of my buddies were. I just wanted some good clothes and hot showers and three decent meals a day and a few dollars for tobacco and beer . . . You found out later that the others wanted other things. One college kid wanted to impress his girl and he was the biggest fool of all. The high school kids wanted adventure, and. . .that is probably what we was all looking for. Not adventure, maybe, but a new life. Same thing.[11]

In 1939 the word 'adventure' had special meaning for the men who enlisted, the men who would build on what G.F.G. Stanley has called

'The Military History of an Unmilitary People'[12]. About two years later the architect and town planner, Humphrey Carver, witnessed an inspection of Canadian recruits for a new armoured regiment at Windsor, Ont., from a nearby rooftop—in the company, inexplicably, of a captured German Luftwaffe pilot.

> For about an hour we were together ... looking down at the raw recruits on the parade ground, an untidy rabble still without any soldier's discipline in their postures and outlook. They were the sons of Canadian immigrants and they had lived as teenagers through the years of the depression that had knocked the stuffing out of Canada. They hadn't been roused by any kind of national zest for life. Their lives had been flat and uneventful like the boring voice of W.L. Mackenzie King, their leader.[13]

The Luftwaffe pilot's impression of this motley unit can be imagined.

Whatever Canadians may have expected in 1939, a war of limited liability was impossible. Instead there would be pain and hardship and permanent tragedy for countless men and women, but by the same token there would be very few flat and uneventful lives. For better or for worse, war would be the means of creating the national pride that young people had missed in the conditions for simple survival in the thirties. In the purposeful atmosphere that the outbreak of war stimulated, even official Ottawa could no longer preserve the 'calculating aloofness' that was evident to pre-war observers. Events were forcing Canada to step out of the shadows.

5 Embarkation of the st Division Canadian Active Service Force (CASF). Halifax, December 1939.

3

THE SINEWS OF WAR

In the Second World War, as in the First, the North Atlantic Ocean played a vital strategic role, one that placed Canada in the forefront of planning considerations by the Allied nations. The Atlantic served as a bridge for the materials and men that were necessary to create Allied superiority over the enemy. Canada's eastern seaports, placed as they were on or near all the northern trade routes between North America and Britain, were obvious convoy routing centres and would become flourishing entrepôts of trade and shipping. The airfields at Dorval, Goose Bay, and Gander inevitably became vital links in the trans-ocean air-ferrying route that came into existence in 1940. If Canada had not taken full advantage of its position at the western end of the Atlantic bridge, Britain (whose survival depended on North American supply) and the United States would have moved in to fill the vacuum: Britain would virtually have bypassed Canada for industrial supply in favour of the United States as soon as American neutrality laws allowed; and the vital bases in Newfoundland would have fallen under American domination during the war and after. Given those possibilities, Mackenzie King's Cabinet exerted every effort to maintain national control of the entrepôts and to ensure that they would be supplied as much as possible with Canadian products, expanding the national economy and its industrial base to meet the resulting demand.

In 1939 Canada was the only Dominion with the potential to produce and supply a wide range of raw materials and munitions, but it was by no means certain that the country—economically weakened by the Depression—could rise to the situation. There was every possibility of its being a client nation, exporting nothing more than relatively unsophisticated munitions, raw materials, natural resources, and men to the principal belligerents, as in the First World War. Whitehall's expectations of Canada in 1939 were summarized in Anthony Eden's telegram of September 6:

> Defence department would like to increase our normal food imports from Canada by a very large amount ... Ministry of Supply wish to purchase large supplies of raw materials, in particular, copper, aluminium, nickel, and perhaps timber. Moreover, Air Ministry in addition to their outstanding commitments, would like to place

very substantial further orders for aircraft and accessories ... In the circumstances perhaps the most valuable immediate assistance which Canada could give in this field would be any steps which are possible to assist us in the financing of desired purchases.[1]

Canadian leaders first needed to know the market potential for all the munitions Canada could manufacture; the exact British requirements in terms of tonnage and costs; the financial resources Canada needed to call upon in order to assist Britain; and the Dominion's industrial capacity.

What responses there were to Canadian enquiries proved tentative. The recent survey of industry had not given British leaders much confidence in Canada's industrial expertise. Furthermore, amazing as it may seem, Britain had no machinery for considering all her import demands together. This was not because she had no experience in these matters—the First World War had given her ample—but because she had no idea that the inadequate utilization of shipping space would create desperate shortages as soon as the nation shifted from peacetime to wartime production requirements. Even after spending years preparing and issuing orders for the use and control of merchant ships in the event of war, British authorities were not adequately informed of the shipping capacity available to them from either British or foreign merchant fleets. Not until war broke out did the government consult the experts in shipping controls, but even then there was serious competition between different departments for the use of space to import urgently needed food and other types of product, with the result that critical shortages developed in several vital industries. Not until May 1941 was the Ministry of Shipping allowed to dictate an equable distribution of shipping space to each government department.[2] Under such circumstances Britain, in 1939, could not have planned a long-term program to justify Canadian industrial expansion, even if she had wanted to. The British decision to exploit what was immediately available from Canada explains the early emphasis on raw materials, finance, and the British Commonwealth Air Training Plan.

Canada was aware that in 1939 British planners were not thinking ahead beyond three years. There could be little development of Canadian industry in that time. A few Canadian firms did have war contracts, but this was only because the Imperial Conference of 1937 had established a principle of fostering the Canadian war potential, not because an urgent need for help was envisaged. John Inglis Ltd, Toronto, had an order for 7,000 Bren light machine-guns; Marine Industries Ltd, Sorel, and the National Steel Car Corporation, Malton, were producing 25-pounder guns and 3.7-inch shells; Canadian Industries Ltd was producing TNT; a central contracting company called Canadian Associated Aircraft had an order for Hampden bombers; De Havilland of Toronto had an Air Ministry contract for 400 Tiger Moths; Canadian Car and Foundry of Fort William had received a separate order for 40 Hurricanes. If Canadian factories were ever to supplement British industry, such 'educational' orders were essential, particularly in the field of aeronautics, even though the cost of production in Canada was much greater than in Britain. Yet the program smacked of tokenism—of abiding by the principle established by the 1937 Imperial Conference. Until the summer of 1940 Britain's munitions production was adequate for her own needs, limited as they were by the desultory warfare, dubbed the 'phoney war', that preceded the German spring offensive. Orders from Britain barely began to tap existing Canadian resources.

The British Commonwealth Air Training Plan was a different matter. It has been said of the BCATP that 'In essence the British had found an idea and they brought it to Ottawa looking for someone else to put up the cash.'[3] There is some truth to this comment, though it was clear that the Air Ministry put a great deal of store in the scheme, and was prepared to give it extensive support as well as to respect Canadian sovereignty when setting up bases in Canada.[4] But the BCATP had a difficult birth, marked by hard bargaining on the part of both British and Canadian members of the negotiating teams. Discussions began in Ottawa on October 15, 1939. They dragged on for over two months, mostly as a result of Canadian refusals to accept British terms. Canada insisted successfully on having administrative responsibility for the plan; however, there were protracted arguments about the sharing of costs. The Canadian Cabinet genuinely believed that the expense would be quite beyond Canada's means. At one point the government tried to make agreement conditional on a satisfactory wheat-purchasing arrangement. It was suggested that, if Britain would accept the Canadian price of 93½¢ a bushel—20¢ more than the current depressed market price—Canada would be prepared to sign the BCATP agreement. It must have seemed to the British negotiators that blackmail was not very far from the minds of their hosts, although from the Canadian point of view such a hard bargain was justified to alleviate the distress of the Prairie farmers. Eventually a price of 82½¢ was settled on through a negotiating team in London, independently of the BCATP negotiations. In the meantime, in Ottawa Canada agreed to contribute $353 million of an estimated $607 million to the scheme. Then there followed several weeks' delay while Mackenzie King stubbornly insisted that, as one of the terms of the agreement, the plan must be accepted as Canada's first priority in the war effort, which would enable King to show the Canadian public that the major Canadian contribution to the war was to be made by the air force and not by what he called 'great expeditionary forces of infantry'.[5]

Undoubtedly the principal advantage of the BCATP to Canada and to the Liberal government was the chance to make a recognizable and significant contribution to the war effort at home rather than overseas. There would be economic benefits from the establishment

6 A drafting room at CAF Headquarters, Ottawa, during the planning stage of the BCATP.

of training bases and the requirement to manufacture training aircraft. And, if the BCATP had priority over an expeditionary force, there would be less likelihood of a reinforcement crisis like that of 1917, demanding some form of conscription to satisfy manpower requirements for the army. The plan also offered a means of furthering Canadian national autonomy. Mackenzie King demanded that it be written into the plan that Canadian graduates of the scheme be incorporated into RCAF units in the field. This eventually produced the following wording in Article 15 of the Memorandum of Agreement:

> The United Kingdom Government undertakes that pupils of Canada, Australia and New Zealand shall, after training is completed, be identified with their respective Dominions, either by the method of organizing Dominion units and formations or in some other way, such methods to be agreed upon by the respective Dominion Governments concerned....[6]

After the negotiations were over, the principals on each side formed a jaundiced view of the motives and methods of the opposite side. When the agreement was signed, the British High Commissioner in Ottawa, Sir Gerald Campbell, commented testily that 'the Canadian Government saw everything in terms of the advantage which might be secured for Canada and themselves.' We certainly know that Mackenzie King thought the British 'seemed to think that all they have to do is tell us what has to be done', and that British negotiators for their part took away unflattering opinions of the Canadian prime minister. Harold Balfour, the British Air Ministry representative, believed (incorrectly) that there was mutual distrust between King and his Cabinet, that King played off one section of opinion against the other, 'thus cunningly holding the balance of power in his own hands'.[7]

The BCATP was not only vitally significant but extremely complex in its organization. Fifty-one air-training schools were created between April 1940 and December 1941. Another great accomplish-

17 Students at No. 4 Elementary Flying Training School, Windsor Mills, Que., about to go up for instruction flights in Fleet Finch aircraft.

ment was the intake of over 39,000 trainees—more than half as many again as originally planned for. Canada contributed over 80 per cent of all trainees until May 1942.

Demographically the most interesting feature of the Canadian contribution to the BCATP was the large proportion that came from Ontario. Numbering about a third of the total population, Ontarians accounted for almost half the aircrew applicants and a proportionate number of graduates, a percentage that helps to explain the origin of the expression 'Royal Ontario Air Force' that was bandied about, only half in jest, by aircrew from that province. The other provinces were represented more or less in proportion to population, with the exception of Quebec.

When the BCATP agreement was renegotiated in 1942 the United Kingdom took responsibility for filling 'not less than 40 per cent of the training capacity'. It subsequently provided about 48 per cent of trainees over the rest of the Plan's life. Between 1942 and 1945 Canada found about 25 per cent, the other Dominions another 25 per cent between them, and miscellaneous Allied countries the remaining 2 per cent. Canada's monthly contributions reached their highest—3,379—in August 1943 and during eight months of that year exceeded 2,000 per month. By the war's end the BCATP had produced 131,553 aircrew, of which 72,835 (51 per cent overall) were Canadians.

During the BCATP negotiations of 1939 Britain suffered her first food crisis owing to the shortage of shipping. In mid-November 1939 some flour mills actually stopped work for lack of grist. Because Canadian supplies were essential, ships were diverted from other destinations in North America to the St Lawrence River on an emergency basis to load up with wheat that had already been purchased by Britain in the form of futures in 1938. Not so urgent in 1939, but just as important, was the need for Canadian timber, because German control of the Baltic had severely restricted the flow from that source of supply. By the end of the year Canada, still Britain's major supplier of nickel and aluminum, had also increased exports of iron and steel and manufactures thereof by more than a third. Generally, however, Canadian productivity and business were not much affected by the 'phoney war'.[8]

Hitler's electrifying campaigns in Scandinavia and France during the spring of 1940 brought an end to the unreal conditions of the 'phoney war'. After the fall of France in June and the successful evacuation of the British Expeditionary Forces from Dunkirk, Britain and her allies found themselves confronted by Fortress Europe. So long as that near and powerful menace to the United Kingdom could be resisted, they could call upon badly needed shipping not available before, some diverted from service to France, some acquired from German-occupied countries. British leaders, therefore, no longer obliged to support a full-scale military effort on the European continent, were free to exploit maritime strengths against the enemy while preparing for an eventual counter-attack against the Axis powers. There was now total dependence on maritime forces and lines of communication, and North American supplies became even more necessary than before.

As soon as war had been declared a British Purchasing Mission had come to North America and acquired a temporary home in Ottawa. When the United States Congress agreed to alterations in the Neutrality Act late in 1939, so that American war supplies could go to Britain, the British Purchasing Mission moved to New York, leaving behind a small British Supply Board in Ottawa. It soon became evident that British authorities preferred to shop south of the border—and for very good reasons. In the first place, Roosevelt had always assured Britain of his eagerness to support the Allied cause. Even before the war, in July 1939, he had told the British ambassador he favoured establishing an American naval patrol in the western Atlantic to prevent the 'warlike operations of belligerents'—and the changes in the Neutrality Act constituted further proof of the transition to something more than benevolent neutrality; to something, in fact, that was more like non-neutral belligerency. In the second place, the United States was believed to be a reliable source of supply and Canada was not—at least not until its industrial potential could be assessed properly. When Britain abandoned all caution in the expenditure of dollars in June 1940, there was no financial reason for choosing doubtful Canadian sources rather than proven American ones, and the British Supply Board was distinctly lethargic in creating orders for Canadian firms. A number of events brought about a change in this attitude. The British government had refused to let Canada supply the Canadian Army Overseas with equipment from Canadian sources but insisted that the letter of a 1939 agreement be adhered to and that orders be placed through the British Ministry of Supply. In April 1940, however, as a result of Canadian pressure, the British agreed to place such orders in Canada—mainly for political reasons because in British eyes there was no requirement to go outside Great Britain. Then the fall of France in June 1940 shattered this preconception: soon after Dunkirk the Ministry of Supply allocated to Canada about a third of its orders for re-equipping the British army.

Canada was now on its way to finding an international market for its war products, and it was essential to organize a massive program for industrial expansion. Under these circumstances the war turned up men of outstanding ability who made great efforts, often at considerable personal sacrifice, to serve the cause. It is not an exaggeration to say that C.D. Howe, Minister of Munitions and Supply, changed the country from a very small producing nation to a respectable industrial power. But even the dynamic Howe could never have done this had not international events created the essential framework for expansion. For example, Dunkirk—where the British army lost so much equipment, particularly vehicles, that British factories could not meet the demand for replacements—created a need that Canada could help to fill because it already had an automobile industry. However, the international framework also imposed limitations on the nature of Canadian production. In the case of the Canadian automobile industry, American domination was so complete that engines—whether for land vehicles or aircraft—were never produced in Canada during the Second World War. Furthermore, it was necessary to resolve two crucial financial problems—exchange barriers with the United States and the British dollar deficits in Canada—before Canada could exploit the urgent demands for goods created by the events of 1940. Finally, Canada had to come to terms with the United States concerning the defence relationships of the two countries. In August 1940 Mackenzie King accepted Roosevelt's invitation to visit him near Ogdensburg, N.Y., where the President and King signed the Ogdensburg Agreement, recognizing joint Canadian and American responsibilities for the defence of North America, to be spelled out in decisions recommended by the Permanent Joint Board of Defence. Although this did not have specific implications for the munitions industry, it provided the machinery for negotiation between the two countries in time of war. Ogdensburg marked an important step in Canada's growing independence of Britain, as well as its new relationship with the United States, and heralded Canadian attempts to obtain a voice in international decisions for countries that were not Great Powers.

Eventually the PJBD made thirty-three formal recommendations concerning North American defence, and all except two were approved by the Canadian and American governments. The board also conducted a great deal of important informal discussion, and worked out the vitally important Basic Defence Plans for North America. A bitter debate over the strategic direction of forces on Canadian territory reached its climax in Washington at the end of

18 A machinist pauses for a snack before he finishes a gun barrel on the lathe at Sorel Industries Limited, Quebec, December 1940.

May 1941, with the temperature at 94° Fahrenheit and the air-conditioning cut off. 'Every so often the American section would break off into a huddle to concert some fresh assault,' recalled General Maurice Pope, 'but we poor Canadians seemed to have nothing to huddle about, save our determination not to give in.'[9] The Canadians won their point. By Joint Basic Defence Plan No. 2, American commanders did not have authority over the administration and discipline of Canadians: each nation maintained strategic direction and command of its own forces. However, tactical command against an enemy threat would be given to one supreme commander.

Even though Roosevelt and Mackenzie King had established an exceptionally friendly personal relationship, Canadian representatives had to employ some deftness in protecting Canadian interests at meetings of this board, and other similar boards, to avoid military, political, and economic domination of Canada by the United States in decisions affecting both countries.

In March 1941 the United States government made the momentous decision to provide war materials to Britain on a lend and lease basis, which allowed American war supplies to reach Britain in exchange for a theoretical deferred payment. This raised difficulties for Canada, which itself had a severe balance-of-payments deficit in the United States. How could Canada pay for U.S.-made components needed to complete existing British orders without accepting lend-lease itself? (To do so might have resulted in the liquidation of Canadian investments in the U.S. and in a poor bargaining position for Canada after the war.) For that matter, why should Britain pay for Canadian products when she could have American ones on credit—a

19, 20 In these two photographs Veronica Foster, named the 'Bren Gun girl', is shown jit-terbugging at the Glen Eagle Country Club near Toronto and pos-ing for the photogra-pher at the John Inglis plant, Toronto, where she worked. May 1941.

most attractive proposition to a country with a dollar deficit in Canada? The Canadian government, helped by the great good will towards both Canada and the Allied cause that was prevalent in the United States, solved both problems in an imaginative and practical way.

Mackenzie King went to Washington. After negotiating with Cor-dell Hull, the Secretary of State, and Henry Morgenthau, the Secre-tary of the Treasury, he visited Roosevelt at his Hyde Park estate. He pressed the argument that if the United States 'insisted upon taking from Canada what few possessions she had in the U.S. [by liquidat-ing investments in order to make U.S. aid possible], it would only give voice to anti-U.S. sentiment in this country.' He proposed that the U.S. should buy from Canada as much as Canada was buying from the U.S. 'On a grand Sunday, April 20, 1941,' in Roosevelt's words, he and King signed the Hyde Park Declaration, which pro-vided for a virtual barter in war materials, the United States paying in dollars for Canadian manufactures and Canada using the proceeds to purchase American war material. 'Roosevelt thought this was a swell idea,' Mackenzie King told the Canadian journalist Grant Dexter.[10] The necessary raw materials, machine tools, and spare parts for the fulfilment of British orders could be considered as lend-lease items and would not affect Canada's balance-of-payment position. In no time large American defence orders began to flow into Canada and by 1942 it had overcome its balance-of-payments problem.

As soon as it became clear that British dollar deficits in Canada would prevent the continuing purchase of Canadian products, C.D. Howe pressed the Cabinet in July 1941 to take radical financial measures to help Britain. 'The time to be generous with Britain is now,' he said, '...rather than in the post-war period when our people will be in a less generous mood.'[11] British dollar deficits in Canada

21 The first Valentine tank produced at the Montreal Locomotive Works inspected by C.D. Howe, Minister of Munitions and Supply, and Lieutenant-General Ken Stuart, Chief of the General Staff. May 27, 1941.

were met by the repatriation of British securities, acceptance of payment in sterling, and payment for as much as possible in gold—which Britain was obtaining in limited quantities from South Africa. When Canadian sterling balances became unacceptably large in London in the autumn of 1941, they were converted into an interest-free loan to Britain of $700 million, and in January 1942 munitions and war supplies, including food, were contributed as an outright gift to the extent of one billion dollars. In 1943, when the credit ran out, an arrangement was made whereby Canada would donate its surplus production to the Allies through a Canadian Mutual Aid Board. (Although aid went to several Allied countries, the bulk went to the United Kingdom, to the value of more than one and a quarter billion dollars.) On learning of the proposal for mutual aid, an official in the Dominions Office commented that Canada's gift would cost, in terms of its population, 'about five times what lend lease cost the United States'.

It would be true, if cynical, to say that Canadians, having produced the goods, gave them away because no one could afford to buy them. But not to have put to use the output of Canadian industry, which was in full production, would have made no sense at all when the demands of war were at their height and when a reduction of output would have brought back unemployment and prejudiced the chances of establishing a strong post-war market. It was none the less a remarkable gift, representing the true spirit of Canadian policy; it embodied the heartfelt concern and support in the nation for the survival and liberation from Nazi conquest of Britain and Europe.

The industrial growth that accompanied these developments could not have occurred without the imaginative use of organizational and technical talent. C.D. Howe's Department of Munitions and Supply, which came into being on April 9, 1940, became the force behind the acceleration, control, and co-ordination of Canadian industry. For Canadian products to meet the exacting standards necessary for munitions production, British expertise was called upon in the form of naval and air technical missions and the Anglo-Canadian Inter-Governmental Inspection Board. Renamed the Inspection Board of the United Kingdom and Canada in January 1941, it made Canada an acceptable alternate source of supply to Britain in many critical areas. But not only to Britain. Canadian fighting services now had to rely on Canadian sources of supply where they had previously relied on British. In fact all the Allied armed forces overseas would come to use Canadian industrial exports.

The Wartime Industries Control Board, created on June 24, 1940, regulated raw materials and services needed by industry. Crown Companies, which involved a large cross-section of industrial and business leaders, were formed to solve production problems beyond the capabilities of existing industry and to overcome difficulties in supply, purchasing, and administration raised by the special circumstances of the time. One such enterprise, Citadel Merchandising Co. Ltd, based in Ottawa, was created to procure some forty to fifty thousand new machine tools urgently required for munitions production. Another company, War Supplies Ltd, created in May 1941 after the Hyde Park Declaration under the formidable direction of E.P. Taylor, drummed up sales for Canadian products in the United States. In less than three months, contracts worth about $200 million had been obtained. Altogether 28 Crown Companies were incorporated: 11 operated plants and the remainder carried out supervisory, administrative, and purchasing functions.

Large-scale production began in July 1940. This was when the new Minister of National Defence, J.L. Ralston, received Cabinet approval to order for the Canadian army 300 25-pounders, 900 2-inch mortars, forty 40-mm guns, and 488 Valentine Tanks complete with armament. From this modest beginning Howe's ubiquitous Department of Munitions and Supply oversaw such growth that by 1945 Canada had supplied more than 815,000 transport and combat vehicles to the Allies, including almost all the transport used by the British Eighth Army in North Africa and Italy. This degree of expansion naturally demanded continual additions to existing plants.

The pattern of such growth is graphically demonstrated by the development of ammunition production between 1939 and 1943. In 1939 the only vestige of Canada's enormous output of ammunition in the First World War was the Dominion Arsenal at Quebec, which had been kept in existence. By reactivating old equipment, it raised its production from 750,000 rounds a month to 12,500,000. In addition, another creation of the First World War, the Dominion Arsenal at Lindsay, Ont., was opened up again. These plants were found par-

22 Lieutenant-General A.G.L. McNaughton, commander of First Canadian Corps, examines a 25-pounder field gun at Sorel, Que., during a visit to Canada on February 9, 1942.

ticularly useful in 1941 because they were the only ones capable of rolling steel, used in the production of shells and cartridges, to the tolerances required by the Small Arms and Ammunition Branch, so they were given responsibility for supplying this product to other plants that were by then in existence. A small plant at Valcartier, a branch of the Dominion Arsenal at Quebec, had been the only one capable of filling ammunition with explosives at the beginning of the war. When more output was needed, this highly skilled and dangerous work was undertaken by firms that were mostly under the direction of Defence Industries Ltd, a subsidiary of Canadian Industries Ltd: the Cherrier plant at Saint-Paul l'Hermite and the Bouchard plant at Sainte-Thérèse, Que. Until 1942 there was no plant capable of making the cores for armour-piercing bullets, and to overcome the tiresome need of importing this item a new government factory, York Arsenals Ltd, began production in February 1942 under the management of the Canadian Acme Screw and Gear Company Ltd of Toronto. When orders exceeded the capacity of government plants, Defence Industries Ltd again took up most of the overflow. New ammunition factories appeared at Brownsburg, Que., which started large-scale production in August 1941; and urgent orders for 9-mm Sten gun ammunition arrived in 1942 at yet another new plant, the Montreal Works. In February 1943 it became clear that a shortage of satisfactory tools might lead to large rejections of ammunition made at such plants, so Defence Industries Ltd set up the Westmount Tool Works. At about the same time new sources of supply were created in a Toronto plant operated by Industrial Associates (Canada) Ltd and by Dominion Rubber Munitions Ltd.

Other areas of production followed similar patterns, each overcoming its special problems with the aid of the Production Branches. Army equipment, for example, was the responsibility of the following Branches: Army, Engineering, and Design; Automotive and Tank; Gun; and Signals. The National Research Council—always an innovative force in Canadian technology—achieved a modest contribution in the development and design of weaponry for land warfare. The GL Mark III C anti-aircraft radar was a successful project, although it did not reach full production. The Ram tank, consisting of an American chassis and a cast-steel superstructure, attempted to combine the best features of U.S. and British tank design in late 1940, but was soon superseded by the American 'General Sherman'—the most successful Allied tank of the war—which had in turn been influenced by an early mock-up model of the Ram. Canadian developers were more successful when, using the Sherman chassis, they produced a number of self-propelled guns, of which the 25-pounder, or 'Sexton', proved to be a highly successful model. In addition the National Research Council developed a method for the large-scale production of the new explosive RDX, using radically new

23   A Canadian-built Ram tank arriving in England on March 2, 1942.

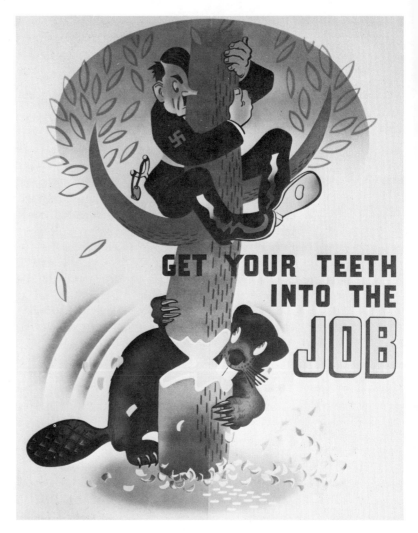

GET YOUR TEETH
INTO THE
JOB

24 A poster issued by the Wartime Information Board about 1942.

techniques, and produced another new explosive called DINA from which it was possible to develop the flashless propellant Albanite for the U.S. Navy.

By the end of the war, equipment produced in Canada for use in land warfare included several weapons for which it was the only reliable alternate source to Britain: Bren light machine-guns, 25-pounder guns, Boys anti-tank rifles and 2-pounder anti-tank equipment (until they were superseded in 1942) as well as 3.7-inch anti-aircraft guns. These were British-designed weapons made to British standards under British tutelage. To have adapted highly developed American industry for these products would have been impractical: thus Canada turned its industrial backwardness to advantage.

The shipbuilding industry had the most startling impact on Canada in its effect on the distribution of Canadian manpower and in its total contribution to the war effort. Canada had built a number of vessels in the First World War and there were fifteen yards scattered throughout the country capable of producing a variety of ship types. But all of them together employed no more than 4,000 men in 1939. Four companies had the capacity to build ships of 10,000 tons deadweight; five others had berths for building ships up to 4,700 tons deadweight. The RCN alone stated requirements for 104 new vessels of all types, and even after the Cabinet reduced this figure for financial reasons, an authorized program received approval in February 1940 for 92 British-designed corvettes and Bangor-class minesweepers. In April 1940 the Naval Shipbuilding Branch came into existence and started placing contracts. By the end of the year 14 new corvettes were commissioned—8 of them into the Royal Navy (although manned by Canadians) and 6 into the Royal Canadian Navy. Britain placed orders for 26 merchant ships of 10,000 tons deadweight in December 1940, but work did not start on them until April 1941, when Wartime Merchant Shipping Ltd came into being as a Crown Company.

Since Canada did not have a code of standards for the construction of warships, the British Admiralty Technical Mission, aided by technical officers of the RCN, had to establish British dockyard standards. The task was enormous. Yards in the Great Lakes and Quebec, where trawlers and corvettes were built, were unbelievably primitive

25 A merchant ship begins to take shape at the Dominion Bridge Company, Montreal, probably in 1943.

to naval officers accustomed to Admiralty standards. 'In one', observed a member of the mission, 'there was no drawing office at all; the percentage of skilled labour was very small throughout; and the Lakes' yards tended naturally to follow Great Lakes' practice which specialized in the reduction of costs. . .[The process of education] was explosive at times.'[12] Procuring the fittings and weapons for ships posed a special problem because most large engineering firms, by July 1940, were committed to orders for the army and air force. The mission was able to surmount this difficulty by sending members of its staff—which in 1943 reached a peak of nearly 2,000 people—across the country to find plants capable of producing the equipment required for the shipbuilding program. For instance, the CPR Locomotive Repair Shops in Calgary became a prime source of naval guns and the Parker Pen Company of Toronto manufactured primers for naval ammunition.

Such things as magnetic compasses, hydraulic steering gears, tachometers and large diesel engines, never before made in Canada, were contracted out to Canadian firms wherever possible; but they often came from the United States because only a limited number of firms in the Canadian electrical industry were able to handle the entire process of design, production, engineering, and manufacture. Steel plates of the size and quality needed for shipbuilding had to be imported from the United States until 1942, when the Steel Company of Canada completed a new rolling mill capable of producing these plates itself.

By 1946 the industry had gone through a rapid apprenticeship, solved problems by extensive improvisation, and found new sources of equipment by persistent searching and a willingness to rely on untried manufacturing plants. The results were modest by British or American standards, but considering that the Canadian industry had been moribund in 1939, the final accomplishment in the space of five years was striking. Canada had built 410 merchant ships, 487 escorts and minesweepers, 254 naval tugs, and 3,302 landing craft. At its peak in 1943 the shipbuilding industry employed 126,000 men. It was the second-largest employer in the country after the manufacturers of industrial equipment and materials.

Like shipbuilding, aircraft production grew out of small beginnings in 1939. There had been some manufacture of aircraft in the First World War and, what was never achieved in the Second World War, a few engines. In the early 1920s orders from the Canadian Air Board sparked a small but fairly lively industry that soon ran into difficulties but managed to struggle through the Depression. The industry's fortunes improved in the late thirties with the decision to spend most of the Canadian defence budget on air-force expansion, and with the consequent show of interest by the mission sent out from Britain under Lord Weir in 1938 to investigate technical industrial potential in North America. This mission resulted in much

26 Delicate fingers were an asset in assembling instruments. This woman is working on airspeed indicators in Winnipeg. May 16, 1942.

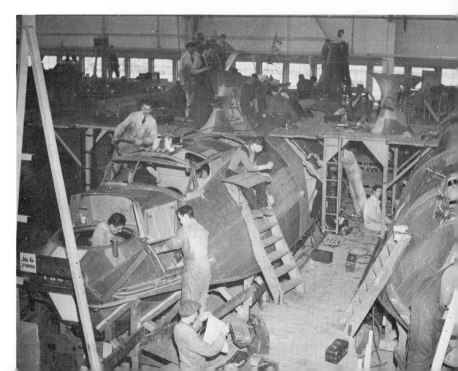

27 Canada produced its own version of the famous Consolidated 'Catalina' flying boat, the Canso 'A' amphibian, shown here in production at Canadian Vickers, Montreal.

more promising 'educational' orders than for other branches of manufacturing in the country. Requirements of the BCATP after December 1939 offered a further shot in the arm. In June 1940 the government provided the co-ordinating services to bring about the rapid expansion of aircraft production when the Department of Munitions and Supply created the Air Production Branch and incorporated the Crown Company of Federal Aircraft Ltd. When a second Crown Company—Victory Aircraft Ltd—was formed in 1942 to take over the National Steel Car Corporation at Malton, Ont., Canadian aviation manufacturers were producing a large range of training and combat aircraft, including the plywood Mosquito and the very large (for its time) Lancaster bomber.

De Havilland Aircraft of Canada provides an example of the Canadian experience in aircraft manufacturing during the war. Situated in Toronto, it grew rapidly in 1940 to fill orders not only for Tiger Moth biplane trainers but for about forty Fairey Battles and 700 Avro Ansons to meet training requirements. In search of workers, the firm went beyond local technical schools to the labour market and recruited totally unskilled men and women who enrolled in crash courses with a token allowance of three to five dollars a week. Their introduction to air frames was the fuselage of a First World War Curtiss JN-4—nothing more than a skeleton strung with some remains of wire rigging. Nevertheless, they were taught to read a blueprint, to work with precise measurements, and how to work with metal. Those with mechanical aptitude went into skilled tasks such as tool-and-die jobs; the others went onto aircraft assembly lines. The training program was almost too successful because the plant was for a time in the embarrassing position of having too many trained employees for the available work. Some simply quit their jobs in disgust because there was nothing for them to do; others discreetly slipped out of sight of the foreman until new bays had been built and the plant had tooled up for the latest production requirements.

In September 1941 De Havilland received the contract to build Mosquito aircraft, which in spite of the gradual expansion of previous years created several problems—some of them anticipated but none the less awkward. Inevitably both British and American parts were used, and since they had different measurements—for screw threads and wrenches, for instance—mechanics had to have two sets of tools. Sub-contracts for fuselages, tail assemblies, flaps, and undercarriages went to the most unlikely places. Cockshutt Plow of Brantford became responsible for aircraft hydraulic parts and had to make considerable adjustments to meet the standards of cleanliness required. Otaco Ltd of Orillia, Ont., manufacturers of farm implements, carriages, and rural hardware, provided undercarriages. (This firm succeeded in building an exceptionally strong landing gear.) By hard work, ingenuity, and improvisation, De Havilland's first Mosquito was ready for its test flight on September 24, 1942. However,

28 This British poster, published and distributed by the Director General of Aircraft Production, was donated to the Canadian war effort by British Aeroplane Engines Ltd, Montreal.

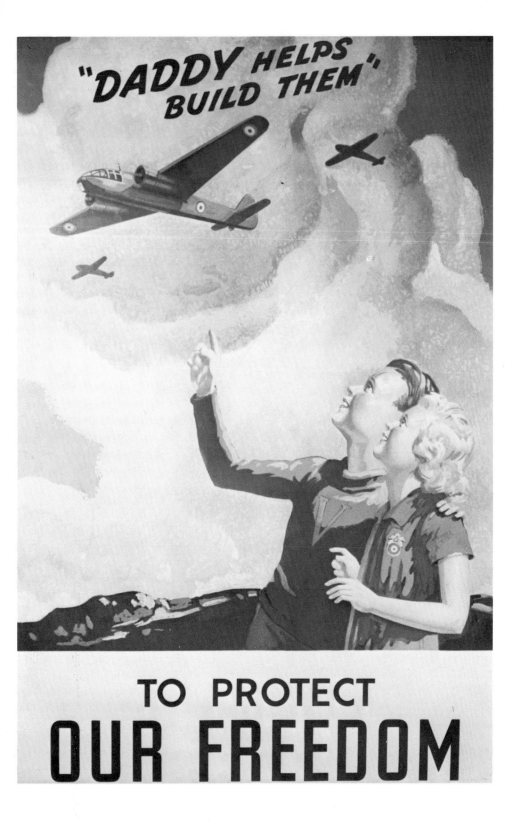

production was disappointingly slow and in 1943 C.D. Howe appointed J. Grant Glassco as controller of the firm to shake up management and meet higher monthly quotas. At the war's end the plant had produced 1,032 Mosquito aircraft. By way of comparison the plant in Britain built 5,200, other firms there built 500, and another 212 came from Australia.

It has been calculated that in terms of weight—which allows for the much larger aircraft being produced late in the war—the last quarter of 1944 saw one hundred times the production achieved during the last quarter of 1939: over 7,000,000 pounds (the weight of the 905 aircraft produced in 1944) as opposed to 70,000 pounds (the weight of the 31 aircraft produced in 1939). Employment in the industry reached its peak of 116,000—something less than the figure for shipbuilding—in August 1944, after all other branches of production in Canada had started to fall off. The achievement of the industry was a triumph because it placed aircraft firms in an exceptionally strong position for postwar manufacture. However, even though the industry had the advantage of a head start with orders received in the late thirties and was able to police its own standards with the cooperation of the RCAF, it still had difficulty in meeting production goals, which took the edge off the triumph.

For Canadian industry as a whole, 1943 was the record year, when the effort reached its peak and the economy was fully committed to the needs of war. Men and women employed in industry numbered 1,239,327, a figure that was not reached again until 1947. The gross value of production was $8,725,350,000, an amount that increased only marginally in 1944 before falling off substantially in 1945 and 1946. The manufacturing production index, set at 100 in 1949, was 104.1 for 1943 and 106.1 in 1944, and this level was not matched until 1950.

The Canadian government had succeeded in exploiting its industrial potential, reserves of manpower, and geographic position not only to preserve national control of the economy but also to establish a favourable position for competing with countries that had dominated world trade before 1939. There was still a military victory to win, however, and Canada was just as preoccupied with its military contribution as with the industrial efforts that supported it.

4

THE ATLANTIC BRIDGE

The sea and air lanes between North America and Europe formed a changeable and grim setting for the battle that in 1939 was about to be fought for Britain's lifeline. The best routes across the Atlantic were the northern ones because they were the shortest and the least accessible to German naval forces. Offsetting this advantage was the terrible climate. The North Atlantic, where it is not tempered by the Gulf Stream, is one of the most inhospitable places on the face of the earth. Fog settles down on the Newfoundland Banks and near the shores of Canada's Atlantic provinces like a cold blanket for weeks at a time, shutting out sight and distorting sound. It is so frequent and widespread that navigation becomes hazardous in the extreme. Gales come almost as a relief because they break up the fog; then, however, the sea and swell often build up to heights of more than 60 feet and the danger of collision or grounding gives way to other perils.

In winter the weather deteriorates for weeks on end into one massive storm system that stretches from North America to Europe. Winter temperatures turn spray and breaking seas into ice that builds up excessive topweight on the superstructure of ships and exposes even the most seaworthy vessels to the possibility of foundering or capsizing. This weather pattern spelled danger for airmen as well as seamen during the war, since it caused the icing up of aircraft in the air and the closing down of their bases. But unlike seamen, airmen welcomed the respites that from time to time brought sunny skies, excellent visibility, and seas that were miraculously transformed to gentle waves or even flat calms. For seamen, especially after enemy submarines were able to extend their patrols well out into the Atlantic after 1940, good weather brought with it the ever-present danger of destruction by torpedo because such conditions favoured the submarine.

Bridging the Atlantic was the key to strategic supply. To transport as much as possible—merchant ships and their cargoes, troopships with their human freight—to Britain, and from there if necessary to various theatres of operations, it was necessary for naval authorities to exercise complete control of ship movements. Loading and unloading had to be carried out with maximum efficiency and every effort had to be made to avoid congestion by large numbers of vessels in port at any one time. It was also necessary to devise means of protecting ships from enemy attack while on passage. For all these reasons the decision was made by the Admiralty to send ships across the ocean in convoy in order to regulate their movements and the more easily to provide escorts both by sea and air.

This did not mean that protection was adequate: not until 1943 were convoys used to their best advantage as a system of mutual defence against submarine attack that offered the best statistical chances of survival. In the meantime there were far too few naval vessels or maritime patrol aircraft available. The first convoys that formed up in Halifax with twenty to thirty ships in the fall of 1939 had no more than an escort of two Canadian destroyers and one flying boat for twenty-four hours. For the rest of the way they were shepherded by an armed merchant cruiser or battleship (types of ship that had no anti-submarine capability). About 500 miles from their destination in Britain, sea and air escorts of the Royal Navy and Royal Air Force joined to provide a measure of anti-submarine protection. Ships with a speed of more than 15 knots often steamed independently because they could outrun an attacking submarine. Even when more ships and aircraft could be found as escorts, the system failed to prevent heavy losses in 1939 and 1940. Moreover, it caused problems in cargo handling by the congestion it created in British ports. As German capabilities improved and Allied fortunes in Europe waned, the rising losses at sea gave the Battle of the Atlantic a desperate character.

German *Unterseebooten*, popularly known as U-boats since the First World War, concentrated at weak points in the naval defences of the Allies with devastating effect until the spring of 1943. There were fewer than 48 operational boats in September 1939; sometimes in subsequent months there were still fewer available, and numbers did not increase dramatically in the first eighteen months of the war. After May 1941, however, the fleet grew rapidly, and by May 1945 Germany had produced 1,170 submarines. At one time the total strength amounted to about 450, though by the end of the war losses had reduced the number of operational submarines to 144. Surface ships and aircraft were also used for attacks on shipping, but only the U-boat posed a deadly menace to lines of communication. 'The only thing that ever really frightened me was the U-boat peril', Churchill wrote. 'Never for one moment could we forget that everything happening elsewhere—on land, at sea and in the air—depended ultimately on its outcome, and amid all other cares, we viewed all its changing fortunes day by day with hope and apprehension.'[1] If Hitler had accepted naval advice in 1942 and concentrated all his U-boats in the Atlantic—rather than also stationing them off Norway, and in the Mediterranean and Indian Oceans—Germany might have won the Battle of the Atlantic and, consequently, the war.

The U-boat attacks began on September 3, 1939, the day Britain declared war, when a German submarine sank the British liner *Athenia* on her westward passage to New York. By May 1943, 2,190 ships had been sunk in the Atlantic. With these disastrous losses the amount of tonnage available for cargo fell off rapidly and new construction did not begin to reverse the trend until late 1942; not until August 1943 did shipyards produce enough ships every month to outstrip sinkings.

Canada participated in almost every phase of the development of anti-submarine warfare, from the planning of convoys to the forming of hunter-killer groups in the last two years of the war. As the navy expanded dramatically from 11 fighting ships and about 3,000 men to 373 fighting ships and about 93,000 men and women in five years, Canadian warships were not only concentrated on the supply lines to Europe. They served with the British fleet off Norway and with convoys to Russia; they went to the Mediterranean, Caribbean, and Pacific theatres; and they were employed extensively for coastal operations off the coast of Northwest Europe in 1944 and 1945. The RCAF increased its squadrons for anti-submarine patrol from 2 to 10 on the Canadian Atlantic seaboard by late 1943, detached one of them to operate under British control from Iceland in 1944, raised 6 squadrons for service with Coastal Command of the RAF (mostly in the Atlantic theatre), and sent many Canadians to serve with RAF Coastal Command squadrons. In the process of this rapid expansion there were severe problems of technical modernization, training, and morale, especially in the navy, so that between 1939 and 1943, when the Battle of the Atlantic reached its climax, the Canadians often did not measure up to the needs of the convoy battles. But it must be added that at a critical moment Canada provided escorts that were desperately needed and Canadians shared the worst of hardships experienced in the war at sea. Even though the Canadian contribution to the escort of convoys before 1943 was not so effective as that of Great Britain, it was both generous and strategically vital. And after 1943 Canadian ships and aircraft achieved results that compared favourably with those of other Allied forces.

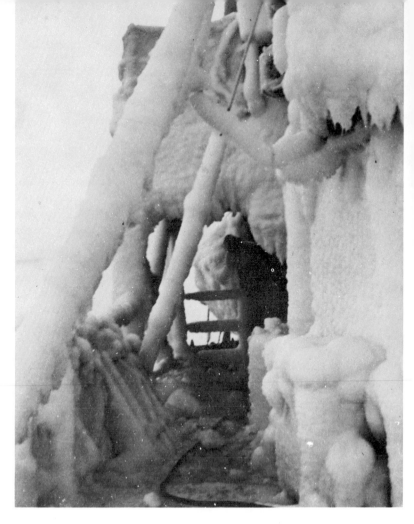

30 Part of HMCS *Noranda*, a Bangor-class minesweeper, iced up from heavy seas breaking over the ship. December 1942.

The predominance of naval ships and personnel has always preserved the memory of the Battle of the Atlantic as a naval achievement, but the parts played by airmen and merchant seamen were indispensable to defeating the enemy attack on shipping. Similarly, because more Canadian ships and naval personnel were involved in the Atlantic than in any other theatre, the defence of convoys has been thought of as the real function of the Canadian navy in the Second World War. In fact the RCN seized the opportunity presented by the Battle to develop new roles for the navy, just as the Battle forced the RCAF to expand its maritime air role.

In 1939 the superb natural harbour of Halifax, already the nation's principal naval base, was the scene of feverish activity as hundreds of ships from North American ports were marshalled there. By the summer of 1940 the number of merchant ships available for convoy became so large that Halifax could no longer efficiently accommodate all the shipping present. The rule that ships must be capable of

1 The corvette HMCS *Chambly*, which had one of the best fighting records in the RCN, convoying in fog. 1941.

speeds greater than 9 knots and that they must steam under 15 knots to sail in convoy had to be bent when shipping needs became critical. Some pretty ancient vessels began to turn up and their masters sometimes untruthfully, or optimistically, claimed higher speeds than their ships could manage. The speed of the main body often had to be reduced to prevent old crocks from becoming stragglers—prime targets for U-boats in the eastern Atlantic. In August 1940, therefore, slow convoys were instituted, and Sydney, Cape Breton, became their rendezvous so long as that harbour was free of ice.

Letters allocated to convoys in the early years of the war indicated their destination or point of departure in Britain. Outward-bound convoys had the label 'BO' or 'O'; homeward bound were 'H' ('HX' from North America and 'HG' from Gibraltar, for instance). Slow convoys from Sydney, Cape Breton, received the designation 'SC', probably standing for 'Sydney-River Clyde'. Troop convoys were given the special designation 'TC', and it was on December 10, 1939 that TC-1, consisting of passenger ships turned troopships—the *Aquitania, Empress of Britain, Duchess of Bedford, Monarch of Bermuda*, and *Empress of Australia*—followed the destroyers HMCS *Ottawa, Restigouche, Fraser*, and *St. Laurent* out of Halifax harbour past Mauger's Beach, Chebucto Head, and Sambro Lightship into the broad reaches of the Atlantic. The Canadian escort parted company the next day, but with the protection of a strong covering force of the Royal Navy, the stately liners filled with men of the 1st Canadian Division brought Britain the first visible evidence that Canada was in the war.

Over the next three years Canada's pre-war fleet was joined by several new types of vessel to meet the requirements of the sea war. Of these, and of all the warships with which the RCN has been identified, the corvette is perhaps the most famous. It was adopted as the result of fortuitous circumstances and not, as it would be natural to assume, on the direct·recommendation of British naval advisers. In August 1939 a mission of the Canadian Manufacturer's Association had brought home from England plans of several new types of ship being developed by the Admiralty. Among them were those for the 'Smith's Dock Patrol Vessel—Whaler Type', which had been approved by the Admiralty in June as the best anti-submarine vessel for rapid production. The shipbuilding representative of the Canadian mission, when he returned to Canada, deposited the plans with the National Research Council in Ottawa. Somebody at NRC phoned Naval Service Headquarters to see whether the navy would be interested in having them and was told it would.[2]

The RCN immediately adopted the design for the patrol vessel because it was easier and cheaper to build than the ships that had previously been under consideration for the anti-submarine role. The corvette, as it was called by the Admiralty, was 190 feet long, carried a 4-inch gun and an asdic set, and was equipped with depth charges for attacking submarines. It had a maximum speed of 15½ to 16 knots. At the same time the navy also selected the Bangor-class minesweeper for construction in shipyards across the country. The Bangor could double as an anti-submarine escort, was 162 feet long, armed with a 4-inch gun, could readily be fitted with asdic equipment, and could reach a speed of 16½ knots. In February 1940 the decision was made to build 64 corvettes, and orders were also placed for 14 Bangors. Another 14 Bangors were ordered before the end of August 1940. By the end of the year the first 14 corvettes were in service, and by December 1941 all except one of the original order had been completed.

The corvette has rightly been lauded for its ability to turn on a dime and outmanoeuvre a submarine. With its long endurance (particularly true of later versions) and its ability to bounce in the water like a cork rather than pound into heavy seas, it made an ideal escort and was an important asset to the Canadian and British navies. However, living conditions on board were terrible. Corvettes were what is known as wet ships. Seas breaking over them would result in salt water seeping in through hatches, ventilators, and leaky seams. For weeks on end their crews lived in a state of continual dampness, usually having to tolerate sea water mixed with food and sometimes vomit sloshing about on the deck. The atmosphere below became progressively more foul from day to day.

32 Bedford Basin, the superb natural harbour where hundreds of convoys assembled before leaving Halifax. 1941.

There'd be about 30 men in our quarters. Once we picked up 12 guys in a lifeboat and most of them came in with us. You could say it was crowded, a room hardly big enough to swing a small cat by the tail. Hammocks everywhere, messing table in the centre, and guys off watch sleeping, guys playing cards, writing letters, just staring at nothing, and half the time the whole goddamned Atlantic was trying to get in at us. That's a mess deck for you. If you opened the portholes any time but a nice summer day you'd freeze, and you couldn't open them at night. Blackouts. God! Just so you wouldn't get fished, torpedoed.

Say, 15 or 20 days across, Halifax, to Londonderry—20 days if you had a few old tubbers doing 8 knots—and the smell just got worse and worse. No showers, you see. The navy rule, no showers on ships at sea. Not even for officers and P.O.'s. You could shave, but some never did and some kids were so young they never had to. Oh, I tell you, it was a grand life, great to be a sailor. The ship was a floating pigpen of stink. You couldn't get away from it. The butter tasted of it. The cooks used to bake bread every night and the bread smelled of feet and armpits. There must be something about eggs. They'd pick up the smell. Everything did, and that goes for meat too.[3]

Until naval construction provided sufficient escorts, armed yachts helped to fill the gap, but since they had little or no anti-submarine capacity they provided only the appearance of a defence against submarine attack, although the experience their crews received was good training. In October 1940, as part of the 'destroyers for bases' deal negotiated between Britain and the U.S., six of the fifty 20-year-old

American destroyers involved came to the RCN as a gift from Britain. Known because of their four funnels as 'four-stackers', they were unstable in heavy seas, as difficult to manoeuvre as battleships and extremely uncomfortable. The ship's wheel, recalled the captain of HMCS *St. Croix*, was 'as large as a normal cart wheel'—what you might expect to find in a Mississippi paddle boat. Rather than the hydraulic lines by which up-to-date ships transmitted helm movements to the steering engine, the four-stackers had wires 'which ran right along the deck ... and were liable to be stuck by ice or even a fender rolling against them'. Ships' captains and engineers lived in a perpetual nightmare because so many things could go wrong; but, as sailors so often do, they developed a perverse affection for their difficult charges.

The American destroyers did not join the fleet until December 1940. By that time Canada's seven original destroyers had all sailed for British waters to assist in the evacuation of forces from France and the protection of convoys in the eastern Atlantic. Canada suffered its first naval loss on June 25 when HMCS *Fraser* was cut in two by the cruiser HMS *Calcutta* while manoeuvring at close quarters by night. Four months later HMCS *Margaree*, a destroyer newly commissioned into the RCN, was sliced in half by a merchant ship when a convoy was altering course at night (an evasive tactic against submarines) on October 23. On the night of December 1 HMCS *Saguenay*—which, with two British destroyers, was defending a homeward-bound convoy from Gibraltar against continuous U-boat attack—surprised an enemy submarine on the surface. The Canadian ship received a torpedo that blew off 40 or 50 feet of her bows as a reward for her efforts. By the time 1940 drew to a close, therefore, the RCN had been tested in combat.

German submarines were attacking merchant ships much further west by this time because they had new long-range submarines and new bases in the Bay of Biscay. For the most part the victims were ships steaming independently, stragglers from convoys, and slow convoys either with inadequate escort or beyond the endurance limits of warships and aircraft based in Britain and Northern Ireland. Escort vessels could not detect surfaced U-boats because their asdic worked only under water, and U-boats could move rapidly into the paths of convoys at night and attack before they had been discovered, creating extreme confusion as they picked off their targets and then escaped in the darkness. Until new tactics could be developed, little could be done about this.

The loss of ships from westbound convoys that had been dispersed because their escorts had reached the limits of their endurance and had to turn back was partly solved by establishing new bases for ships and aircraft in Iceland and Newfoundland early in 1941. The Newfoundland bases, after considerable negotiation, became a Canadian responsibility, and the Newfoundland Escort

33   This photograph, taken on the bridge of HMCS *Barrie* in the North Atlantic in June 1945 (with the war just over in Europe), shows what conditions were like on a relatively calm day. The man on the left holds a cup of hot, sweet cocoa ('ki'). The staple remedy for cold, weariness, hunger, and thirst, it revived the energy and spirit of men on watch.

34   On board the corvette HMCS
Kamsack in August 1942. Men
slung their hammocks over the
tables in the messdecks of British-
and Canadian-built warships.

Force—or, as it was later called, the Mid-Ocean Escort Force—was placed under the command of a Canadian officer, Commodore L.W. Murray, who reported to the British Commander-in-Chief, Western Approaches, in Liverpool. The first seven RCN corvettes arrived at St John's on May 27, 1941, and in June all Canadian destroyers were withdrawn from British home waters for service with the Newfoundland Force.

The navy had been preceded in Newfoundland by the RCAF. Canadian aircraft had been flying patrols from Gander since 1939, and the first detachment of 10 Bomber and Reconnaissance Squadron (the term used for maritime patrol squadrons) had been stationed at Gander since June 1940. By June 1941 the squadron, with its 16 Douglas Digby aircraft, provided a limited adjunct to the Newfoundland Escort Force. In July four Catalina Flying Boats of 116 Squadron began operations from Botwood, the seaplane base near Gander. By this time naval and air staffs in Britain had devised tactics for both ships and aircraft to deal with night attacks by submarines, Canadians had received briefings on the new developments, and the likelihood of Canada's making a major and autonomous Canadian military contribution to the Battle of the Atlantic had suddenly become very strong.

At this stage in the war both the navy and air force had to lean heavily on a small nucleus of trained personnel, especially the few who now had first-hand experience of anti-submarine warfare. Destroying submarines was not a pastime for novices. It demanded instinct based on familiarity with the prey and had to be done in all kinds of sea and weather conditions. The vast majority of ships' companies were totally inexperienced—innocents abroad. The captain of one corvette has written:

> With more than three-quarters of the complement as fresh to the sea as the ship herself, it was hard to perform our simple task; hard to keep steam up, avoid the shoals or even steer a straight course. Had anything warlike occurred there would have been a shambles.[4]

The RCAF had less difficulty because aircrew training, although no less demanding mentally than basic naval training, did not involve the fundamental readjustments necessary to living and working at sea. Unlike the navy, however, the ranks of airmen flying with Eastern Air Command of the RCAF had not been bolstered by men who were familiar with the war against U-boats in the eastern Atlantic. British officers from Coastal Command of the RAF as well as Canadian naval officers had visited Canadian squadrons and lectured on the newest anti-submarine tactics, but Canadian airmen had no opportunity to experiment with them until a U-boat ventured into their patrol area, within 600 miles of the east coast of Newfoundland.

The first such U-boat was detected by shore-based radio direction-finding stations on May 21, but neither ships nor aircraft were able to

locate and attack it. In the following months there was an increasing number of contacts in the Northwest Atlantic, but not one U-boat was destroyed. Sometimes sheer bad luck robbed the Canadian naval and air forces of success; more often unfamiliarity with their duties and inexperience in identifying targets were the cause of failure.

On September 11, 1941, the corvettes *Chambly* and *Moosejaw* abandoned a training cruise in order to defend SC-42, a convoy of 64 ships and 4 escorts attacked by 8 submarines off the east coast of Greenland. This led to the first successful Canadian attack on a submerged U-boat, U-501 (which was on her first operational cruise)—the result of wise decisions by the commanding officer, Commander J.S.D. Prentice, pinpoint navigation by an officer brought up in the merchant service, efficient classification of the underwater contact by a well-trained sonar team, and a measure of luck. When U-501 blew her tanks and surfaced, *Moosejaw* fired only one round with her 4-inch gun because the next shell jammed in the breach. The first lieutenant of *Chambly* then led a group that attempted to retrieve the U-boat's papers, but the sea-cocks were open and the vessel quickly sank, one Canadian stoker in the boarding party being drowned. Commander Prentice, who had come out of retirement in the Cariboo country after twenty years' service in the Royal Navy, was reported to have stood nonchalantly on the bridge of *Chambly* issuing orders, his monocle at the right angle. 'Not once did it fall out,' an officer commented. 'It looked as if it were part of his face.'[5]

In October 1941 Canadian naval forces were put under American 'co-ordinating supervision', as it was tactfully described, even though the United States was officially neutral. This arrangement made tactical sense in so far as it replaced control by the British Commander-in-Chief, Western Approaches, based in England with an American commander in Argentia (one of the British bases exchanged for destroyers), who would be much closer to the situation. But Canada was not consulted. Murray was most unhappy about the decision. He believed that the British were prepared, in his words, 'to sell us down the river' in order to keep the Americans on the western side of the Atlantic by giving them full responsibility in Newfoundland.[6]

American warships of both the Navy and Coast Guard now began to convoy shipping from American ports and sometimes found themselves in combat with U-boats far out in the ocean, even though ships in American waters were immune from attack because Hitler did not want to provoke Roosevelt. After the United States became a belligerent on December 7, German U-boats were let loose in American waters. American ships withdrew from the Newfoundland bases to supplement the Atlantic and Pacific fleets, leaving behind only a few Coast Guard cutters, and the 11 Canadian destroyers and 43 corvettes remaining in Newfoundland were faced with almost impossible demands on their services.

35 HMCS *Sackville* was typical of the unimproved corvettes the RCN put up with long after the British had made significant improvements in the construction and equipment of such vessels.

36 HMCS *St Croix* entering Halifax harbour after a storm on December 18, 1940. The ship had broached to and nearly capsized in a hurricane.

37 Commander J.S.D. Prentice, well known for the monocle he wore even at the height of battle, engineered the first submarine kill by Canadian forces.

Early in 1942 the centre of gravity for the Battle of the Atlantic shifted to the American seaboard, where coastal shipping sailed without protection. American naval doctrine held that convoys without protection were far more dangerous than no convoys at all—a plausible view. Why place a lot of defenceless ships together and provide submarines with a huge target? Furthermore, the U.S. Navy, with its Pacific responsibilities, was desperately short of escorts. Unfortunately this strategy took little account of the British experience, which had shown that the rate of sinkings among ships in unprotected convoys was incomparably smaller than among individual merchant vessels.

The result was that in the first half of 1942 the American coastline took on the nature of a shooting gallery. U-boat commanders called this period the 'Goldene Zeitalte', which has been loosely translated as the 'Happy Time'.[7] Night after night submarines rose to the surface, almost at leisure, and picked off ships, many of them silhouetted against the undimmed lights of the shoreline, with torpedoes or gunfire. From January to July 1942 nearly 400 ships were sunk between the latitude of Cape Cod and the equator, west of the

40th meridian, for the loss of only 7 U-boats. The benefits of convoys—even with inadequate sea and air escorts—were finally acknowledged by U.S. naval authorities, and normal traffic resumed under a convoy organization. In March 1942 the first convoy sailed from Halifax to Boston; in July convoys began to sail further down the coast. Such was the shortage of escorts that Canada's small and already overburdened fleet was called upon to protect southward-bound shipping. Thus in August HMCS *Oakville* found herself in the Caribbean, where she sank one U-boat.

The Canadian coastline was not immune from the enemy onslaught. By the end of July about 42 ships, including 6 in convoy, had been sunk in the waters off Canada and Newfoundland, while only 3 U-boats had been destroyed. Between May and September 3, U-boats sank 19 merchantmen and 2 escort vessels in the St Lawrence. With its heavy shipping, the river was of course thronged with targets, but other conditions also accounted for the heavy losses. Warm and cold currents, combined with the constantly changing density of the river's mouth, built up layers through which sonar could not penetrate and there was a scarcity of escort vessels. A continuous U-boat offensive resulting in many sinkings within sight of land would no doubt have brought down the wrath of the voters on the government, so in September 1942 the gulf and river were closed to overseas shipping. The amount of cargo shipped out of Canada fell by more than 25 per cent, which amounted to a victory for the U-boats won at virtually no cost to Germany.

The Canadian naval service, with 188 warships and 16,000 men serving at sea, could now provide nearly half the surface escorts for convoys from North America to Britain. (Because of the availability of tankers that could fuel escorts at sea, Londonderry in Northern Ireland—rather than Iceland—became the eastern terminal for Canadian warships in February 1942.) The RCAF, with 8 maritime patrol squadrons and 78 aircraft on the Atlantic seaboard, was carrying out increased air surveillance of the Northwest Atlantic. But as yet air support for convoys was insufficient. That section of the mid-Atlantic called by the Germans the Black Pit, where no available shore-based aircraft could fly because of their limited endurance, harboured packs of U-boats that gathered on the surface to co-ordinate their attacks. The only aircraft that could cover the region were VLR (Very Long Range) Liberators, which were Consolidated-B24 bombers with modifications that increased their endurance to 16 hours. The first squadron of Liberators, based in Britain, was not available until December 1942. But weather conditions often kept them from flying, so that at the crucial moment a number of British and Canadian convoys were deprived of air cover.

During the winter of 1942-3 the performance of both the Canadian navy and the air force was clearly less effective than that of British forces in the same period. Only 7 of 79 submarine sinkings on the

9 Depth charges being dropped over the stern of HMCS *Saguenay* before her final accident.

8 Survivors from the torpedoed merchant ship S.S. *Eurymedon* coming on board HMCS *Ottawa*, September 1940.

North Atlantic convoy routes could be attributed to Canadian forces, 3 by ships and 4 by aircraft, and in January 1943 the British Director of Anti-Submarine Warfare observed: 'Eighty per cent of all ships torpedoed in the last two months were hit while being escorted by Canadian groups.'[8] There were good explanations for this dismal situation, but they did not make the criticism any more palatable.

Rapid expansion of the RCN from a small nucleus meant that the training and the maintenance of morale of a large number of inexperienced men became increasingly difficult. The service grew from 3,000 men in 1939 to 40,000 men by the end of 1943. Inevitably the large intake of recruits led to a decline in selection standards, and the quality of instruction suffered when operational demands reduced the available training time.

Another difficulty for the Canadians was poor equipment. Well after the time that the Battle of the Atlantic was at its height, Canadian ships were still without the latest improvements fitted in British escorts. Canadian corvettes did not have the extended fo'c's'les and modern bridges that afforded a little more protection for men against the elements and thus allowed them to function effectively when they contacted the enemy. Canadian warships did not have the latest radar equipment, so that only rarely could they detect submarines on the surface. Asdics were primitive in comparison with the new models in British ships. The only weapon Canadian ships had against submerged U-boats was the depth charge. Filled with high explosive, this 400-pound cylindrical bomb—looking more like an oil drum than a deadly missile—was dropped over the stern or thrown over the side; as it sank, a hydrostatic valve triggered the firing mechanism at a pre-set depth. If close enough to the submarine, two or more depth charges could crush a pressure hull; but to attack, the warship had to pass right over the submerged U-boat and in the process was likely to lose contact with it. British ships had been fitted with the more advanced hedgehog, which launched twenty-four 50-pound bombs or grenades ahead of the ship, and which exploded only on actual contact, thus avoiding the constant noise and disturbance of the water from the explosion of depth charges that had missed their target. Because of this, and because it was not necessary with an ahead-throwing weapon to pass right over the target, the ship had a much better chance of remaining in contact.

Canadian ships faced other difficulties, as a corvette captain recalled:

> To attack a submarine I had to station myself in the asdic house, watch the compass and direct the steering of the ship from this position, since there was no compass outside on the bridge. This was a bad arrangement and was subsequently altered.
>
> To begin with it was a bit of a squash inside the asdic house, and there always seemed to be wires leading from the compass in every direction, some attached to headphones; there was a drop-leaf table on one side and a folding stool which seemed to open up when trodden on; and there was my collapsible bunk which I had had fitted against the other side of the little compartment. Once wedged in alongside the compass it was a job to get yourself out. And to be able to make an exit was important. It was almost better to crane your neck in from outside through an open window. But that would have given you a distorted view of the compass card, and you would have needed the sight of a seagull to read the degrees.[9]

Canadian corvettes lacked gyro compasses and relied instead on the magnetic compass, whose needle wanders even in the calmest sea. Steering a precise course to attack a submarine was thus next to impossible. Many Canadian ships were without high-frequency direction finders or 'Huffduffs' (H/F/DF), which provided a rough bearing on the wireless communications of U-boat packs. Without Huffduffs, Canadian escorts had no way of locating submarines preparing to attack the convoy.

These deficiencies amounted to an equipment crisis of major proportions. After the Admiralty authorized innovations, there were long delays in processing them through Naval Service Headquarters in Ottawa. (These appear to have been caused by the shortage of personnel, the inadequacy of staff training, and the total absence of liaison with the Admiralty on technical matters.) The result was that alterations and additions in the RCN were a year or more behind those made for the Royal Navy.

The RCN was not blind to the situation. Staff and training organizations in Ottawa, Newfoundland, and Londonderry had been trying since early 1942 to improve fighting efficiency in Canadian ships. Their efforts had been frustrated in part by the constant distractions afforded by the need for more escorts, so that Canadian ships had less time than British in harbour and had to cut short more of their training periods. The strain of being at sea continuously for more than a year affected men's efficiency and sapped their morale.

> The worst time was dusk, when the dull day was fading and another ominous night was bearing down. I hated the sight of the yellowish-grey light, the dun seascape, the cold, curling waves as the evening dissolved into blackness.[10]

The shortage of equipment, the inadequacy of training, and the consequent shortcomings in performance remained unsolved problems until mid-1943, when the RCN began to catch up with the Royal Navy. Yet this atmosphere of gloom was occasionally brightened by recognized achievements and individual successes. The constant demand on escorts made it difficult to keep Canadian ships together in permanent groups. When they could be put into a group, their efficiency improved with teamwork and the morale of their personnel rose accordingly. HMCS *Skeena* and *Saguenay* were charter members of the 'Barber Pole' Group—so named after the red-and-white markings on the funnels of the vessels—which was recognized by British and Canadian naval authorities alike for its successful protection of convoys. Lieutenant-Commander K.L. Dyer, while captain of *Skeena*, invented a technique for breaking up U-boat night attacks with the simultaneous firing of 'starshell' by all escorts at the crucial moment when all submarines had gathered for the kill. The starshell released lighted flares that descended by parachute, lighting up the surrounding sea and forcing the U-boats to submerge.

Because of such accomplishments some Canadian naval officers in key positions were confident of the potential within the RCN and waged an ultimately successful campaign to have Canada's efforts in

41 Survivors from torpedoed merchant ships arrive at St John's, Nfld, in the British rescue trawler HMS *Northern Gift*, April 25, 1943.

the Battle of the Atlantic recognized by the creation of an autonomous Canadian command in the Northwest Atlantic. If this seems anomalous, or at least premature, when the efficiency of Canadian forces was in the main so questionable, it was no more anomalous than having the Canadian ships and aircraft based on Newfoundland under the control of an American officer. In 1941 the Canadians in Newfoundland had initiated the Americans into the complexities of convoy organization and anti-submarine warfare. Co-operation had been excellent and the American staff had been willing pupils. Their commander had exercised his authority with tact and offered useful assistance out of his own limited resources. By late 1942, however, American forces had dwindled away to a mere 2 per cent of the naval escorts on the Mid-Ocean Escort route, compared with 48 per cent now provided by the RCN. Canadian aircraft squadrons in the region outnumbered American squadrons by eight to three. Thus Task Force 24, under American Command, had more Canadian than American content. And whatever the shortcomings in the fleet, there were no complaints about the efficiency of the command and staff organizations at St John's or Halifax.

As a result of the convoy conference held in Washington in March 1943, Rear-Admiral Murray, with his headquarters in Halifax, became Commander-in-Chief Canadian North West Atlantic on April 30, 1943, the first and only theatre commander in the history of the Royal Canadian Navy. His appointment proved that the Allies recognized not only Canada's right, but also its ability, to control the sea and air forces operating in the region closest to its own territory.

An important and not sufficiently recognized contribution to the Battle of the Atlantic was the ferrying of aircraft across the ocean. In 1940 Britain's Minister of Aircraft Production, the Canadian-born Lord Beaverbrook, persuaded Churchill to support his scheme for an Atlantic Ferry Organization (ATFERO) over the protests of the Air Ministry (which advocated transporting all aircraft by sea). Pilots from the British Overseas Airways Corporation and other sources were to fly badly needed bombers and flying boats—made in the U.S.A. and Canada—from ATFERO's base in Montreal to Britain, by way of Gander, Nfld.

In August 1940 Sir Edward Beatty, president of the CPR, took the responsibility of setting up the scheme with a staff of men experienced in transport and aviation. Besides prominent Canadian executives in business and industry who offered their services as 'dollar-a-year' men, the staff included D.C.T. Bennett, later famous for his exploits in the Pathfinder Group of Bomber Command, four other British and American pilots who were all first-class navigators, and a number of Canadian radio operators. P.D. McTaggart-Cowan of the Canadian Department of Transport was ATFERO's chief meteorological officer, perhaps the most important person in an organization that depended so much on the weather.

Flying the Atlantic in 1940 was a new and dangerous business. Since the first crossing by Alcock and Brown in a Vickers Vimy in 1919—a crossing that ended with a forced landing in an Irish bog—there had been many attempts and few successes. Charles Lindbergh's dramatic exploit in *The Spirit of St. Louis* in 1927 still ranked as the greatest of transatlantic flying achievements. Not until 1939, however, did the British Overseas Airways Corporation begin limited flying-boat services across the Atlantic. Nothing was known about the behaviour of upper air currents over the ocean: before McTaggart-Cowan there was no meteorological forecasting service. In wartime there could be no assistance from ships stationed along the route to stay in communication or help guide aircraft.

Equally there was a dearth of pilots with sufficient ability in navigation to know their exact position after flying for many hours beyond sight of land. There were not enough to be found in the British Overseas Airways Corporation or from American sources to maintain a continuous ferry service on a large scale. Fortunately the few who were available proved so effective, and the civilian pilots

42 A Lockheed Hudson of 11 Squadron patrolling off Halifax in 1940.

who joined them, including many Canadians, proved so adaptable that the actual navigation and flying problems were resolved.

There were other difficulties—deliveries from the factories to Montreal were slow, and the organization of flights was not at first very efficient—but by May 1941 the system was working reasonably well. By August ATFERO had delivered 315 aircraft to Britain, leaving a backlog of 133 at Dorval and Gander still awaiting pilots to fly them across the ocean. The once-revolutionary idea of risking military aircraft in direct transoceanic flights to their far-off destinations had taken firm hold. This being the case, and a massive flow of such aircraft now being expected, British and American air force authorities no longer thought such an informal arrangement as ATFERO would be adequate to handle the large number of aircraft now expected to pass through the system. In August 1941 the RAF established Ferry Command under Air Marshal Sir F.W. Bowhill, thus replacing the civil organization with a service one. Civilians and servicemen alike worked for the new command in both operational and military capacities, while new air and meteorological stations sprang up on both sides of the Atlantic to provide facilities for handling increased deliveries and the weather forecasting that consequently became necessary.

As crucial sea battles were being fought beneath them, aircraft flew from Newfoundland to Northern Ireland or Scotland in a steady stream; and by a southern route from New York to Africa, overland to the Mediterranean theatre, and even to India. Lockheed Hudsons, the first large group of aircraft ordered from the United States, were used for British Coastal Command. (It may be asked why, if they could fly the Atlantic, they could not provide coverage over the Black

Pit in 1942 and 1943. The answer is that, although their overload fuel tanks gave them the range to fly the 1,500-mile distance from Gander to Northern Ireland, they had an effective patrolling range with all their fighting equipment of only about 450 miles.) Consolidated Catalina Flying Boats, a longer-range aircraft (about 600 miles), were also delivered for Coastal Command. There were four-engined bombers, Liberators, and Flying Fortresses, including late in 1942 the VLR Liberators, which would play an important part in the defeat of the German attack on shipping.

The pilots included British, Canadian, and American civilians and servicemen—some experienced airmen and others fledglings from the BCATP. By June 1943 Ferry Command had delivered 2,241 aircraft, besides many important persons, mail, and much-needed equipment. In terms of tonnage and men, however, the achievement was small compared with that of the convoys.

The importance of shipping to the defeat of the Axis powers had never been more evident. At the great strategic conference at Casablanca in January and at the so-called Trident Conference at Washington in May, the first object the Allies agreed to strive for in the coming year was control of the Atlantic. Upon this depended the success of the other three aims: the strategic air offensive against Ger-

A British Liberator shepherding an Atlantic convoy in 1944. It was the very long-range maritime patrol aircraft that closed the gap in the mid-Atlantic, making U-boat attacks on convoys in what was known as 'the Black Pit' hazardous in the extreme.

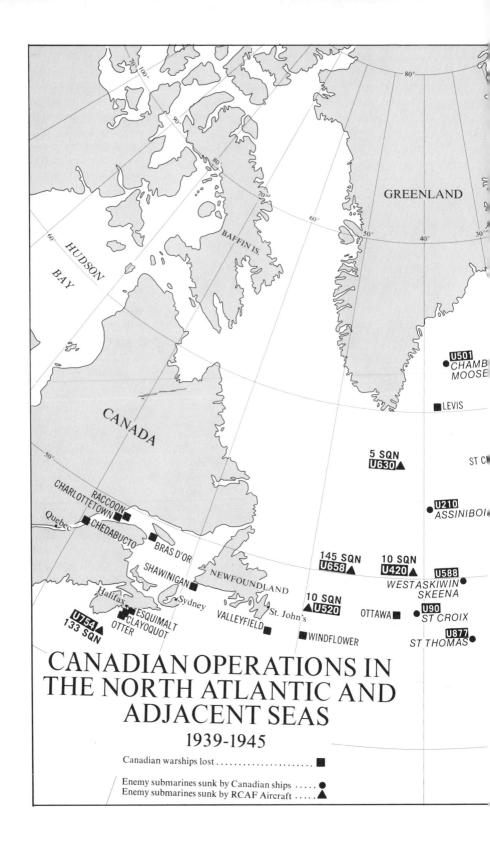

GREENLAND

HUDSON
BAY

BAFFIN IS.

CANADA

U501
●CHAMB
MOOSE

■LEVIS

5 SQN
U630▲

ST C

U210
●ASSINIBOI

RACCOON
CHARLOTTETOWN■
Quebec ●CHEDABUCTO
BRAS D'OR

145 SQN
U658▲

10 SQN
U420▲

U588

WESTASKIWIN●
SKEENA

SHAWINIGAN■
NEWFOUNDLAND
10 SQN
▲U520

OTTAWA■
U90
●ST CROIX

Halifax■
Sydney
VALLEYFIELD●
St. John's

U754▲
133 SQN
ESQUIMALT
CLAYOQUOT
OTTER
WINDFLOWER

U877
●ST THOMAS

CANADIAN OPERATIONS IN THE NORTH ATLANTIC AND ADJACENT SEAS

1939-1945

Canadian warships lost . . . . ■

Enemy submarines sunk by Canadian ships . . . . . ●
Enemy submarines sunk by RCAF Aircraft . . . . . ▲

(Note: U-484 was sunk by HMCS Hespeler and Dunver in co-operation with 423 Squadron RCAF.)

(NOTE: U-94, sunk in the Caribbean by HMCS Oakville in co-operation with U.S. forces, is not shown) many; a full-scale invasion of Europe from Britain; and a campaign in the Mediterranean theatre to eliminate Italy from the war. The military supplies needed to take these initiatives demanded a surplus over the minimum shipping requirements for survival not only in Britain but also in parts of the Mediterranean theatre and for the starving populations of India. For three years British and American specialists in shipping control had struggled to meet increasing worldwide commitments when submarine losses constantly reduced the number of ships available to them. Increasing productivity in American shipyards and the defeat of the submarine in the Atlantic brought a dramatic change in the situation. The Atlantic bridge was now on a firm foundation. For Canada this marked the end of a severe apprenticeship and the beginning of much-improved effectiveness in the war at sea.

The Canadian achievements of the next two years resulted from the ability to take advantage, for the first time, of the latest developments in anti-submarine warfare. In 1942 operations research scientists had demonstrated the simple mathematical truth that if you doubled the number of merchant ships, you did not have to double the number of warships needed to defend the convoy. Larger convoys became more common and in the spring of 1943 there were some escorts to spare. These formed roving 'Support Groups' that—instead of being tied to one convoy—could sail rapidly to any spot where submarines were attacking. Support Groups were particularly lethal when they included the aircraft carriers converted from merchant ships in North American shipyards and known as 'Woolworth' or Escort Carriers. Air reconnaissance for convoys was also made possible by the British invention of small flight decks on merchant ships, known as MAC (merchant aircraft carriers) ships, or catapults on CAM (Catapult Aircraft Merchantmen) ships from which aircraft flew off as needed. Other inventions, including improved airborne radar and 'Leigh Lights' (high-powered floodlights) fitted in maritime aircraft, exposed surfaced U-boats to devastating surprise night attacks.

By September 1943 there were over 21,000 Canadians at sea, most of them in the RCN's 229 major fighting ships and largely concentrated in the Western or Mid-Ocean Escort Forces. In Eastern Air Command there were 165 aircraft in 11 maritime patrol squadrons, 7 of them based on the Canadian mainland or Prince Edward Island, 4 based on Newfoundland. In the United Kingdom's Coastal Command, of 40 anti-submarine squadrons 3 were Canadian, while 2 of the 7 squadrons used for air strikes against enemy shipping off the north coast of Scotland, in the North Sea, the English Channel, and the Bay of Biscay were also Canadian. In addition, many individual Canadians flew in British squadrons.

Several 'River' class destroyers had been acquired from the Royal

44 Beaufighters attacking enemy shipping in the North Sea. 1944.

Navy and a few of the new British-designed frigates, developed as a result of experience in the war, were beginning to join the fleet. Escort and Support Groups usually included one or two destroyers, and 13 Canadian destroyers were still used in this role. As for aircraft, one Canadian squadron was now flying VLR Liberators from Newfoundland, two were flying Cansos (the Canadian amphibian version of the Consolidated Catalina flying boat), and the other squadrons of Eastern Air Command were flying twin-engined Hudson or Ventura planes. The RCAF squadrons with Coastal Command flew Sunderland flying boats and twin-engined Wellington bombers for anti-submarine work; and Bristol Beaufighters, Wellingtons, or Hampden bombers were used for anti-shipping strikes. The navy was catching up slowly with British equipment as ships went into refit. Eastern Air Command squadrons were behind, in that none of their aircraft yet had the Leigh Light and the latest radar equipment was not always available, but in other respects they were up-to-date.

Both organization and training had improved immensely. Because Nova Scotia and Newfoundland weather was usually too dirty for efficient training conditions the Canadians, with extensive British support, set up a base in Bermuda. But the most famous and possibly

45 Two of the aircrew of a Sunderland flying boat in 422 Squadron snatch a few moments' sleep. 1944.

the most effective training for ships' companies was provided in the ordinarily sleepy little harbour of Tobermory, Scotland. There a retired rear-admiral of the Royal Navy, in his wartime rank of commodore, established a reputation for rapid results by means of merciless driving, surprise, and a perverse sense of humour. Gilbert Stephenson, 'The Terror of Tobermory', was one of the unforgettable experiences of all those Canadians who had to work up their ships on the eastern side of the ocean.

RCAF personnel in training did not receive the same sort of shock treatment—the needs of fighting an aircraft with a crew of six or eight men were different from those of a warship. Flying skills, navigating, gunnery, and bombing were the vital requirements, carefully nurtured by hours of flying training in Operational Training Units and then in the squadrons themselves.

On September 16, 1943, the 9th Support Group (EG-9) was en route to the Bay of Biscay. One of the first groups with Canadian ships, it included the destroyer *St. Croix* and the corvettes *Chambly*, *Sackville*, and *Morden*, all with good combat records. As was often the case, the senior officer was in a British ship, the frigate *Itchen*. A pack of 19 U-boats was at this same time moving into a line across the path of 3 convoys at sea or about to sail. Alerted by daily German position reports, British naval authorities eventually diverted EG-9 to the defence of 2 westbound convoys leaving Liverpool. These convoys, ONS-18 and ON-202, joined forces and by September 20, 68 merchant ships found themselves under the protection of 7 British, 7 Canadian, and 3 French escorts. Air cover was plentiful. VLR Liberators from Britain and, as the ships moved further west, from New-foundland carried out aggressive sweeps over and around the convoy. A MAC ship ensured the availability of Swordfish aeroplanes for local reconnaissance.

The Germans were hoping for a breakthrough with their new acoustic torpedo, which homed on the noise of ships' engines and was designed to neutralize the escorts before submarines tried to attack the convoy. By the time EG-9 arrived, two escorts had already been damaged in engagements with submarines and forced to return to harbour. On the other hand, a Canadian Liberator, carrying out a sweep on its return to base from Britain, had attacked and destroyed U-341 on September 19. Then a British Liberator sank U-338 with a new type of British acoustic torpedo on September 20; and the British destroyer *Keppel* sank U-229 two days later. Two more U-boats were seriously damaged. In exchange, 6 merchant ships and 3 escorts —HMCS *St. Croix*, the British corvette *Polyanthus*, and HMS *Itchen* —were sunk.

This convoy was the occasion of one of the most remarkable survival experiences of the war. When the *St. Croix* was torpedoed on September 20, Able Seaman Fisher, a stoker, obeyed orders to abandon ship and took charge of the ship's whaler. Amid the confusion and shock of sudden disaster—among several explosions, he heard the torpedoing of *Polyanthus*—he and his companions hauled men out of the water until there were twenty-four in the 27-foot boat. Constantly taking seas over the side and leaking from several holes, the vessel drifted all night. Then the survivors were rescued by *Itchen*. The next day, September 22, *Itchen* attacked a submarine:

> There were a lot of bubbles and oil and we were sure we had got a sub and we were happy. We all went below and tried to sleep. About a quarter to nine, 22nd. September, action stations went again. We went to the upper deck where it was quite cold and very dark. Around nine our searchlight went on and there was a sub in the beam. . . .Then the forward gun went off but the shell landed short and the bridge gunners started to fire. There was an explosion. We had been torpedoed. I was blown about thirty feet and landed against a gun deck. I got up, the ship was listing and I could hear water rushing in. I couldn't see a thing. . . .Just before I jumped over the side I called my chum Mackenzie, but there was no answer. So I dove over the side. As I hit the water there was a terrible explosion. I was sucked under and nearly lost consciousness. My insides seemed to be squeezed out of me. I was choking as I struggled back to the surface again, got a breath of air, and a wave took me under. . . .I came up. . .and swam about thirty or forty feet and looked back at the propellers of the *Itchen* which were just disappearing. She had gone down in about forty seconds.[11]

A board floated by and Fisher hung on to it with another man, but his companion went under after about an hour. 'Then. . .I started to

46 The naval dockyard, Halifax, April 27, 1944. A MAC ship is at anchor behind the vertical crane boom, three frigates are alongside, and two frigates are manoeuvring with tugs. Also to be seen are minesweepers and a boom gate vessel.

run into quite a few bodies,' he recalled, 'and the convoy started to pass us. The wash from the ships would wash us back and forth, we would go under and choke and there was a lot of oil and small boards that would slap us in the face. Then the star shells stopped going up and it got very dark.' Miraculously he was plucked out of the sea by Polish hands from a merchantman in convoy some time in the following hour. All his shipmates died, as did all but two of the combined ships' companies of *Polyanthus* and *Itchen*.

Terrible sacrifices: yet in the harsh currency of war they were far from worthless. After analysing the experiences of this convoy it was easy to devise a means of diverting acoustic torpedoes by towing a noise-maker astern of each warship, and the merchant shipping lost in September was replaced without difficulty. Convoy SC-143—39 merchantmen and one MAC ship—sailed from Halifax on September 28 to run the gauntlet against 18 U-boats. Although one of the escorts, the Polish destroyer *Orkan*, was torpedoed on October 8. British Liberators destroyed U-419 and U-643 astern of the convoy, and a Canadian Sunderland flying boat of 432 Squadron sank U-610

35 miles away. After the air escort departed that night a submarine managed to hit one merchant ship, which sank—the sole reward for the Germans.

The centre of gravity in the anti-submarine war now shifted because operations in the mid-Atlantic failed to produce results for the anti-shipping efforts of submarines. In three months only 9 of 2,468 merchant ships had been sunk in exchange for 25 U-boats—5 destroyed by warships, 6 by United States naval carrier-borne aircraft, 13 by shore-based aircraft (including 2 Canadian), and one by warships and shore-based aircraft combined. The German navy could not stand such heavy losses any longer. This spelled the end of wolf-pack tactics on northern routes and the renewal of efforts against Gibraltar convoys with the help of aircraft based in France.

The Luftwaffe had not co-operated very well with U-boats over the years, largely because of inter-service rivalry. All the same, developments by the Germans in combined sea and air attack against naval forces in European waters amounted to a serious potential danger in late 1943. Their newest weapons were glider bombs. With a speed of 300-400 knots, and carrying 1,100 pounds of explosive, they could be directed towards their targets by radio control. Their first use in the Bay of Biscay in August 1943 had resulted in the destruction of the destroyer HMS *Egret* and in serious damage to HMCS *Athabaskan*. Now glider bombs were about to be used against convoys.

The first potential victim of the new German offensive was a convoy of 66 ships and 7 escorts sailing from Gibraltar on November 14. Three lines of U-boats—a total of 28 submarines—lay in wait across the convoy's path. German reconnaissance aircraft made contact on November 16, and attacks began on the 18th. Three days later the convoy emerged from its ordeal, which included a glider-bomb attack on the 21st, with one escort damaged, two British aircraft shot down by submarines under attack, one merchantman sunk, and another damaged. The escorting forces had in turn sunk three U-boats, damaged a fourth, and shot down five enemy aircraft.

The first Canadian ships to share in the triumph of this important battle were in the 5th Support Group. On November 20 the corvettes *Snowberry* and *Calgary* combined with the British frigate *Nene* to sink U-536. HMCS *Prince Robert*, an armed merchant vessel converted to an anti-aircraft ship, appeared on the scene when Heinkel 177s were in the act of unleashing their glider bombs on the 21st. Her powerful armament provided a barrage in the convoy's wake.

By this time more and more effective Canadian naval forces were gravitating to the eastern Atlantic. This was a trend that had begun to increase in momentum late in 1942 when Canadian corvettes first went to the Mediterranean. There had also been a very small Canadian component among the flotillas of landing craft for the North African invasion in November 1942. In 1943, 25 landing craft of the 55th and 61st Canadian LCA (Landing Craft, Assault) flotillas and 24

47 U-744 surfaces near HMCS *Chaudière* after a hunt of 29½ hours. March 6, 1944.

craft of the 80th and 81st LCM (Landing Craft, Mechanized) flotillas landed British infantry and mechanical equipment for the invasion of Sicily that would take place on July 10.

It was still necessary to protect ships on the North Atlantic sea lanes, but there were very few U-boats left in the western Atlantic. Since the October battle not one submarine had been sunk by Canadian forces west of the 27th meridian, although a Canadian frigate, HMCS *Valleyfield*, had been sunk just off Newfoundland on May 6, 1944. However, Canadian sea and air forces working in the eastern Atlantic, in the Arctic, and in British home waters were extremely active against the enemy. The Canso flying boats of 162 Squadron RCAF, transferred from its Newfoundland base to Iceland in January 1944, did especially well as the Germans tried desperately to move submarines based in Norway against invasion forces in June 1944.

On April 17, 162 Squadron achieved its first success, convincingly illustrated in a series of five photographs of a U-boat's ordeal and the oil patch that marked its grave. In June the squadron's aircraft attacked 6 U-boats and destroyed 5 of them—one with the help of another squadron. In exchange 3 aircraft were destroyed, 13 airmen were killed and one was taken as a prisoner of war to Norway. Another aircraft was damaged by enemy fire. 'I am much impressed by the spirit of the aircrews, who appear to be quite undaunted by the odds they are facing,' wrote Sholto Douglas, the Air Officer Commanding British Coastal Command, of the squadron.[12]

On June 24 one of the two Victoria Crosses awarded to members of the RCAF was earned by a member of the squadron. David Hornell, who came from Toronto (where he had worked in the laboratory of the Goodyear Company and had been a Sunday School teacher), took his Canso flying boat in against a U-boat sighted just as the aircraft was about to turn home for base. The German fire became extremely heavy and accurate at a range of about a thousand yards. While Hornell concentrated on the best positioning for his attack, the starboard engine was hit, the wing caught fire, and as the fabric burned away, leaving nothing but the ribs of the wing, the aircraft began to shudder unbearably. It was necessary to shut down the starboard engine, which meant added difficulty in controlling the machine. Meanwhile the submarine was turning to port and Hornell had to alter course violently before dropping his depth charges. The manoeuvre demanded exceptional strength and skill by both pilot and co-pilot. Hornell then achieved a perfect 'straddle' before having to 'ditch'.

His problems had barely begun. As he completed the attack, the starboard engine fell off. At the best of times the Canso was a heavy machine to handle and alighting on rough seas was always a terrifying ordeal. On the first attempt Hornell's doomed Canso bounced from a wavetop, 150 feet into the air. On the second attempt it hurtled another 50 feet. Finally Hornell came in on a glide, hauling back with every ounce of strength on the control column, and came to rest in waves about 12 feet high. His crew managed to get out in spite of some minor injuries, but one of the dinghies overinflated and blew up, so eight men had to share one five-man dinghy.

Their plight seemed hopeless. Not one of their radio signals had been received ashore, so nobody knew where they were, let alone in

8 U-624 sinking after an attack by aircraft of 22 Squadron. March 30, 1944.

50 Searching a survivor of U-448 on board HMCS *Swansea*, April 14, 1944.

49 Survivors of U-448 scrambling aboard HMCS *Swansea* in the North Atlantic, April 14, 1944. *Swansea* shared the credit for sinking this U-boat with the British sloop *Pelican*.

what condition. By simple good luck a flying boat from a Norwegian squadron, on a routine patrol, saw one of their distress rockets and was able to send for help. This aircraft was also able to confirm that the submarine had been destroyed. Before a rescue could be effected, twenty-one hours after ditching—the weather becoming worse all the time—two of their number died and Hornell himself lapsed into a coma from which he could not be revived.

Most Canadian naval forces were in the English Channel and the Bay of Biscay to prevent German submarines and ships from attacking cross-channel shipping. Canadians tried to remain distinct from the British in their own escort groups and in their own motor torpedo boat and minesweeping flotillas. Some of their efforts cannot be measured by results—there were times when the simple presence of naval formations may have been enough to inhibit enemy activity—but RCN escort groups sank three submarines in July and August. It is noteworthy that on each occasion HMCS *Ottawa*, commanded by Commander J.S.D. Prentice, was in at the kill. Prentice, it will be remembered, had engineered the first Canadian U-boat sinking in 1941.

The Canadian Tribal class destroyers *Haida, Huron,* and *Athabaskan* were making their reputations in coastal warfare. In the early morning hours of April 29, 1944, *Haida* and *Athabaskan* engaged two small Elbing class destroyers off the French coast. In a furious battle *Haida* drove one of the Elbings ashore and destroyed it with gunfire, but *Athabaskan* was sunk by a German torpedo with the cost of 144 men. *Haida* conducted a daring rescue operation within range of the enemy's shore batteries and retrieved 38 survivors, but she had to leave the rest behind when daylight came. She also left behind her motor cutter with several volunteers to pick up more survivors. The vessel rescued 6 of the 91 men in the water, eluding capture by enemy minesweepers, and after an adventurous journey across the Channel returned to safety. A relatively small incident—repeated, matched, and surpassed elsewhere, no doubt —but for a young navy the kind of thing on which the pride of service is built.

The two Canadian MTB flotillas also took an active part in coastal warfare during 1944. Manned by personnel who had for the most part served an apprenticeship with British coastal forces, they began Channel operations in May. From the D-Day landings until late summer the 29th Flotilla covered the beaches near Le Havre, while the 65th engaged in search and pursuit in the western Channel. They were responsible for the destruction of four enemy ships in convoy and the damaging of several others, besides sinking and damaging a few enemy torpedo and gun boats. Two Canadian MTBs fell victim to mines. On February 14, 1945, the 29th Flotilla was destroyed when high-octane fuel in Ostend Harbour suddenly caught fire and spread, burning 5 of the flotilla's 8 boats and killing 26 men.

In August 1944 the RCN embarked upon naval air operations. HMS *Nabob*—which, although a British escort carrier, was commanded and for the most part manned by Canadian personnel—joined the Home Fleet for air strikes against German targets in Norway. After only three weeks she was the victim of a U-boat attack. Brilliant damage control saved the ship from destruction and aircraft from her British Fleet Air Arm squadrons, flying off a crazily angled flight deck, drove off a second submarine attack, but when *Nabob* got to dry dock she seemed to have reached her journey's end. She never again went to sea as a warship. (Initially sold as scrap after the war, she was resold to German and then Chinese owners, who renamed her the S.S. *Glory* in 1968.) HMS *Puncher*, the second British escort carrier commanded and manned principally by Canadians, had been used to transport aircraft across the Atlantic before she began air operations in February 1945.

The U-boats had to abandon all their Biscay bases by September 1944, but they moved to Norway and to North Sea bases and continued to threaten lines of communication. A revolutionary new development, the 'Schnorkel' mast, allowed air to be drawn into a submarine under the water and exhaust fumes to be expelled, thanks to a valve arrangement that, when waves broke over the mast, also prevented water from pouring into the vessel. Thus it became possible for new U-boats to run diesel engines while submerged, and consequently to charge batteries and proceed under water at speeds previously limited to surfaced submarines. As 1944 drew to a close, new and very large Type XXI U-boats with Schnorkels were coming into service for distant operations. (Other similarly fitted but smaller Type XXIII boats were also approaching completion.) Had it not been for the disruption of factories, shipyards, and canals by strategic bombing, and the capture of industrial towns by advancing armies in Europe, these new vessels would have been ready in large numbers early in 1945, providing a serious new threat because they were so difficult to find. Only after they had attacked could convoy escorts realize their presence—a throwback to the dark days of 1940.

The continuing danger of submarine attack ensured the continuing demand for Canadian anti-submarine sea and air forces in European waters. In trying to visualize Canadian efforts here, one must resort to statistics. At least 25 per cent of the 426 escort vessels in British home waters in 1945 were Canadian. W.S. Roskill, the British official historian, observes that the RCN 'thus came to carry as large a share of the struggle for control of Britain's coastal waters as it had borne in the Atlantic convoy battles of earlier phases.'[13] Results show that the effort in the eastern Atlantic late in the war was in fact much more significant than earlier convoy battles. Of the 27 U-boat kills credited to the RCN between 1939 and 1945, 20 occurred east of the 35th meridian of longitude, and 17 of those took place after November 20, 1943.

51 Survivors of HMCS *Esquimalt*, which was torpedoed off Halifax in April 1945.

52 U-190, which sur-
rendered at Bay Bulls,
Nfld, on May 14, 1945.

The air effort showed similar tendencies. In May 1945 there were 784 aircraft of Coastal Command, 511 of them used in anti-submarine warfare and the remainder for attacks on enemy shipping. They flew from bases as far north as Iceland and as far south as Gibraltar. A measure of the Canadian contribution to Coastal Command must include all Canadians who took part in its activities. Canadian squadrons formed just under 10 per cent of the total force; in addition, many RCAF aircrew were to be found in British squadrons. Of 178 submarines destroyed by aircraft of the Command during the whole course of the war, 16 were credited to Canadian squadrons. Of 110 U-boats not sunk but put out of action, 10 were damaged by RCAF aircraft. In anti-shipping operations, Canadian squadrons participated in the destruction or damage of 85 vessels, or 17 per cent of the total for Coastal Command. Most of the successes took place towards the end of the war: all the submarines sunk or damaged in the eastern Atlantic by Canadian aircraft met their fate after May 1943, and 67 of the 85 surface vessels sunk and damaged were a result of operations in 1944 and 1945. Like the RCN, therefore, the RCAF was proving itself a highly effective force now that it was on the enemy's doorstep.

Convoys still sailed across the Atlantic in 1945 and Canadian forces still provided a very large proportion of the escorts. Besides 10 squadrons of Eastern Air Command there were 8 escort groups of minesweepers and corvettes and 3 support groups of destroyers and frigates based on Halifax. Other small ships based on Halifax, St John's, Newfoundland, Saint John, Sydney, and Gaspé looked after coastal convoys or patrolled coastal waters. In the last year of the war they were roughly handled by U-boats returning to the North Atlantic. As already noted, HMCS *Valleyfield* was torpedoed off Newfoundland on May 6, 1944. The corvette *Shawinigan* in the Cabot Strait on November 24, 1944, and the Bangor minesweepers *Clayoquot* and *Esquimalt* on the Halifax approaches on December 23, 1944 and April 16, 1945 respectively all fell victim to torpedoes. U-boats off

Canada remained completely unmolested. Sea and air forces close to home were therefore not as effective as those overseas. Were they less efficient too? Possibly. But a categorical 'yes' or 'no' to this question cannot be given. There were too many variable factors to take into account, especially climate and water conditions affecting the peformance of equipment.

After May 8, 1945, victory in Europe gradually reduced the hectic pace. The navy immediately declared more than half its ships 'surplus to requirements' and all except two squadrons of Eastern Air Command could now be disbanded. On May 19, 1945, a Liberator from 10 Squadron sighted U-889 on the surface, 250 miles south-east of Cape Race. Two Bangor class minesweepers hove in sight and began to escort the submarine to harbour. The frigates Buckingham and Inch Arran took over the task and on the afternoon of May 13 received the U-boat commander's official surrender just off Shelburne, N.S. Two days earlier U-190 had surrendered at sea to the frigate Victoriaville and the corvette Thorlock. On the other side of the ocean, on May 19, a support group including one British and four Canadian frigates escorted fifteen surrendered U-boats into Loch Eriboll, Northern Ireland. The long black hulls aroused feelings of revulsion in the men who had been fighting them for so long, but they must also have felt a sense of relief. Even though the war against Japan still had to be won, the return to Europe was finally complete, unhampered by that tenacious German menace to the sea lanes.

Canadian seamen and airmen had played a memorable part in the sea war against Germany. Bridging the Atlantic would have been a longer and, perhaps—given the strategic importance of Newfoundland and the Mid-Ocean Escort Force—an impossible task without them. Their efforts are remembered in Canada every May, on Battle of the Atlantic Sunday. But the truth is, Canadians did not achieve their potential until after that battle had been won in 1943. It was not until the last year of the war against Germany that Canadian airmen and seamen—following British techniques and trained to a very large extent by the Royal Navy and Royal Air Force—proved themselves in versatile combinations of long-range patrol aircraft, anti-submarine escort groups, MTB and destroyer flotillas skilled in coastal warfare, and carrier task forces operating in the crowded waters of the Northwest European littoral.

5

THE ARMY OVERSEAS 1940-1943

The 1st Division, still largely untrained and unequipped, sailed for England in December 1939—training could be better carried out in the milder English winter climate. It soon settled in at Aldershot, the Victorian garrison town on Salisbury Plain, and training began during the second week of January. The Chief of the Imperial General Staff, General Sir Edmund Ironside, informed McNaughton that it would not be required in France 'until early May'.

The British had entered upon their coldest winter since 1894. While to the Canadians it was mild enough in terms of temperature, they were used to a drier cold and to insulated houses, storm doors and windows, and central heating. The Aldershot barrack blocks in which they found themselves housed were bleak and frigid structures of Boer War vintage, with one tiny open fireplace—for which there was never enough coal!—to heat each spartan barrack room. There was no provision for hot water or showers and even the cold-water supply was limited. There was also a shortage of equipment for training, and imagination was a poor substitute. As they practised the esoteric art of gunlaying without either guns or targets, Canadian gunners found themselves 'in odd postures making strange movements in response to barked out orders, the centre of attraction being a particular individual who would squat on an airy seat, twiddle his fingers and stare fixedly at nothing.'[1]

Another problem arose over the fact that the British were still relying on much of the tactical doctrine developed during the First World War. Military theorists like Liddell Hart and J.F.C. Fuller had long been advocating more modern techniques of warfare based on mobility, flexibility, speed, and co-operation of all arms. They were largely ignored by the British General Staff (though their ideas were enthusiastically adopted by the Germans). Canadian doctrine and training faithfully followed British practice. For the Hastings and Prince Edward Regiment 'the 1918 Pamphlet of Field Engineering was the Bible ... Miles of trenches grew and spread across Salisbury Plain and the pathetic futility of it went quite unnoticed. No voice cried out against that monumental folly.'[2]

On April 9 the 'phoney war' came to a sudden and violent end when the Germans launched their invasion of Norway and Denmark. Caught badly off balance, the British and their French allies responded in a confused and ill-considered fashion. They hoped to stop the enemy somewhere in central or northern Norway and hastily put together an expeditionary force to do so. The Canadians were caught up in the prevailing tumult. General McNaughton agreed that his troops might be used in an amphibious attack on Trondheim, a key port in central Norway. Control of Trondheim would block the German drive to the north and secure the light railway that brought Swedish iron ore—which could be worked into particularly highgrade steel—to tidewater at Narvik.

McNaughton, who never lacked drive and enthusiasm in these early days, accepted the British plan without referring it to Ottawa for Cabinet approval. Lester B. Pearson, then a foreign-service officer on the staff of the Canadian High Commissioner in London, felt that 'if the whole thing turns out badly ... then I would not wish to be in McNaughton's shoes if he agrees to the use of Canadians in this way without prior authorization from Ottawa.'[3] Nevertheless, by April 19 a contingent 1,300 strong, composed of the most advanced units in training, was waiting to embark at Dunfermline, Scotland, expecting to be the first Canadian ground forces to see action in the Second World War.

Perhaps luckily for McNaughton their hopes were soon frustrated. The Trondheim plan was changed and the Canadians found themselves back on Salisbury Plain. British and French forces bumbled ineffectually about the Norwegian coastline for another five weeks. The last British troops left Narvik on June 8, but by that time a far greater disaster had overtaken the Allies and the chaotic Norwegian operations had faded out of the headlines.

On May 10, 1940, the Germans had launched their attack in the west. Panzer divisions, supported by dive-bombers, swept across the Netherlands, Belgium, and northeastern France and ripped great holes in the British and French defences. The main thrust came through the tangled hills and forests of the Ardennes, which Allied strategists had dismissed as quite unsuitable for a major armoured attack. The Germans then swung north to cut off the British Expeditionary Force and the northern group of French armies from the main French forces in the south.

Again a scheme to employ the Canadians was quickly initiated. They would be landed at Calais to secure a port through which the BEF could be evacuated to England if necessary. General McNaughton, who was to command British troops in the Calais area as well as his own men, had orders to keep open the coast road to Dunkirk. However, only hours after an advance party consisting of McNaughton himself, four staff officers, and ten 'Mounties' of No. 1 Canadian Provost Corps arrived at Calais, the road was cut by German Panzers. At almost the same moment Canadian units began to arrive at Dover

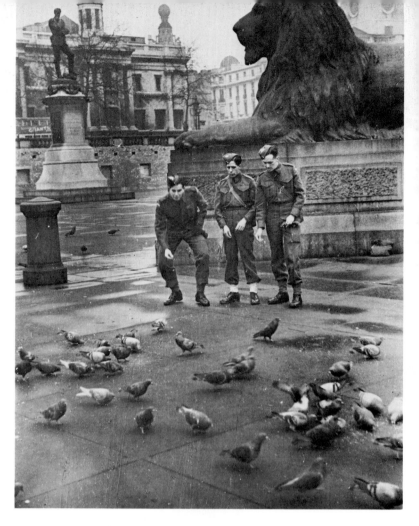

53 At the end of a brief leave, Canadians feed the early-morning pigeons in a deserted Trafalgar Square, London.

and by 11:00 a.m. on May 24 the first of them were embarked and ready to sail. They waited the rest of that day while the War Cabinet and War Office debated what should be done. The eventual conclusion was that there was now no purpose in sending the Canadians across the Channel. That night they were ordered back to Aldershot. 'A very flat feeling for all of us who had been highly keyed up,' recorded the 1st Brigade's diarist.[4]

As for the isolated BEF, a combination of luck and dogged determination enabled the greater part of it to escape by way of Dunkirk. Between May 26 and June 4 the Royal Navy, and what the Admiralty euphemistically described as 'other little ships', lifted more than a quarter-million men (including 70,000 Frenchmen) from the harbour quays, and another hundred thousand off the open beaches to the east of the town, and took them back to England. All Britons rejoiced at this 'miracle of Dunkirk', but Winston Churchill grimly reminded them that 'We must be careful not to assign to this deliverance the attributes of a victory. Wars are not won by evacuations.'

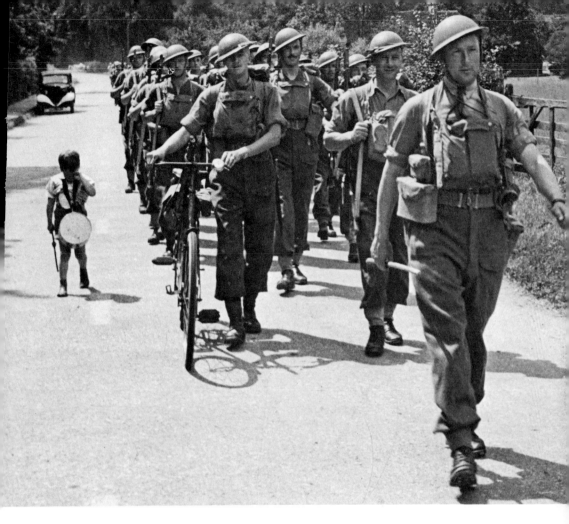

54 Major B.M. Hoffmeister (who as a major-general was to command a Canadian armoured division before the war ended) leading B Company of the Seaforth Highlanders of Canada down an English road in the summer of 1940.

With the British gone and the French thoroughly demoralized, the German blitzkrieg fanned out to the south and west, bypassing Paris. The Italians, anxious for a share of the spoils, declared war on Britain and France and invaded France from the south on June 10. It still seemed possible, however, that a western redoubt might be established in Brittany and early in June the two divisions in England still fit to move and fight—one British and one Canadian—were dispatched to Brest. The 52nd (Lowland) Division, already under orders to move, started to cross on June 7 and five days later the Canadians began to follow them. 'The general idea . . . was that these troops would not be available for operations until the Division had concentrated,' McNaughton recalled later,[5] but the now customary incompetence of British planning and staff work ensured that the first Canadians to land were sent forward piecemeal towards Le Mans, sometimes with neither officer nor senior NCO in charge. Wine was plentiful and the Canadians were popular; not all of them arrived in a soldierly manner and there were 'some reports of drunkenness and reckless driving'. Perhaps fortunately, the German spearheads were still more than 40 miles away.

On June 14, the day Paris fell, the British War Office came to terms with reality and ordered the evacuation of this second Expeditionary Force. The Canadians withdrew, leaving behind most of the 1st Brigade's transport and heavy equipment but bringing off their own guns and a number of invaluable Bofors anti-aircraft guns belonging to British units that had abandoned them in Brest. The French were now out of the war, except for that gallant minority that chose to follow Charles de Gaulle into exile and form the genesis of Free France.

Back in England and concentrated once again, the Canadians found themselves the only division in the country equipped to fight as a formation and still mobile enough to move quickly to any threatened point. They promptly became the mobile reserve—'McNaughton's travelling circus', they called themselves. They were held ready to counter-attack any landing on the British coasts as the islanders, now isolated by the fall of France, buckled down to fight a serious war. While strong points and anti-tank defences were hurriedly constructed along 'stop-lines' throughout the south and east of England, while young boys and old men flocked to join the Home Guard and the RAF and the navy guarded the Channel, the army's training was stepped up to an unprecedented intensity and degree of toughness. Only two months earlier, in April, Ironside had confided to his diary the wish that 'our commanders had the terrific energy of McNaughton in the Canadians'.[6] Now Prime Minister Chamberlain had been replaced by Churchill, Ironside by Sir John Dill. McNaughton was given a key appointment: command of the newly formed British VII Corps, which included his own division—now under Major-General G.R. Pearkes—the British 1st Armoured Division, and two brigades of New Zealanders. VII Corps formed GHQ Reserve south of the Thames, the most vital assignment in the defence of the Channel coast.

The concepts of the First World War were entirely abandoned. The countryside erupted in a rash of tank-traps, road blocks, machine-gun nests, strong points, and barbed-wire obstacles. The whole shape of infantry training changed with a new emphasis on air defence, dispersal, and the use of one-man slit-trenches instead of elaborate trench systems. Nothing typified this realistic approach to war more than the forest of steel posts that sprouted on British army parade grounds, intended to destroy any troop-carrying enemy gliders that might attempt to land there. Drill—the foundation of good soldiering at any time—did not stop but was carried on between and around the posts.

At the same time equipment began to arrive in increasing quantities. The worst English winter in half a century was followed by one of the finest summers and Canadian morale rose even as rations were reduced. Having reorganized his forces after the defeat of France,

55 Canadian soldiers cross an obstacle while training at a battle-school in England. They were kept moving by instruction staff—one can be seen in the second line not carrying a rifle.

Hitler was now planning the invasion of Britain. The first step was to establish air superiority over the Channel and southern England. The Battle of Britain began on August 13, but the Royal Air Force—with more Canadians flying in its fighter squadrons than in those of their own RCAF—drove the Luftwaffe from the skies, during daylight hours, by the end of September. Without air superiority the enemy could not land an army on English shores with any prospect of success.

As the year wore on, a steady flow of additional units from Canada to the United Kingdom made practicable the formation of a second Canadian division and the creation of a Canadian corps, which on Christmas Day 1940 inherited the VIIth's commander and its GHQ Reserve role. But the possibility of a German attack receded rapidly in 1941. Before long the Canadians were training for an eventual return to the European mainland—though no one yet knew how they would be transported there or established once they arrived. 'A dagger pointed at the heart of Berlin,' McNaughton called them, in a melodramatic phrase that was quickly picked up by the media. For

Canadians at home and abroad his words echoed through the next two years—proudly at first, then with an ironic note, and finally with a kind of forlorn and increasingly vocal resentment as British, Australians, New Zealanders, Indians, South Africans, and eventually Americans went into battle on different fronts all over the world while Canadians still languished at garrison duties in England.

A tank brigade (complete with Canadian-built tanks) reinforced the infantry divisions already in Britain during June 1941, followed by the 3rd Division and then the 5th Armoured, while the 4th Division was retained for home defence in Canada. The routine of training at individual, unit, and formation levels in turn was broken briefly only after Hitler had attacked the Soviet Union on June 22. A balanced force of brigade strength went off in late July to the Norwegian-owned Spitsbergen archipelago. From these remote islands in the Arctic Ocean, which lay close to the now-vital convoy routes to Murmansk in northern Russia, radio stations had unwittingly been aiding the anti-shipping operations of the Luftwaffe with their weather transmissions. After a landing that was unopposed and bloodless, the Canadians evacuated the total population of the islands and destroyed all stores and facilities. In September they were back in southern England.

On the other side of the globe from Spitsbergen lay Hong Kong. The British chiefs of staff had long recognized that their Chinese outpost was indefensible in the event of war with Japan. In the summer of 1941 the colony was garrisoned by four battalions of British infantry, hostages to fortune who were there primarily for reasons of prestige, morale, and the maintenance of civil order. However, when Major-General A.E. Grasett, the Canadian-born British officer who had just relinquished the Hong Kong command, returned to Britain via Canada in August 1941, he discussed the colony's situation with Major-General H.D.G. Crerar, who was then the Chief of the General Staff. In England he went on to convince the War Office of the desirability of increasing the Hong Kong garrison, a reinforcement that the British subsequently argued 'would have a very great moral effect in the whole of the Far East and ... show Chiang Kai-shek we really intend to fight.' Perhaps Grasett also mentioned his chat with Crerar on the subject, for the British asked Ottawa to 'give consideration to providing for this purpose one or two Canadian battalions from Canada.'

There were two good reasons why this should not be done, the first being the vulnerability of Hong Kong and the second that there were no adequately trained and uncommitted troops in Canada at the time. However, the Canadian prime minister's comprehension of strategy and logistics was not very profound and in this essentially military situation his customary political insight deserted him. For Colonel J.L. Ralston, the First World War veteran who was now the

56 After landing at Victoria, the capital and port of Hong Kong, on November 16, 1941, men of the Royal Rifles of Canada and the Winnipeg Grenadiers march through the streets watched by a thin crowd of curious Chinese. A month later Japanese assault troops were ashore on the island.

Minister of National Defence, and for Crerar it is less easy to find excuses. On their advice the Canadian government agreed to send two battalions to Hong Kong.

The best-trained units in Canada were those of the 4th Division, now preparing to join McNaughton's forces in the United Kingdom. At the other end of the scale were nine battalions which, 'due either to recent employment requiring a period of refresher training, or to insufficient training, are not recommended for operational consideration at present.' Two of the latter, the Royal Rifles of Canada (despite their name, primarily a French-speaking unit) and the Winnipeg Grenadiers, had already served overseas in Newfoundland and Jamaica respectively. General Crerar, however, apparently chose not to distinguish adequately between garrison duties in islands remote from the prospect of battle and the hard realities of combat. He noted that they 'are both units of proven efficiency' and assigned them to Hong Kong. When they sailed, on October 27, 1941, neither unit had had any consistent training at the battalion level, nor had all their men completed their Tests of Elementary Training for all weapons. Both units had needed large drafts to bring them up to strength and now found themselves, in the words of their brigade commander, with 'a number of men who did not know, and were not known by, their officers.'[7]

However, their battle worthiness was an academic question under the circumstances they were soon to encounter. Not even Panzer Grenadiers, or Guardsmen or Marines in such meagre numbers could have withstood for long the blow that was about to fall on Hong Kong. The Canadians landed on November 16 and the Japanese launched their attack three weeks later. In ten days they were across the straits that separated the New Territories from Hong Kong proper and began to push their way inland. By December 23 the battle-weary garrison was split in two and pinned into peninsulas on the south and west of the island. There was no air cover or support and the defenders had no more than a dozen anti-aircraft guns. 'Very heavy shelling, mortaring and dive bombing all morning and extremely difficult to maintain communication,' radioed the senior British naval officer. 'Further fighting will be uncontrolled. . . .No water in hand and all men physically exhausted after days of continuous fighting.'[8]

The initial attack on the island had been borne, in part, by the Canadians, but after seven days of brutal and almost uninterrupted fighting the Royals' War Diary could still optimistically (and quite incorrectly) confide that 'Lack of ammunition [is] all that saves the Nips from being shelled off the island.' The fighting got closer and closer until ammunition was hardly the most important factor. On Christmas Eve a subaltern of the Winnipeg Grenadiers found himself probably the first Canadian to engage in hand-to-hand combat with the enemy in the Second World War.

Ke hands with us !!
is the only and best way remained for you !

握手吧！

67 A Japanese propaganda leaflet dropped on Hong Kong during the battle for the Crown Colony. Despite its crudity, it provides a substantially accurate impression of the situation that actually existed.

I was able to knock his rifle and bayonet out of the hands of one of the Japs, and with my new weapon managed to run through another of the enemy. Unfortunately I had difficulty withdrawing the blade and while endeavouring to do so I was lucky enough to catch the flash of a sword being raised to strike.

Quite subconsciously I jumped for my assailant, grasping the blade with my right hand, and circling his neck with my left arm, forcing his head against my chest....While struggling in this fashion we both lost our footing and rolled down a small slope for about ten feet....I managed to regain approximately the same standing advantage I had enjoyed earlier, except that by now we had both lost our grip on the sword. Since my opponent's face was tucked against my chest I endeavoured to turn his head in such a way as to enable me to deliver what I hoped would be a knockout with my fist. Unfortunately, I failed to notice that I had forced his steel helmet down over most of his face and the net result of a terrific uppercut was a sprained thumb for me....I had completely forgotten that I carried a pistol up to this moment and in something of a frenzy I endeavoured to reach it ... Complications arose here for I found after inserting my right forefinger through the trigger guard [that] the cut I had received on this finger when I had first grasped the [sword] blade had deprived it

Remember HONG KONG!

THE ROYAL RIFLES OF CANADA

WILL BE RECONSTITUTED ONE HUNDRED PER CENT

Follow their glorious example

ENLIST NOW

APPLY TO THE NEAREST RECRUITING STATION IN YOUR DISTRICT

of the necessary strength to squeeze the trigger. Still further difficulties arose when I attempted to withdraw the finger and found that the flesh, acting much the same as the barb on a fish-hook, rendered it difficult to remove that finger from the trigger guard. However, I did manage and pressing the pistol to the base of my opponent's neck, finally ended the struggle.[9]

Very early the next morning, as a company of the Royal Rifles organized themselves for a last stand at Stanley Barracks, a telephone call from the senior British officer in the vicinity ordered the re-siting of their reserve platoon, which was occupying the Officers' Mess. 'I have a definite promise from the Brigadier that no troops will be allowed in the Officers' Mess,' he announced, according to the regimental records.[10] Only hours later came the inevitable order to surrender and the guns fell silent.

The Canadians had lost nearly 300 killed and 500 wounded in the course of the fighting. Company Sergeant-Major John Osborn of the Winnipeg Grenadiers won, posthumously, Canada's first Victoria Cross of the war. 'An inspiring example to all throughout the defence,' ran the citation in the *London Gazette*, four years later, '...in his death he displayed the highest quality of heroism and self sacrifice.' Those who survived were marched into Japanese prison camps. There, under atrocious conditions, another 260 died during their years of captivity. In Canada a Royal Commission appointed to investigate the circumstances under which the Canadian force had been dispatched eventually decided that the expedition had not been either 'ill-conceived or badly managed', a delicately phrased verdict that seems to have evaded the real questions of competence and judgement at the highest level.

In England fatigues and 'duties' (which took up at least half of every regimental soldier's time) followed monotonously on one another and drills followed drills. Unsuccessful exercises brought numerous repetitions in their train, while successful ones brought only more advanced exercises. Thus First Canadian Army, formed in April 1942, practised its assigned 'break-out' role for the still-distant but now inevitable bridgehead that would eventually be established somewhere on the coast of western Europe. Some day, somewhere, somehow Allied troops would have to create a 'Second Front' to ease the pressure on Russia, which was still trying vainly to stem the German assault in the east. Before that day arrived, however, the Canadians were to be involved in one more combat situation even briefer and more costly in human terms than the Hong Kong débâcle.

The Russians were continually demanding that their allies open a Second Front and relieve the German pressure on them. Churchill would have liked to oblige them but felt (probably rightly) that such a project was still beyond the scope of Anglo-American resources.

8 When the Royal Rifles were re-formed after the fall of Hong Kong, a poster previously used by the regiment was reworked.

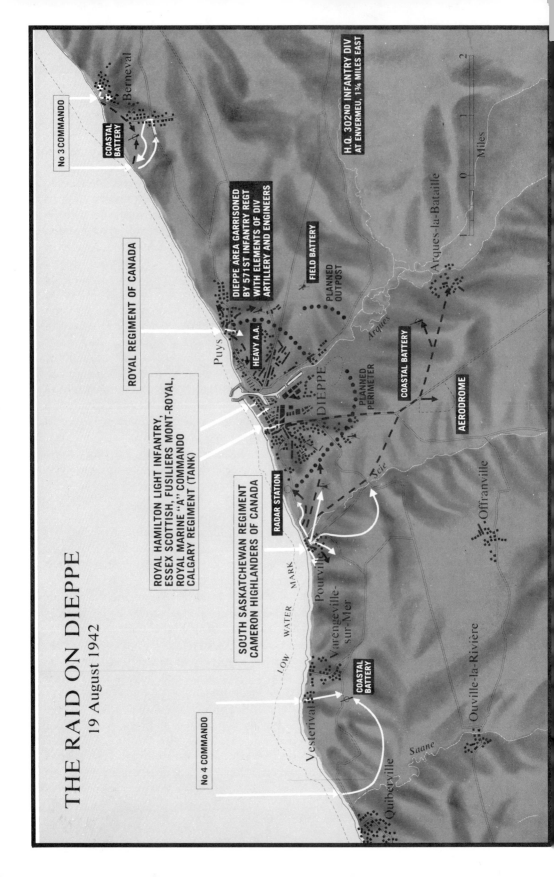

THE RAID ON DIEPPE
19 August 1942

No 3 COMMANDO

COASTAL BATTERY

Berneval

H.Q. 302ND INFANTRY DIV
AT ENVERMEU, 1¾ MILES EAST

Miles
0   1   2

ROYAL REGIMENT OF CANADA

DIEPPE AREA GARRISONED
BY 571ST INFANTRY REGT
WITH ELEMENTS OF DIV
ARTILLERY AND ENGINEERS

FIELD BATTERY

PLANNED
OUTPOST

Arques-la-Bataille

HEAVY A.A.

Puys

Arques

PLANNED
PERIMETER

COASTAL BATTERY

DIEPPE

ROYAL HAMILTON LIGHT INFANTRY,
ESSEX SCOTTISH, FUSILIERS MONT-ROYAL,
ROYAL MARINE "A" COMMANDO
CALGARY REGIMENT (TANK)

AERODROME

RADAR STATION

Scie

Offranville

SOUTH SASKATCHEWAN REGIMENT
CAMERON HIGHLANDERS OF CANADA

Pourville

LOW WATER MARK

Varengeville-
sur-Mer

Ouville-la-Rivière

Vesterival

COASTAL
BATTERY

Saane

No 4 COMMANDO

Quiberville

However, a really large, successful raid would worry the Germans and compel them to strengthen their Channel defences at the expense of the Eastern Front. An outline plan for such a raid was prepared and on April 30 General Montgomery, the British officer commanding Southern Command, broached to McNaughton the idea of employing Canadians, telling him he believed they 'were those best suited'. After learning more about the plan, McNaughton agreed that Canadians could be used.

Amphibious landings on a hostile shore have long been accepted as one of the most difficult and dangerous of all operations of war. British Commandos had been nibbling at the coasts of Europe since the last days of 1940, but it was recognized that even the biggest of their bites—such as the raid on St Nazaire in March 1942—was so insignificant in scale that it added little to the body of knowledge and doctrine necessary to launch a Second Front. A 'reconnaissance in force' was necessary to attain that knowledge, and since the planners then believed that the immediate capture of a moderately large port would be essential to success, it was decided that the reconnaissance should be made against Dieppe under the code-name Operation *Rutter*. The Canadians would provide the main assault force and the 2nd Division, commanded by Major-General J. H. Roberts, was selected to form it. By May 20 the troops were on the Isle of Wight to begin intensive training in amphibious operations that culminated in two full-scale 'dress rehearsals' on a stretch of the Devonshire coast resembling the Dieppe area.

Only when they embarked on the ships that were to carry them across the Channel, on July 2 and 3, were they told what their objective was. But unsettled weather now interfered with the mounting of *Rutter* and the ships never left their harbours. On July 8, after the troops had been held on board in their cramped quarters for five or six days, the project was reluctantly abandoned and the men marched ashore. Over the next three weeks, however, the proposal for another *Rutter*—this time code-named *Jubilee*, but still with Dieppe as the objective—was gradually revived.

There was a clear possibility that by now the enemy knew about *Rutter* and that Dieppe had been the target. But for that very reason, it could also be argued, the Germans would not expect Dieppe to be the objective again. And in fact post-war research has revealed that the Germans attached no more significance to Dieppe than they did to the other ports of the Pas de Calais. However, there was every reason for them to believe that a major raid—perhaps even an attempt at a Second Front—would come *somewhere* along the coast before the summer was out. On that basis they were maintaining all their coastal defences at a high level of readiness.

The main attack was to be launched against the town itself, along a three-quarter-mile arc between the harbour mole and a point just west of the Casino, a large white building standing in solitary splen-

59 Landing craft carrying Les Fusiliers Mont-Royal race for the beaches of Dieppe when the reserve wave of infantry was ordered in.

dour on the promenade, behind a low sea wall. In front of the wall a shingle beach sloped down quite steeply to sand or water, depending on the state of the tide. As six squadrons of fighter-bombers hit the buildings closest to the beach, the eastern half—code-named 'Red Beach'—was to be assaulted by the Essex Scottish; the western half—'White Beach'—by the Royal Hamilton Light Infantry. Behind them would land the tanks of the Calgary Regiment, while a floating reserve of Les Fusiliers Mont-Royal and a Royal Marine Commando would be committed as required. A mile away to the west, at the hamlet of Puys, the Royal Regiment of Canada and three companies of the Black Watch of Canada were to land on 'Blue Beach' and hook inland, towards the town; on the other flank the South Saskatchewan Regiment would land on 'Green Beach' at Pourville and swing west into Dieppe, while the Cameron Highlanders of Canada were to drive south nearly 4 miles as far as Arques-la-Bataille, where the local German headquarters was believed to be located.

As the assault force closed the French coast in the early hours of August 19, 1942, a part of it encountered a small enemy convoy en route from Boulogne to Dieppe. In the brief but violent fire-fight that followed, one German ship became 'a total loss' and three British escort vessels were 'seriously damaged'. More important, the sounds of battle alerted some coastal defences in the eastern part of the area to be attacked, but no special precautions seem to have been taken in the central or western sectors. In the event, however, no special precautions were needed. The customary German state of dawn readiness was to prove quite enough to handle the raiders when, supported directly only by light naval gunfire and six squadrons of fighter-bombers, the first of almost 5,000 Canadian soldiers began to land on the beaches in front of Dieppe. By an hour after noon nearly 900 of them were dead or dying and over 1,000 were wounded. 1,900 were prisoners of war and only 2,200 of those who had landed were on their way back to England.

Only at Pourville were the Canadians lucky enough to achieve some degree of surprise. At Puys the Royal Regiment and the Black Watch were virtually annihilated by 150 German soldiers admirably placed on a cliff to one side of the beach. Only a score of men got over the sea wall. Of those that landed 200 were killed and 20 later died of wounds. All the rest were taken prisoner. In Dieppe, where the landings were timed to take place a half-hour later than on the flanks, German soldiers in the windows of buildings beyond the promenade and in concealed vantage points on the cliffs on each side of the town waited for the raiders to land.

The fighter-bombers arrived early, three minutes before the landing craft touched down, so by the time the Canadians began to storm ashore the Germans had recovered from the momentary bombing and strafing of the aircraft. The overwhelming impression as the first troops landed was one of horrendous noise, which stunned the mind and made it difficult to formulate or comprehend the simplest sentence. High explosive bursting on shingle, the rattle of small-arms fire, the dull roar of distant naval guns and sharp report of high-velocity field pieces, the howling of aircraft engines, the screams of wounded men—these sounds in deafening combination numbed the minds of soldiers who had never before been under fire. 'People had shot over us and around us,' recalled the battle adjutant of the Royal Regiment, landing at Puys, 'but nobody had ever shot at us—and

This German photograph of the Dieppe beach—from the West Headland, where the Germans had machine-guns entrenched—was taken within a day or two of the raid. The casino and the buildings behind it (extreme right) were subsequently demolished by the Germans to improve their fields of fire in the event of another attack.

61 During a rehearsal for Dieppe, a Landing Craft (Assault) carries Canadian infantry towards an English beach.

there's a big difference, a very big difference. . . . as I left the assault craft I saw perhaps a hundred dead men.'[11] His reaction was common to those landing on every beach.

In the centre 'it was unbelievable that anyone survived', according to a platoon commander of the RHLI. His landing craft was still nosing into the beach when 'we were hit; the Bangalore torpedoes exploded among the toggle ropes and grappling irons. I only remember the sound because I was blinded. The boat filled with water and I was soon up to my neck. I couldn't hear at all after that for a long while but later there were faraway noises as if I were listening to something over a very poor connection on a long distance "phone call".'[12] Blinded for life, he and one private were the only survivors of his platoon.

Alongside the Hamilton men the Essex Scottish were faring even worse. Thirty-two officers and 521 other ranks had embarked for Dieppe, but only two officers and 49 other ranks (27 of them wounded) sailed home again. On all the beaches except the one at Pourville, where the initial opposition was less ferocious, masses of men, stupified by the intensity and brutality of battle, huddled behind derelict tanks and landing craft or under the sea walls. Enfiladed by machine-guns and scythed by mortar shrapnel and splintered flints

42 An infantry land-
ing craft after the battle
at Dieppe, with most of
its overhead cover rip-
ped off and the interior
—littered with bodies and
equipment—destroyed,
most likely, by a mortar
bomb exploding inside
and setting off more
explosives carried on
board.

from explosions on the pebble beach, they were slaughtered where
they lay.

A warrant officer of the Essex Scottish led a dozen men in pushing
a Bangalore torpedo—lengths of pipe filled with explosive that could
blow a gap in wire entanglements when the contents were
detonated—through the barbed wire on the top of the sea wall.
When the torpedo exploded, the group made a mad dash across the
promenade. It entered a number of buildings and cleared them of the
enemy, working its way down to the harbour, but there were too few
men to continue the attack or to hold their positions once the Germans began to concentrate against them. Most of them were eventually captured, but the sergeant-major and a couple of others succeeded in fighting their way back to the beach after a desperate half-
hour. Some of the Hamilton men got into the lower floor of the Casino, where they fought the Germans from room to room for several
hours. While that struggle went on, another little group burst into
the town, penetrated as far as the church at St Rémy, and established
itself in a theatre that it held until 10:00 a.m. Then it struggled back
to the Casino, part of which continued to be occupied by Canadians
until the evacuation from the beaches was under way.

The tanks of the Calgary Regiment were not able to make much

63 The RHLI's padre, the Rev. John Foote, won his Victoria Cross dragging and carrying wounded men across this Dieppe beach to Tank Landing Craft No. 5, where the battalion's wounded medical officer, Captain D.W. Clare, had established a makeshift regimental aid post. Note how the tank has bogged down in the shingle.

headway. Most of those that got ashore were stopped on the beaches either by shingle banks, the sea wall, or enemy guns. Nevertheless the tank hulls were proof against any weight of fire that the local defences could bring to bear and no crewmen were killed or wounded inside their machines. Some tanks continued to fight even though immobilized; some surmounted the sea wall and reached the promenade. But the crews found the narrow roads leading into the town blocked with concrete and their tank treads were soon broken by anti-tank gunfire. One tank on the promenade flushed some German infantry and 'made a dash for them ... Both gunners opened up and we got plenty of them. Even had the pleasure of running down one who tried to dodge us.'[13] But it too was immobilized before very long.

Offshore, aboard the headquarters ship *Calpe*, General Roberts had little idea of what was happening. Many of the radio operators on the beaches were being picked off by German snipers. Others had their radios destroyed by shrapnel, and even when communication with *Calpe* was possible, the confused, smoke-shrouded fighting was difficult to comprehend from disjointed wireless conversations. A garbled message suggested that the Essex Scottish were making headway on 'Red' beach and Roberts ordered the Fusiliers Mont-Royal to reinforce them. In fact the remnants of the Essex regiment were still pinned against the front of the sea wall.

It made little difference. Most of the Mont-Royals were landed by some mistake on 'White' beach, behind the RHLI. A warrant officer remembered afterwards

> the wounded and dead who lay scattered on the beach. Some of the wounded were trying to swim out to the boats [and] many were bleeding heavily, reddening the water around them. [Once ashore,] mortar bombs are bursting on the shingle and making little clouds which seem to punctuate the deafening din . . . close to me badly mutilated bodies lie here and there. The wounded scream . . . the blood flows from their wounds in a viscous, blackish tide . . . . For myself, I am absolutely astounded to have reached the shelter of a building. I was certain that my last hour had arrived.[14]

A dozen men of the Mont-Royals, led by a sergeant, got into the maze of ancient streets behind the promenade and fought their way through them to the dock basins behind the harbour. Then, when their grenades and ammunition had been all used up, they were forced to surrender. Their captors stripped the Canadians of their weapons and outer clothes, left them in the hands of a single armed guard, and went in search of other prey. The Canadians' leader induced the guard to come within arm's reach by begging for water and then grappled with him. Another of the group killed the German with a piece of iron pipe. The Canadians dashed off, each man for himself. The spectacle of unidentifiable unarmed men in their underwear sprinting through the middle of a battle apparently unnerved every German they passed because they got back to the beach unharmed.

One man who seemed impervious to his own danger and to the sights and sounds of conflict that engulfed him was the RHLI's chaplain, John Foote. He picked up the wounded, man after man, and carried them to the Regimental Aid Post established in the lee of a grounded, burning Tank Landing Craft. Not a bullet or a splinter touched him. During the evacuation he helped carry more wounded to the boats but in the end chose not to leave himself, explaining that the men who were being left behind needed him more than those returning to England. He won the only Victoria Cross ever awarded to a Canadian chaplain.

At Pourville, on the right flank where the South Saskatchewans and the Cameron Highlanders had landed between 4:52 and 6:00 a.m., the initial opposition was light. Really serious fighting developed only as the South Saskatchewans crossed the River Scie (Lieutenant-Colonel Cecil Merritt leading them with a reckless bravery that earned him a VC) and hooked left towards Dieppe proper. They were stopped well short of the town. The Camerons pushed 2,000 yards inland before the evacuation order was issued. As the two battalions withdrew, 'the wide concrete promenade was strewn with bodies,' wrote Wallace Reyburn, a war correspondent. When his turn came to leave,

> the beach was dotted with prone figures on the sand and men running out to the boats....From each end there was the raking fire of machine guns. ∴.Mortar shells exploded on the beach and sent cascades of sand and pebbles far and wide. Snipers picked off men as they ran. Focke-Wulfes came roaring down low and spat their machine guns and cannon fire at us. I watched a Junkers 88 that had managed to slip through our fighters, come trundling (it seemed so slow and laborious compared to the speed of the Focke-Wulfes) along about a hundred feet above the beach and drop its bombs as it got over the boats.[15]

The struggle for air superiority did not begin with the first landings. Two RAF squadrons cruised over Dieppe for half an hour until the Luftwaffe appeared. Then, as the numbers of enemy aircraft increased, 50 squadrons of fighters, including 6 Canadian ones, fought in relays to maintain a local air superiority that would protect the troops below from enemy air attack and permit the fighter-bombers providing direct support for the ground forces to work without Luftwaffe interference. At times during that disastrous morning the haze over Dieppe was full of wheeling and diving aircraft as German and Allied pilots chased each other around the sky. Two more Canadian squadrons formed half the wing assigned to tactical reconnaissance duties. Their work required that they fly low, in pairs—easy targets for prowling German fighters or for anti-aircraft fire. Their Mustangs ranged fruitlessly over the surrounding countryside, searching for approaching reinforcements (which the Germans did not need) and suffering a higher casualty rate than any other air units engaged in the battle.

Altogether the RCAF squadrons lost 13 aircraft and 10 pilots in the total Allied air losses of 106 aircraft and 81 pilots and aircrew. Ninety-two German aircraft were alleged to have been 'destroyed' and another 39 were claimed as 'probables', so that the air battle over Dieppe was not a resounding success in 'win/lose' terms. However, the Allies were far more able to bear such losses as occurred and their record looks better than that of the Germans when the ratio of losses to sorties flown is examined. They lost only one fighter for every 27.2 sorties flown but the enemy lost one per 7.6 sorties. German losses actually totalled 78—a third of their fighter force in the west at that time—while the Allied loss of 88 fighters amounted to less than a tenth of the fighter strength based in the United Kingdom. Since the fight took place over German-held territory or close to the coast, the Germans probably recovered more of their airmen.

Dieppe was not the unmitigated disaster that Hong Kong had been, despite the fearsome losses. This time men had died to some purpose in establishing the principles that were to break the Atlantic

64 Luftwaffe soldiers, probably from an anti-aircraft unit, examine the personal papers of a Canadian wounded at Dieppe.

Wall two years later. Objectives must be more realistic, tactics more sophisticated, and training more rigorous. Communications must be more comprehensive, equipment more appropriate, and, most of all, fire support by sea and air must be overwhelming. Moreover, some method would have to be found to put vast numbers of men and matériel ashore on open beaches, for the prospects of taking an established port by storm were obviously dim. The 'boffins' —research scientists and engineers—went to work on AVRES (Armoured Vehicles, Royal Engineers), amphibious (DD) tanks, 'Mulberry' pre-fabricated harbours, and 'PLUTO' (Pipelines Under The Ocean) that could pump fuel directly across the Channel. Casualties were replaced from the reinforcement depots and the men who had been lucky enough to get away from the beaches went back to the apparently endless cycle of training, fatigues, 'duties', and exercises, benefiting from the trial by fire at Dieppe—and remembering, perhaps, that it is the last battle that decides every war.

In Canada the first reaction to the news of Dieppe was one of pride and admiration for the heroic conduct of the troops, as it was described by war correspondents such as Ross Munro, Wallace Reyburn, and the American, Quentin Reynolds. Families were left to mourn their dead or worry over sons and brothers in German prison camps as the full casualty figures were released gradually, over the better part of a week. Subsequently public opinion began to veer towards uninformed and emotional criticism of the Establishment —politicians, senior civil servants, and general officers—for sending Canadian soldiers on such an ill-starred endeavour. The first faint criticisms came from the Toronto *Globe and Mail* (August 23), which questioned whether the methods used at Dieppe were really the best ones. The Montreal *Gazette* headed its first editorial on the raid 'The Dagger is Whetted', but by September 17 it was asking if the dagger had been blunted at its first thrust. *Saturday Night* (September 9 and October 23) carried articles suggesting that the Dieppe concept and the planning of it were almost exclusively the work of Canadian officers and that the failure of the raid demonstrated the bankruptcy of Canadian generalship. Neither allegation was true. It might have been more effectively argued that the army should never have accepted an invitation to send its untested troops into such a potential killing ground. But how could any Canadian general have refused to commit his men to battle when so much of the country's leadership, media, and public had been pressing to see Canadians in action?

Despite the criticism, the government refused to provide scapegoats, although General Roberts was relieved of his appointment shortly afterwards and never held another operational command. The strictures gradually died away, leaving in their wake (in the words of the official historian) 'something to undermine the hitherto unassailable position of General McNaughton with the public'.

5 Prisoners are marshalled in the streets of Dieppe after the battle. The Canadian in his underpants may have abandoned his battledress trousers in a last-minute and unsuccessful attempt to reach the departing ships.

6

SICILY AND SOUTHERN ITALY

By Christmas 1942 elements of the RCN and RCAF had had a considerable amount of battle experience in their respective spheres: a growing number of Canadian sailors and airmen could now match themselves against the men of Allied sister services. But the Canadian army was relatively inexperienced. The British—after defeats in France, Greece, Crete, Malaya, and Burma—had swept across North Africa to link up with American forces in Tunisia; the United States had been in the war for only a year but already its Fifth Army had had several months of combat experience in the Mediterranean theatre; the Russians, having stemmed the German juggernaut at Stalingrad, were flinging it back through eastern Europe in the course of the most massive battles the world has ever known. The Canadian army, however, lacked either a record or the immediate prospect of sustained action. To be still 'a dagger pointed at the heart of Berlin' was an unsatisfying role when other armies were actually lunging at the Germans day by day. Only a combination of common sense and tightening discipline kept the troops' morale at a satisfactory level.

At home discontent was much more apparent and vociferous. Perhaps the emotional need to hear of Canadian troops in action reflected problems of national identity and the uncertain direction of society—problems that the uniformed soldier overseas did not have. As Dieppe faded from Canadian headlines, demands for a more active role for our ground forces became insistent. During November 1942, in the space of five days, the *Winnipeg Free Press* editorialized that Canada should 'send a full division to some theatre of war' at once; the *Vancouver Sun* reported a decorated veteran of the Great War harrumphing to his old comrades of the Canadian Corps Association that 'soldiers sitting idle in England ... [were] ... the greatest disgrace of the war'; the Montreal *Gazette* exaggerated the situation with a caustic story headlined 'Mental Illness in Overseas Army Laid to Inactivity and Anxiety' (such cases were very few). Nearly every daily newspaper and radio station in the country quoted former prime minister R.B. Bennett's needling comment that he knew of 'no good reason why the Canadian Army should have to spend its fourth Christmas in Britain without firing a shot'—the last phrase of which must have grated on the survivors of Dieppe. Moreover, despite General McNaughton's well-known concern for holding the Canadians together in one unified (and Canadian) command, there were now very senior officers under him who shared Bennett's view. The Chief of the Imperial General Staff, General Alan Brooke, wrote in his diary for February 10, 1943: 'Harry Crerar to dinner, and a long harangue from him as to the necessity of getting some Canadians fighting soon for imperial and political reasons.'[1]

Hume Wrong, the Assistant Under-Secretary of State for External Affairs, expressed similar opinions in a memorandum to the Prime Minister. In the middle of March, Mackenzie King set about defusing this potentially explosive issue by rejecting McNaughton's view and notifying Churchill that Ottawa would now favour the employment of some Canadians in extended operations. It was still understood, however, that troops sent to combat theatres (the Mediterranean was, in effect, the only possible one) would be returned to First Canadian Army before the opening of a Second Front. On April 23 the British formally responded to King's signal by asking permission to employ a Canadian infantry division and a tank brigade 'to undertake certain operations based on Tunisia'. The Canadian government approved the request. General Eisenhower, the Supreme Allied Commander in the Mediterranean theatre, intended to capture Sicily as a base for further operations against southern Europe and to secure the Mediterranean shipping routes. He would do so using British, American, and Canadian forces. The formations assigned by General McNaughton to join the famous Eighth Army under General Montgomery were those that had been overseas longest: the 1st Division and the 1st Army Tank Brigade.

These Canadian troops moved north to Scotland for special training in amphibious and mountain operations. Meanwhile it was decided that Major-General H.L.N. Salmon, the divisional commander, should go at once to Egypt, where the Eighth Army's share of the Sicilian landings was being planned. His aircraft left on April 29 but crashed into a Devonshire hillside shortly after take-off with the loss of all on board.

Into his place as commander of the Mediterranean contingent stepped Canada's youngest general, Guy Granville Simonds. Promoted to command the 2nd Division only a few days earlier, at the age of 39, the hard-driving Simonds had begun the war as a captain on the staff of the Royal Military College at Kingston. His subsequent meteoric rise had culminated in his appointment to a divisional command, after a spell in Tunisia as a senior staff officer with a British corps to gain a little of the battle experience the Canadians were still so sadly lacking. Simonds therefore already knew the Eighth Army, its generals, and something of its methods. Within twenty-four hours of his arrival in Cairo he had been briefed by General Oliver Leese, the commander of XXX Corps in which the Canadians would serve, made a Canadian plan, and cabled it back to Britain so that his staff could start organizing the combat loading of the assault ships for Operation *Husky*, the code-name for the Sicilian landings.

The Canadians sailed from the Clyde in several convoys towards the end of June, still uncertain of their destination—although the fact that they had been issued with Sherman tanks, which were now standard in the Mediterranean theatre, instead of their Canadian-built Rams, must have given them an idea. They were told their objectives on July 1, 1943, and for the next ten days they drilled, exercised, studied the assault plans, and played endless games of bingo (legally) and poker (not so legally). On July 4 and 5 the convoys passed Gibraltar and entered the dangerously enclosed waters of the Mediterranean. While they steamed towards Sicily, the Allied air cover—including the RCAF's 417 Squadron, which had been serving with the Desert Air Force since April—kept them free from any attentions of the Luftwaffe. Enemy submarines did succeed in sinking three vessels en route, all of them off the North African coast between Oran and Algiers, and of the 900 Canadians on board 58 were lost.

The initial landings on Sicily were made by British and American airborne troops in the pre-dawn darkness of July 10. Unexpected winds left many of those who jumped from aircraft scattered over a wide area. Others, who were in gliders being towed by Dakota aircraft, were drowned after poor navigation led to their gliders' being cast loose far out to sea. These misfortunes might have had serious repercussions for the seaborne assault forces if opposition to the landings had been strong. But the bulk of the quarter-million men in Sicily were second-line Italian garrison troops. The Germans were holding two of their finest divisions—the 15th Panzer Grenadiers and the Hermann Goering Panzers—in reserve for a possible counter-attack as they waited for a point of Allied main effort to become apparent.

In fact there was no single point of main effort. Just after dawn the Canadians, forming the left flank of five British landings that spread over 40 miles of shoreline, landed near Pachino close to the southern tip of the island, while the American Seventh Army, under General George Patton, established three more beach-heads spread over another 40 miles of coast as far again to the west. The opposition was negligible everywhere on the Anglo-Canadian beaches and, although some of Simonds' troops were up to two and a half hours late in getting ashore, by 6:45 a.m. the general was able to report to XXX Corps HQ that 'all Canadian objectives had been taken'. Twenty minutes earlier General Eisenhower had broadcast from Algiers an announcement of the initial assault that made no mention of Canadian participation: inexplicably, Eisenhower claimed that 'security requirements made it inadvisable to mention the Canadians by name'. The omission, which was instantly picked up by the Canadians, was corrected within ten minutes by another announcement from the Pentagon in Washington, but it provided a disturbing background to the more

66 In the grey Sicilian dawn the first Canadian infantrymen to land in Europe since Dieppe plunge through the shallow water of a Cape Passero beach on July 10, 1943.

significant issue of Allied relationships that was to be raised within the next few days.

On the Canadian beach everything was tranquil. A private in the Seaforth Highlanders of Canada—a Canadian-born Tennessean who had gone north to enlist in 1939—has described the scene:

> We were ordered now to advance. The cane-brakes ended and farm fields began. We walked through the fields of ripe tomatoes, stopping momentarily to pick a few. . . . Two houses loomed ahead. Near the large white house on the right was a heavy middle-aged man, dressed in dark pants, white shirt, and black vest. He merely looked at us with a little interest before he resumed his work of repairing a window. . . . We passed on through another cane-brake and into another field.[2]

Two days later the Canadians were more than 30 miles inland, despite a shortage of wheeled transport and an enervating combination of heat, humidity, malarial mosquitoes, and fine white dust. Soon they were moving up into the mountainous centre of the island, but it was not until the fifth day, just outside the village of Grammichele, that they first came under German fire. Men of the 1st Infantry Brigade and tanks of the Three Rivers Regiment took the village by noon at a cost of 25 casualties. The next day, on July 16, fighting over higher, rockier ground unsuitable for tanks, the infantry lost another 27 men clearing Piazza Armerina.

The Germans, recognizing the inability of their two divisions to throw ten times their number of Allied soldiers back into the sea,

ITALY
3 September 1943 –
25 February 1945

0 20 40 60 80 100
Miles

GULF OF GENOA

• Genoa

EMILIA

Bologna•

Reno

GOTHIC LINE

Senio •Ravenna

Pistoia•

Pisa• *Arno*

Florence• •Rimini

Tomba di Pesaro

TUSCANY *Foglia* Pésaro•

Arezzo• *Metauro*

•Siena FIRST CANADIAN CORPS

L. Trasimene •Ancona

ELBA

Perugia• MARCHES

CORSICA ADRIATIC

UMBRIA SEA

Viterbo• *Tiber*

LATIUM WINTER LINE

ROME ABRUZZI •Ortona

Villa Rogatti•

FIRST CANADIAN CORPS &

Sangro

Anzio• *Biferno* Termoli•

SIXTH U.S. CORPS JAN 1944 Ceprano• MOLISE

Liri Cassino• Campobasso•

ADOLF HITLER LINE Vinchiaturo•

GUSTAV LINE *Volturno* Foggia•

TYRRHENIAN SEA APULIA

Naples• SEVENTY-EIGHTH BRIT DI & FOURTH ARM'D BDE 22 - 23 SEP 1943

CAMPANIA •Melfi

Salerno• Bari•

Gulf of Salerno FIFTH U.S. ARMY SEP 1943 Potenza•

SARDINIA LUCANIA Taranto•

FIRST BRITISH AIRBORNE DIV 9 SEP 1943

GULF OF TARANTO

CALABRIA

Catanzaro•

SICILY
10 July – 6 August 1943

Trapani•

•Palermo

Marsala•

Sciacca• Messina• Strait of Messina

Agira Mt Etna Reggio•

Leonforte• Regalbuto•

Valguarnera• Adrano•

Piazza Amerina•

Licata• •Catania

Grammichele•

SEVENTH U.S. ARMY 10 JULY 1943 •Augusta

Ragusa• Syracuse•

Modica• Rosolini•

Ispica•

0 10 20 30 40 50 Pachino•

Miles EIGHTH BRITISH ARMY 10 JULY 1943

EIGHTH BRITISH ARMY 3 SEP 1943

•Messina

FIRST CANADIAN DIVISION

Reggio•

67 During the first day of the Sicilian landings, shipping steadily piled up off the beaches and a stream of transport and mechanized equipment poured inland along bulldozed tracks. In the foreground one of the first Italians to surrender stands unguarded and ignored.

had resolved to withdraw into the mountain bastion around Mount Etna. Field Marshal Kesselring's tactics were to establish numerically weak rear-guards in naturally strong positions, to have them resist fiercely for a stipulated time and then disengage quickly and fall back through the next selected strong point. The battlefield, like most modern battlefields, seemed deserted—sunburnt hillsides lashed by sudden bursts of machine-gun fire and the sporadic 'krr-umph' of exploding mortar shells. In a matter of days the men of the 1st Division learned more about the practice of their trade as they pushed forward than they had in the previous three and a half years.

Another cause of Allied dissension now cropped up. General McNaughton had arrived in Algiers on the first day of the landings,

68 Sherman tanks of the 12th (Three Rivers) Armoured Regiment drive through the shattered streets of Regalbuto. The capture of this key point, defended by men of the crack Hermann Goering Division, gave the Canadians their hardest fight of the Sicilian campaign.

bent on visiting the Canadians in Sicily as soon as possible. But on July 17, when the Canadians were moving on from Piazza Armerina, he learned from General Montgomery that, 'owing to shortage of transport no visitors will be allowed on the island during active ... operations.' When McNaughton argued his case with General Alexander, the Deputy Supreme Allied Commander, that suave soldier backed Montgomery. The Canadian, a crusty character at the best of times, went fuming back to London to express irascibly to the Chief of the Imperial General Staff his commitment to the principle that 'representatives of Canada could visit Canadian troops at their discretion.'[3] Montgomery subsequently claimed that he was primarily concerned with keeping from General Simonds the additional strain of entertaining his superior officer while fighting his first battle as a formation commander—'For God's sake, keep him away,' he reports Simonds as saying[4]—but his brusque and mendacious refusal exacerbated a difficult situation. This controversy, involving McNaughton with all three top British commanders, was to play its part in events later in the year.

While the American forces, under the swashbuckling Patton, were swinging around the western coast of the island, Montgomery's battle-weary Eighth Army was not performing as well as expected in the narrow Catanian plain, under the southeastern flank of Etna. Only the Canadians, high in the central mountains, were still pushing forward. Kesselring, intent on maintaining his perimeter and thereby control of his withdrawal, began to strengthen his mountain line. The best part of two more German divisions had now reached him from the mainland and in the battles of Agira and Regalbuto the 1st Canadian Division, reinforced by a British brigade, had to meet and overcome the stiffest opposition of their campaign. The Canadians were beset by problems of command and control: some of their inexperienced regimental officers responded uncertainly to the concentrated pressure of battle, maps were read wrongly, and their radios too often failed them at vital moments. On the positive side, however, they had courage, tenacity, and the resolute energy of General Simonds to carry them through, plus an enormous weight of fire power: the complete divisional artillery, ninety bombers, and more than a hundred fighter-bombers were allocated to support one battalion attack by the Royal Canadian Regiment. Agira was taken on the 28th, after five days' hard fighting and at a cost of 438 casualties. With its fall, and as Patton made rapid progress along the northern coast of the island, the Germans began to scurry back towards the Straits of Messina.

Their departure was hastened by the dramatic news that Mussolini had been deposed by a *coup d'état*. Marshal Pietro Badoglio, the leader of the ministry that replaced him, announced that the war would go on, but Hitler was under no illusions regarding the peaceful intentions of the new régime. On July 30, before Badoglio could even open negotiations with the Allies, masses of German troops were sent south through the Alpine passes to ensure that Italy remained a German satellite. The formal Italian surrender to the Allies did not come until September 8, when the Italians adopted a policy of 'co-belligerency', but the change came too late for the Allies to derive any real military advantage from it. By then northern and central Italy were firmly in German hands.

For the Canadians, the Sicilian campaign ended on the banks of the Upper Simeto River, west of Adano, when they were withdrawn from combat on August 7 to rest and prepare for the assault on the Italian mainland that was now being planned. In his *Memoirs*, Montgomery remarked that 'the Canadians were magnificent in the Sicilian campaign' and his praise was well warranted. They had fought their way across 150 miles of mountains, outflanking the Germans who had tied down the British divisions on the coastal plain, and progressed from the status of military apprentices to journeymen soldiers at least, at a total cost, in the 1st Division, of 562 killed, 1,664 wounded, and 84 taken prisoner by the enemy.

On August 10 the Germans began to evacuate across the Straits of Messina the 60,000 troops they still had on the island. Messina itself fell on August 17, the Americans entering the town from the northwest only four hours before the British arrived from the south.

The capture of Sicily reinforced and made irrevocable Allied control of the Mediterranean, but the decision to continue the fight onto the Italian mainland was questionable. Militarily the 'soft underbelly of Europe' was a myth. Churchill's vivid metaphor was intended to win converts to a political strategy aimed at reaffirming British influence in southern Europe. The British were eager to continue the campaign up the Italian 'boot' and overcame American reservations about the purely military problems involved. The nature of the ground—a central mountain spine with a succession of steep and rugged ridges dropping towards the sea on both sides of the peninsula—would favour the defence. It would also ensure that the Allies' overwhelming technological and numerical superiority was largely negated. Even along the narrow coastal plains the 'closeness' of the country—village and walled field, river and ravine—meant that armoured forces could rarely be deployed en masse; nor could their inherent mobility be properly exploited.

Anglo-American armies were to force their way northwards for the next eighteen months, breaking through the Gustav/Hitler, Caesar, Trasimene, and Gothic Lines with an enormous toll of Allied resources in both men, including a substantial number of Canadians, and matériel.

The successes of the 1st Division in Sicily had been properly celebrated at home and the Cabinet apparently felt that much of the glory was reflecting on them. Now, instead of reuniting the division with the remainder of the overseas army, still in Britain, it was proposed to add a second division, together with a corps headquarters, to the Canadian forces in the Mediterranean: more troops in action would bring more favourable publicity. McNaughton objected, further irritating those who were critical of his attitude as commander of First Canadian Army. Having a corps in Italy would permit Canadian commanders to gain battle experience at a more advanced level, but as the army would then be split almost equally between the Mediterranean and Northwest Europe theatres, the prospect of ever reuniting it would become much more unlikely than it was with only one division separated from the main force. McNaughton's objection had little effect, however, in the face of his political masters' determination. Preparations were begun to increase the Mediterranean contingent to corps strength.

The Eighth Army's attack on Reggio di Calabria at the very tip of the Italian 'toe' on September 3, 1943, was preceded by an immense artillery bombardment from the Sicilian shore, although the enemy had already made a strategic withdrawal from the vicinity. Kesselring

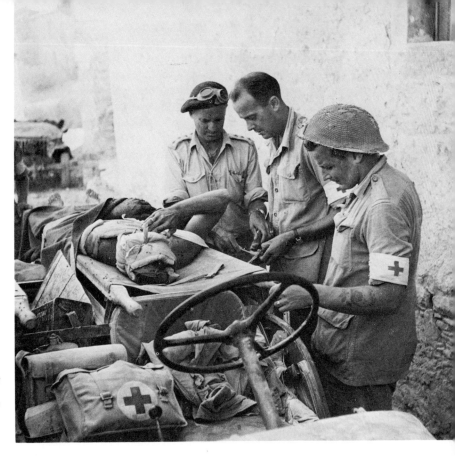

9 A badly wounded German officer is given immediate treatment by two Canadian medical officers while an orderly waits to drive him to the nearest field hospital.

had no intention of offering serious resistance within the limits of effective Allied fighter range because of the danger of a second Allied landing at some point further north on the Italian peninsula protected by air cover operating from Sicily. Marching ashore at Reggio with the British 5th Division, the Canadians met the only actual opposition shortly after they left the beaches. 'There is a zoo in town and our shelling broke open some cages,' Montgomery wrote to Alan Brooke. 'A puma and a monkey escaped and attacked some men of the HQ, 3rd Canadian Brigade, and heavy firing was opened by the Canadians. It is a curious war. ...'5

While the Fifth U.S. Army stormed ashore at Salerno on the 'shin' of the boot—justifying Kesselring's strategy in withdrawing—the Canadians swept up the mainland by way of the 'sole', heading towards the great naval base at Taranto. High in the 'instep' they swung inland, north towards Melfi, which was reached on September 26. With them were the tanks of the Calgary Regiment; of the other units of the 1st Tank Brigade, the Ontarios were with the British 5th Division on the western coast and the Three Rivers Regiment, which had borne the brunt of the Sicilian fighting, remained in Sicily until September 24. The ease of the initial advance during the Canadians' first three weeks on the mainland of Europe was reflected in their light casualties—32 killed, 146 wounded, and 3 taken prisoner. But north of Melfi the Germans began to stiffen their resistance and the rate of advance slowed noticeably.

During October the Canadians found themselves pushing into the central mountain range as the Allies drove north from Naples and Foggia, the American Fifth Army on the left of the Appenines and the British Eighth on the right. The October mornings were heralded by thick, heavy mist that quickly soaked clothes and equipment and, as often as not, each day brought a steady drizzle of cold rain. War artist Charles Comfort wrote of his visit to a regiment of field artillery: 'Officers and men, wearing all the clothing they possessed, mud to the knees, huddled about small charcoal fires, made in biscuit tins or oil cans. In our improvised lean-to, we felt that the limit for resistance had been reached.'[6] For the combat infantrymen, who were skirmishing still further forward and were about to find themselves up against the Gustav Line—the forward edge of the Germans' first major defensive position—things were even worse.

A thousand miles to the north-west, in London, General McNaughton found himself being pressured out of the command of the army he had built so carefully. At 56 he had been doing two men's jobs for nearly four years, as a formation commander and as senior Canadian officer overseas, and undoubtedly he was tired. He had still never led men in battle on a formation level—his First World War reputation had been built on impeccable staff work and an innovative technical approach to gunnery—and it was claimed by higher British commanders, who may have been influenced by a personal dislike of McNaughton, that his battle-command capability was doubtful. He seemed to them to lack both operational understanding (a judgement based solely on training exercises) and the capacity to deal ruthlessly with his subordinates in the demanding circumstances of the complex mobile campaigns expected in Northwest Europe.

Could McNaughton have served under the domineering Montgomery, especially after the Sicilian episode? Probably not. But perhaps a more significant factor in his removal from the scene was his concern with maintaining Canadian autonomy in the maelstrom of military intrigue that swirled about the British Cabinet and chiefs of staff once the United States was in the war and eventual victory was assured. He was also at loggerheads with his own superior, the Minister of National Defence, who 'clearly favours early action for all or most of our men', as Mackenzie King confided to his diary.[7] Ralston did not object to splitting Canadian forces and putting parts of them under British control.

The Prime Minister agreed with McNaughton on the subject of a united Canadian army. He might have been willing to cross swords with Ralston, but he was clearly not prepared to question the British military assessment of McNaughton's fitness to command. At the end of December 1943 McNaughton went, as gracefully as circum-

Men of the Carleton and York Regiment hunt snipers in the narrow, stepped streets of Campochiaro in October 1943. The body lying across the street, between the first two soldiers, is that of an Italian civilian, caught in the cross fire.

stances permitted, into semi-retirement. (It was announced that he was taking sick leave.) In Ottawa Lieutenant-General K. Stuart, Ralston's right-hand man, relinquished his appointment as Chief of the General Staff to go to London as Chief of Staff, Canadian Military Headquarters. As the *Manchester Guardian* astutely observed at the time, 'General Stuart comes to England as Colonel Ralston's senior service lieutenant and thus will bring Canadian troops overseas under the direct control of the Minister.'

The Gustav Line was the southern edge of a defence in depth intended to hold the Allies at least for the rest of the winter. Stretching across the narrowest part of the peninsula, its eastern half was based on the virtually impregnable peaks of the Abruzzi in the central mountain spine and on a succession of swift-flowing rivers that cut across the coastal plain to the Adriatic. Once again the 1st Division, now commanded by Major-General Chris Vokes, found itself in mountains, threatening an attack across the upper Sangro—the first of the river barriers—while the British V Corps (which included the Canadian tank regiments, now remustered as the 1st Canadian Armoured Brigade) 'hit the Germans a colossal crack' (in Montgomery's words) further downstream. At the end of the month the whole of

71 General Montgomery, General Crerar, and Colonel Ralston, outside Montgomery's tactical headquarters at San Pietro in November 1943, immediately after the arrival of First Canadian Corps in Italy.

the ridge commanding the lower Sangro had been taken and the Canadians were ordered down into the plain, slated to spearhead the drive for Ortona with their own Canadian Armoured Brigade in support.

Along the coast the weather was milder but wetter and the heavy clay soil was churned into a thick, voracious slurry by the passage of hundreds of vehicles. Towns and villages—key points in the flow of battle—were reduced to heaps of rubble by the bombing and shelling of both sides. The fields and vineyards between them were cut by deep gullies that created natural traps for attacking armour and provided convenient entrenchments for the German infantry. Air support was inevitably sporadic and uncertain in the cloudy, rainy weather. The Canadians slogged forward against a resolute and well-conducted German defence from the Moro to the Riccio Rivers, covering only a distance of less than 5 miles in more than a month. The padré of one of the armoured regiments remembered later how 'we used to watch the infantry going up into the line. Single file they trudged along, guns carried anyhow, ammo slung round them, trousers bagged and down at heels. No war loan posters at home would show them that way. The P.B.I. [Poor Bloody Infantry] going into the line.'[8] The Canadians lost 2,400 killed, wounded or taken prisoner, and over 1,600 sick. In the third week of December cases of battle

2 Men of the
Edmonton Regiment
move down a street in
Ortona to take their
turn at 'mouse-holing'
and sniper hunting.

fatigue (included in the sickness statistics) rose to 20 per cent of all casualties, and every rifle company in the division had lost at least 50 per cent of its original strength.

As the Canadians fought their way into Ortona, Captain Paul Triquet of the 'Van Doos' won French Canada's first Victoria Cross of the war at Casa Berardi on December 14—the first of three to be awarded to Canadians in Italy. The taking of Casa Berardi settled the possession of the Ortona-Orsogna road and ensured that supplies and reliefs could move up steadily to the infantry pressing north. In Ortona, against most stubborn German resistance, the Canadians perfected a technique of street fighting that would become standard for the rest of the war. Since anyone on foot was a sure target in the rubble-strewn streets, which were mostly impassable to armour, groups of three or four men—a half-section at the most—moved through the shell- and bomb-blasted houses on each side, 'mouse-holing' with high explosives the stone walls of each top floor and then clearing them of German paratroopers from the top down with grenades and sub-machine guns. Only those who were quick, care-

73 A street in Ortona as the battle ebbed away. A Canadian Bren carrier and two motorcycles are damaged while a truck and jeep burn as a result of German mortaring.

ful, and lucky survived to tackle the next street. Booby-traps were common and sometimes the enemy mined a house before leaving through his own 'mouse-hole'.

The fighting increased in intensity. It was 'a carnival of fury', said the CBC correspondent Matthew Halton, who was there on Christmas Day. 'Christmas dinner in the shelled, broken church in Ortona. Candles and white tablecloths ... not four hundred yards from the enemy, carol singers, the platoons coming in in relays to eat a Christmas dinner—men who hadn't had their clothes off in thirty days coming in and eating their dinners, and carol singers singing "Silent Night" '!⁹

Ortona fell officially two days later. As the West Nova Scotia Regiment moved through the town, on its way to the line, on December 29, it found that 'the stench of rotting bodies arose from the ruins like an all-but-invisible mist'. By then the country immediately beyond 'was a desolation of shattered farmhouses and villas, burnt haystacks, and shell-pocked fields, sodden with the winter rains, and befouled with unburied German dead and a litter of equipment, shattered cannon, burnt-out tanks and vehicles.'¹⁰

4 Christmas in a part
f Ortona taken by the
llies (not quite as close
) the front line as the
cene described by
Matthew Halton). The
rigade headquarters
taff enjoy their Christ-
nas dinner in the
hurch of Santa Maria
vhile the signals
fficer plays carols on
ne organ. The men are
)oking happy partly
ecause it is Christmas
nd partly because they
re not in one of the
ifle companies actually
n the line.

The 5th Armoured Division, placed under the command of General Simonds, had arrived in Italy on November 8, 1943. Two divisions in the field now justified the creation of a corps headquarters, over 10,000 strong, including four regiments of artillery and all the usual support units, among which were two General Hospitals of 600 and 1,200 beds respectively. On December 23 command of the new corps was given to Lieutenant-General Crerar, who was being groomed to take McNaughton's place at the head of First Canadian Army. When the 5th Division began to filter into the front around Orsogna in early February 1944, an entire Canadian corps was in action for the first time since the First World War, under circumstances not too unlike those their fathers had known in Flanders. The weather had shown no signs of improvement and the cold winter rain was saturating everything and everybody. When General Crerar, who could now claim at least a brief acquaintance with command of a corps in battle, paid his last visit to the line in February 1944, he looked at the ground north of Ortona and recalled the morass of Passchendaele in 1917.

In mid-February the offensive finally petered out on the high

75 When Ortona became a battlefield in December 1943, this Italian family moved out into the countryside and dug caves in a sandy hillside. They were still living there in mid-February 1944 when this picture was taken by a *Toronto Star* correspondent.

ground overlooking the Arielli—the next river north—and Allied planners began to turn their attention to the western flank of the Appenines. General Montgomery had already left for the United Kingdom to play his part in Operation *Overlord*—the invasion of Northwest Europe—and during the rest of the winter three veteran British divisions of the Eighth Army followed him. The failure of the Canadian government to ensure that their two divisions also went back when Generals Crerar and Simonds left to join the *Overlord* team made it seem most unlikely that the Canadians would ever fight as an army in Northwest Europe. Montgomery was succeeded by General Leese, in whose XXX Corps the Canadian 1st Division had fought in Sicily. Major-General E.L.M. Burns, who had commanded the 5th Armoured Division since General Simonds' departure, was promoted to command the Canadian Corps in March. A dour, introverted intellectual, Burns might have established an adequate command relationship with Montgomery but was a poor choice to work with the huntin'-shootin'-and-fishin' extrovert, Leese. Burns was nicknamed 'Smiling Sunray' by his troops because he never smiled. ('Sunray' was the radio code-name for any commander.)

In the spring of 1944 the Germans had stopped the Allied armies

5 Men of the Saskat-
hewan Light Infantry
ortar German posi-
ons as a prelude to a
ight attack in the
rtona salient.

in their tracks across the whole width of the Italian peninsula. The
only prospect of breaking the deadlock seemed to be at the western
end of the Gustav Line, where the geography was less unfavourable.
There the comparatively broad valley of the southward-flowing Liri
River pierced the German defences before joining the Rapido to
become the Garigliano. A drive up the Liri appeared to offer the best
possibility of breaking the enemy front—if only the enduring bastion
of Monte Cassino, which dominated the mouth of the valley, could
be subdued. Moreover, on January 22 an amphibious landing had
been made by two corps—one American (which included the élite
Canadian-American First Special Service Force, a commando-type
unit) and one British—at Anzio, 34 miles south of Rome. But the
Germans had kept them pinned into a small perimeter, where a
counter-attack might easily throw them back into the sea at any time.
In order to relieve the Anzio bridgehead, concentrate as much pressure as possible on the Germans' weakest point, and force them 'to
commit the maximum number of divisions in Italy at the time that
Overlord is launched' (in the words of General Alexander's Chief of
Staff), it was decided to move part of the Eighth Army onto the western flank and launch a major attack in the Liri valley.

77 Under enemy observation and fire, an artillery FOO (Forward Observation Officer) with the PPCLI sprints across 50 yards of open ground that was once the vineyard and olive grove of an Italian farm. The two wine bottles in the lower left corner had been carefully 'booby trapped' by the Germans.

In April the Canadians began their move across the Appenines, leaving behind them in Ortona the graves of 1,372 of their comrades—nearly a quarter of the total number of Canadians who were killed in the Mediterranean campaign. On May 11 British, French, and American troops attacked the western flank of the Gustav Line, which marked the opening of the battle for Rome. The Canadian Corps was held in reserve, but the independent 1st Canadian Armoured Brigade played an important role in providing close support fire for the initial crossings of the Garigliano by the 8th Indian and 4th British Divisions.

In a night attack the British and Indians established precarious footholds on the northern bank, but the crossing-points were dominated by German guns, and getting reinforcements across to expand the bridgeheads would be difficult. One prefabricated 'Bailey' bridge was erected by dawn, but to put up another in daylight seemed impossible. Then two tanks of the Calgary Regiment appeared, bearing between them a complete 100-foot span of bridging that had been put together well behind the front. Alongside both tanks—the first of which was turretless—walked an officer of the Royal Canadian Electrical and Mechanical Engineers, coolly controlling their speed and direction by telephone, although he was wounded before very long. Driving up to the river bank under heavy fire, the first tank went straight into the water, its crew escaping just as it became submerged to the top of its hull. The rear tank kept going and the bridge slid over the top of the first tank to the far side

78

"YOU SCRAM! THERE AINT ROOM FOR THREE HERE."

of the river. The pusher tank then disconnected and presto!—a new method of bridging small rivers had been proven in the field. It was no fault of the Canadian inventor and director of this bridging operation that the bridge was temporarily put out of action by German shellfire after only four of the Calgary's tanks had crossed.

Eventually, however, sufficient of the Canadian armour was got across and the bridgeheads were secured. Cassino finally fell to the Eighth Army's Polish Corps. (Its thousand-year-old abbey was pulverized by Allied bombing.) Then the Canadian infantry was thrust into the mouth of the Liri valley to 'open up' the hole appearing in the Gustav Line. It was spring and the countryside was at last beginning to resemble that sunny Italy beloved of peacetime travel agents. Armour and air support was plentiful. The fighting bore little resemblance to the prolonged winter battles around Ortona, although it was just as bitter. In two days the Canadians stabbed forward 5 miles and were pressing against a new set of German defences. On their right the British 78th Division kept abreast of them, while on the left a Free French corps and the II (U.S.) Corps of the Fifth Army were also across the Garigliano and driving north towards Anzio and Rome.

The new obstacle was the Hitler Line, another prepared defensive position. Immensely strong but quite shallow, it split off from the Gustav Line in the central mountain massif and, where it crossed the Liri valley, lay about 6 miles further north. Overcoming it demanded a major, carefully co-ordinated set-piece assault and this time General Leese assigned the leading role to the Canadians. General Vokes, whose 1st Division was to lead the way, selected a 2,000-yard-wide axis of advance on the east bank of the Liri where the ground seemed most suitable for the tanks of the 5th Armoured Division, which would follow through to exploit any success. The 5th was commanded by Major-General B.M. Hoffmeister, a pre-war militia captain who had distinguished himself in command of an infantry brigade and who was to be the only Canadian militia officer to achieve general-officer rank in an operational command during the Second World War.

Beginning on May 19 an artillery bombardment of 1,000 shells per hour crashed down on all known enemy strong points, while each night, after dark, infantry and engineer patrols cautiously probed the forward edge of the German defences, lifting mines and reconnoitring tank routes. On May 22 the chaplain of the Seaforth Highlanders noted in his diary that 'my boys move in tonight. ... New boys with fear and nerves and anxiety hidden under quick smiles and quick seriousness. Old campaigners with a far away look. It is the hardest thing to watch without breaking into tears.'[11] He might indeed have cried had he known what was to follow. The next morning Vokes's men charged forward under a barrage of fire from more than 800 guns and every available plane of the Allied tactical air forces. By nightfall the Seaforths had lost more than a quarter of the battalion killed, wounded, or prisoner, the heaviest losses they suffered in one day throughout the war. The 2nd Brigade's losses totalled 543, the Division's nearly 900. Once again flaws in control and communications at various levels, coupled with the initial failure of the British 78th Division to take their objective on the Canadians' right flank, served only to emphasize the effect of a masterly German defensive plan. The supporting armour was devastated by a combination of well-sited minefields, enemy artillery concentrations, and the fire of 'Panzerturm'—tank turrets, sunk into reinforced concrete, whose 75-mm guns commanded nearly every line of advance with their interlocking fire. The Ontario Regiment, for example, lost twelve tanks to the Panzerturm and one to mines, while all its other tanks took one or more direct hits from high-explosive shells. The infantry were left to plunge forward without immediate fire support, funnelled into 'killing grounds'—a hail of mortar bursts and machine-gun and rifle fire. The Seaforth Highlander whose description of the Sicily landing has already been quoted was wounded in this attack only seconds after the events he describes:

> My mind had but one thought; get through the barrage, get through the barrage. . . . No one except the wounded or the dead stopped. . . . Over to the left a German jumped up and seemed to be raising his hands when he was killed by one of our fellows. Directly ahead and about fifty yards away a Jerry stood up and held his machine gun in his arms. A long burst tore into eight platoon to my right. I fired two rounds from the hip at the same time that others must have fired. The Jerry folded up and fell. I stepped on his bloody head as I passed over the position a few seconds later.[12]

The Hitler Line was broken on May 23, 1943. 'I send my greetings and congratulations to your magnificent fighting men . . . ', signaled General Juin, the commander of the Free French corps, who had watched the Canadian attack from the high ground on the other side of the Liri. 'You have done great things in this valley.' The 5th Armoured Division began to move forward, to exploit the break.

As the Germans were forced back on May 23 and the breach deepened and widened, General Leese inserted his XIII Corps into it on the Canadians' right. This was a mistake. The valley became too nar-

80 A photograph of Adolf Hitler and two pictures of himself taken in happier days lie beside the body of this Luftwaffe sergeant of the Hermann Goering Division.

row to carry two corps abreast, each under its own entirely separate headquarters. (If more troops were necessary, they should all have been put under one command.) Nevertheless they poured through the hole punched by General Vokes's 1st Division, which found itself with the Liri on its left and the British 6th Armoured of XIII Corps on its right.

Hoffmeister's men set off in fine style. On May 24 the Lord Strathcona's Horse were leading in their Sherman tanks. A tank commander has recalled the advance:

> 'Push on now' came the Colonel's voice over the wireless and sixty tanks began to roll forward, spreading out into formation. ... a feeling of exhilaration began to take hold. Others had been hit but I was indestructible. Then it happened. One moment, the world around me was full of vivid colour ... and then suddenly, in the fraction of an instant, everything had turned to inky blackness .... At that same instant, from what seemed a long way off, there came a mighty metallic clang as though some great anvil had been struck by a giant sledgehammer.
>
> I think I knew right away what the trouble was. This was not the blackness of unconsciousness or the blackness of death. I was alive, that was certain, but I was blind. ... I slumped forward in the turret,

hands rubbing at eyes, trying to brush away the veil, trying to see something, anything, that would tell me it wasn't true.[13]

But it *was* true. In a Caserta hospital a doctor told him, 'I'm sorry, but we have had to remove both eyes. You see, there was no hope of saving them.' By then his division had forced a crossing of the Melfa, a tributary of the Liri, where Major J.K. Mahony of the Westminster Regiment won a Victoria Cross. But when the British armoured division was stopped by a German rear-guard in a defile and forced over to the left; the 5th was ordered to sidestep to the left also, thus compressing the Canadian front.

Jammed against the Liri, with the British squeezing in from the right and the 1st Division following up immediately behind, the 5th (and Corps headquarters) got into something of a tangle in this extraordinarily crowded valley. Relatively inexperienced commanders and staffs were put under tremendous pressure. The advance lost momentum and the control problem was further complicated by a botched bridging job that held up Hoffmeister's armour for twenty-four hours as it tried to move to a new axis of advance across the Liri. On May 28 the Canadians finally crossed. However, on June 3 General Leese ordered them 'pinched out' of the front so that Juin's Free French, moving up on the left, might slide on to the Canadian axis and press the pursuit.

The operations of the Canadians in the race for Rome demonstrated their lack of experience in fluid battle conditions. At Ortona they had proved themselves in 'static' fighting as bitter and vicious as that at Stalingrad a year earlier, although it had been on a much smaller scale. The Hitler Line, too, had been a set-piece affair. Fluid battle, however, involved much more complex military problems. On May 23 General Burns had been in command of the corps for only ninety days. Hoffmeister had never handled a division of any kind, never mind an armoured one, until he replaced Burns as commander of the 5th Division in March. Their staffs were also lacking the practical experience of handling mobile operations at their respective levels. These weaknesses—based on inexperience and greatly exacerbated by General Leese's blunder—made the Canadians the last choice to pursue the Germans further.

The Americans on the left of the French linked up with their troops in the Anzio bridgehead on May 25 and Rome fell to them on June 4. Its capture was quickly overshadowed by the launching of Operation *Overlord* just two days later.

7
OPERATION 'OVERLORD'

Planning for the invasion of Northwest Europe had begun in October 1941 the principle of an invasion through France had been confirmed. The Americans suggested that such an operation might be the mainland from which the BEF had so recently been ejected at Dunkirk. By December 1941 it had outlined an assault—for which the raid on Dieppe in August 1942 was a dress rehearsal—on the French coast between Dieppe and Deauville at some unspecified time in the future. When the United States entered the war in December 1941 the principle of an invasion through France had been confirmed. The Americans suggested that such an operation might be mounted during 1943, but the British were chary of mounting a premature attack and, as we have seen, were anxious to reaffirm their influence in the Mediterranean. Bowing to British experience, their allies had reluctantly accepted the postponement of a cross-channel assault in favour of the attack on Sicily and Italy.

In March 1943 an Anglo-American planning staff began to consider in detail the strategy and logistics of invading France. The requirement for air cover from fighters limited the possible area of assault to the French and Dutch coasts between Cherbourg and Flushing. The knowledge and technology that had developed from the Dieppe experience meant that the attack need not be launched through a port, but not every beach would be suitable. Such technical considerations as tides, beach slopes, roads, and regional topography soon narrowed the possibilities to two main areas: the Pas de Calais and the Baie de la Seine.

In many ways the Pas de Calais was the most suitable, but for those very reasons it was also where the German defences were strongest. Moreover, major port facilities would eventually be needed and their capture from the Calais beaches would involve taking either Antwerp on one side—a strategy that would demand the crossing of several major water obstacles—or Le Havre on the other, a medium-sized port more than 60 miles to the west. The Baie de la Seine, on the other hand, was much more lightly defended and the great port of Cherbourg lay only 25 miles from its western end; furthermore, a short thrust across the Cherbourg peninsula would isolate it from further reinforcement.

On August 15, 1943, in the course of the second day of the Anglo-American summit conference ('Quadrant') at Quebec, the plan for

Operation *Overlord* was accepted by the Combined Chiefs of Staff. It outlined an assault on Northwest Europe via the Baie de la Seine to take place in late May or early June 1944. Ten months of detailed planning and meticulous rehearsal followed. On Christmas Eve 1943, General Eisenhower, who had been commanding the combined Allied forces in the Mediterranean, was appointed Supreme Commander, Allied Expeditionary Force. Air Chief Marshal Sir Arthur Tedder became his deputy, Admiral Sir Charles Little was to command the combined naval forces, and Air Marshal Sir Trafford Leigh-Mallory was appointed air commander-in-chief.

Perhaps because of the violent personality clashes with which Montgomery was often involved, no commander-in-chief was appointed for the ground forces. General Omar Bradley would take command of the American 12th Army Group, while the far more experienced Montgomery would lead only the British 21st Army Group of the Second British and First Canadian Armies. However, Montgomery would be responsible for planning and for the tactical co-ordination of all ground forces during the initial stages of the assault until the number of men ashore and security of the bridgehead justified setting up two army group establishments.

The landing phase of *Overlord*, called Operation *Neptune*, was postponed for twenty-four hours by forecasts of poor weather. But in the early hours of June 6, 1944, 5,000 ships of every conceivable function, shape, and size were moving steadily into the Baie de la Seine. Far out on each flank, 9 Canadian destroyers of the River class, 11 frigates, and 19 corvettes, together with 6 RCAF coastal reconnaissance and strike squadrons, shared the task of protecting the vast armada from German interference. In mid-channel, Tribal-class destroyers of the naval covering force, including HMCS *Haida* and *Huron*, kept their stations along each side of the invasion 'corridor' ready to repel attacks by anything that might evade the outer defences. A U-boat commander was to write in his autobiography of 'a steel screen of ships and guns . . . a dark umbrella of aircraft. Sixteen of the latest Snort [Schnorkel] boats sailed out to meet the allied armada. One got through.'[1]

Fleet-class destroyers assigned to beach bombardment duties led the long lines of landing craft and assault transports, among them the Canadian ships *Prince Henry* and *Prince David* and five flotillas of Canadian landing craft, totalling more than forty vessels. In the van steamed the little minesweepers, including the 31st Canadian Minesweeping Flotilla. Scattered among the other sweeping flotillas were six more Canadian minesweepers. Working to precise limits under the most exacting conditions, every sweeper faced not only the danger of being mined itself but also the possibilities of shore gunfire, air attack, or the onslaught of German E-boats—extremely fast, heavily armed motor launches. One in three of the ships in the minesweeping force sailed as a reserve against expected casualties. As things turned out, the reserve was not needed. 'In the early evening we were still 40 miles off the French coast,' a Canadian sailor wrote in his diary.

> We hadn't met any opposition at all so far. We couldn't understand it ... The sky was still overcast, but an hour or two after nightfall we could just make out the deeper darkness of the French coast, now only 14 miles away off our starboard bow ... Then in the flat perspectiveless light before dawn we could see the ships that had followed us in. They'd found the channel all right. ... There were ships everywhere, big troop transports, cruisers, destroyers, and landing craft of every description. Soon we could see that the landings had indeed begun. The shore was lined with beached craft, and beyond them the land lay under a pall of smoke. Cruisers were pouring out salvo after salvo in support of the troops, but I couldn't see any answering fire at all.[2]

Self-propelled assault artillery in the landing craft also blazed away at the coast ahead, along with amphibious tanks that had slipped into the water a mile offshore. Vessels bearing batteries of 1,100 3-inch rocket tubes—each firing a salvo equivalent in explosive power to the gunfire of a hundred medium cruisers—drenched selected areas with fire. Supported by this overwhelming weight of firepower and led by flail tanks and the armoured Assault Vehicles of the Royal Engineers, the first troops stormed ashore. 'We are getting close now and the bombardment stops,' wrote a subaltern of the Regina Rifles; 'so far not a shot has been fired from the defenders on the beach. Will it be a pushover? We soon have the answer in the form of machine gun fire and shells from pill boxes which are apparently still open for business despite the terrific pounding they have taken.'[3]

VICTORY IN EUROPE
6 June 1944 – 8 May 1945

0   50   100   200
Miles

CANADIAN ASSAULTS "D" DAY

German resistance nests...

THIRD CANADIAN INFANTRY DIV.
H.Q. 2 ARMOURED BRIGADE

NINTH INF BDE

7 INF BDE   8 INF BDE

FIFTH BRIT INF DIV

BEACHES   MIKE

la Rivière

Courselles-sur-Mer   St Aubin-sur-Mer

Ste Croix-sur-Mer   Bernières-sur-Mer

Banville

THIRD BRIT INF DIV

Beny-sur-Mer   Tailleville

Lion-sur-Mer

Creully   Seulles

FRONT LINE 6 – 1 JUNE   Anguerny

Benouville

Villons-les-Buissons

0   1   2   3
Miles

716TH INFANTRY DIVISION   21ST PANZER DIVISION

Authie

BAYEUX   Caen   Orne

Map labels

Liverpool
Birmingham
N
Cardiff
Bristol
LONDON
I. OF WIGHT
ENGLISH CHANNEL
Dover
Calais
Boulogne
Ostend
Cherbourg
Le Havre
Dieppe
FIRST U.S. ARMY
SECOND BRIT ARMY
6 JUNE 1944
Bayeux
St-Lô
Caen
Rouen
Thury-Harcourt
Falaise
Mortain
Argentan
Le Mans
PARIS
Reims
Troyes
St-Nazaire
Orleans
Loire
FRONT LINE, 25 AUG 1944
Seine
Dijon
Vichy
Bordeaux
FRANCE

NORTH SEA
FRISIAN ISLANDS
Wilhelmshaven
Cuxhaven
Wismar
Emden
Hamburg
Groningen
Oldenburg
Bremen
NETHERLANDS
Zwolle
AMSTERDAM
Apeldoorn
Utrecht
Weser
BERLIN
Rotterdam
Arnhem
Nijmegen
Wesel
Dortmund
Dusiburg
Dortmund
WALCHEREN
Antwerp
Scheldt
Düsseldorf
BRUSSELS
Maas
BELGIUM
Rochefort
Remagen
LUX
Frankfurt
Rhine
GERMANY
Karlsruhe
Nancy   U.S. ARMY
Strasbourg
SEVENTH   FIRST FRENCH ARMY
Munich
Danube
Basle

FIRST CANADIAN ARMY
SECOND BRITISH ARMY
FIRST U.S. ARMY
THIRD U.S. ARMY

EASTERN FRONT 6 MAY 1945
WESTERN FRONT, 6 MAY 1945

The Americans would land on two beaches, 'Omaha' and 'Utah' at the western end of the Baie, and the Commonwealth forces on 'Gold', 'Juno', and 'Sword' to the east. The 3rd Canadian Division, under Major-General R.F.L. Keller, was assigned to 'Juno', with the British 3rd and 50th Divisions to their left and right on 'Gold' and 'Sword'.

The Canadians on 'Juno' met the stiffest resistance of any of the Commonwealth assaults. The padre of the North Shore Regiment recalled that 'the beach was sprayed from all angles by the enemy

> the beach was sprayed from all angles by the enemy machine guns and now their mortars and heavy guns began hitting us. Crawling along in the sand, I just reached a group of three badly wounded men when a shell landed among us killing the others outright. As we crawled we could hear the bullets and shrapnel cutting into the sand around us. ... A ramp had been placed against the [sea] wall by now. Over it we went ... two stretcher bearers ahead of us stepped on a mine ... half-dazed, we jumped down again behind the wall.[4]

A sergeant in the British engineer company neutralizing mines watched two Canadians bash in the skull of a German:

> We were up in the dunes at the top of the beach, just on the other side of the Seulles river ... and as we got to the top of a rise I saw my first German. He was alive but not for very long. These two Canadians who were with me were running up the beach behind me with their rifles. Just as they went up behind me through this opening in the sea wall, the Jerry came up out of the emplacement with a Schmiesser [sub-machine gun]. I thought—Christ! They haven't seen. I hadn't got a Sten gun, it had gone in the drink. But they just didn't stop running, they just cracked their rifle butts down on the German and that was that.[5]

On the extreme eastern flank of the Commonwealth bridgeheads some elements of the 21st Panzer Division came into action against the British during the afternoon. On the whole, though, the German reaction was untypically slow. Their commanders were at first uncertain whether this was a subsidiary attack to one that might come further east at any time, or whether it was in fact the opening of the Second Front. This uncertainty the Allies had fostered with complex deception schemes.

At the end of the day the Allies had succeeded in establishing themselves on all five beaches, but they had not reached any of their assigned objectives several miles inland. Nor had they achieved the intended build-up of men and matériel. Plans had called for 107,000 men to be put ashore with 7,000 vehicles and 14,500 tons of supplies, but only 80 per cent of the men, 50 per cent of the machines, and 30 per cent of the supplies had been landed. However, the enemy was unable to exploit the situation, since their front-line defenders had sustained heavy losses in both men and equipment. Furthermore, Allied tactical air power prevented the Germans from quickly filling

2 Men of the Royal Winnipeg Rifles plunge ashore from a Landing Craft (Assault) on D-Day. Within minutes they—together with a squadron of the 6th (1st Hussars) Armoured Regiment—were attacking a strong point that had not been put out of action by the preliminary bombardments. In the words of the official historian, 'When the strong point was clear, "B" Company had been reduced to the company commander and 26 men.'

the vacuum immediately behind their front caused by placing their reserve divisions too far back. The Canadian spearheads dug in at nightfall 3 or 4 miles inland, ready to call down upon any counter-attack an overwhelming weight of naval gunfire. Six battleships, two 15-inch gun monitors, 23 cruisers, and 77 destroyers assigned specifically to fire-support duties were cruising off the beaches all night.

The next morning the Canadian 7th Brigade reached its D-Day objectives before noon, the first Allied formation to do so. The 9th Brigade, however, pressing towards Carpiquet airfield, met with a reverse. Elements of the 12th S.S. Panzer Division came into action, driving them back several miles to a point only slightly further inland than the one they had reached the day before. Here, just north of Carpiquet, the Canadians fought, and lost, their first real battle in Northwest Europe. They fought 'with courage and spirit but somewhat clumsily',[6] as when their supporting artillery regiment found itself too far back to supply covering fire at the vital moment. They showed weaknesses that were to bedevil most of the Allied forces throughout the Northwest Europe campaign: a ponderous approach to battle, poor co-operation between infantry and armour, a failure of regimental or battalion commanders to keep their superiors quickly and fully informed of what was happening, and a disconcertingly unprofessional approach that too often expressed itself in a tendency to rely on raw courage and self-confidence without employing adequate planning and judgement. These last two weaknesses were perhaps more in evidence among the Canadians (and continued to be evident throughout the rest of the war) than among any other Allied forces.

A certain ruthlessness was exhibited by both sides. On D-Day a

British seaman on a landing craft unloading at Courseulles watched Canadian soldiers march six Germans behind a sand dune some distance away. Bent on getting a souvenir from the prisoners, he ran up the beach only to find the six 'all crumpled up. ... Every one had had his throat cut.'[7] And Kurt Meyer, the commander of the 12th S.S. Division, which joined the battle on June 7, was convicted of countenancing the killing of Canadian prisoners by men of his division at a court martial held in December 1945.*

The first few weeks of fighting in the bridgehead were probably as bitter and malevolent as anything seen on the more notorious Eastern Front. The German formations were soon greatly outnumbered by the Allies, but a very high percentage of the enemy officers and NCOs had seen hard fighting in the east and their battle leadership did much to compensate for their comparative lack of men and matériel. Moreover, the enemy's Panther and Tiger tanks were superior both in armour and armament to the Allies' Shermans and Churchills (although their turrets had to be cranked around by hand), so that in this respect too the numerical imbalance in favour of the Allies was largely cancelled out. The scale was turned by Allied airpower—particularly by tactical airpower. 'On the morning of June 10,' wrote Gehr von Schweppenberg, the commander of the Panzer army in Normandy, ' ... I saw a Panzer Regiment in action against the Canadians. It was hellish but in this case the hell came from the sky.'[8] Three hours later he was being helped wounded from the ruins of his headquarters after an attack on it by British and Dutch light bombers and fighter-bombers of the 2nd Tactical Air Force.

The foundation of Allied air superiority had been laid long before D-Day. For the past two years 'rhubarbs' and 'circuses'—the fighter pilots' terms for massed fighter sweeps over Northwest Europe—had been paring away at the German fighter strength in the west, while the Allied bomber offensive over Germany pinned the largest part of the Luftwaffe's fighter arm to the defence of the Fatherland itself. By D-Day the Luftwaffe in France had been reduced to only 319 aircraft in a state of operational readiness, less than 100 of the total being fighters. Against them were ranged some six to seven thousand Allied aircraft, including more than 3,000 fighters and fighter-bombers. Three RCAF fighter wings of Spitfire IXs—each three squadrons strong and led by Canadian Wing Commanders Lloyd Chadburn and George Keefer, together with the British ace (and one of the top-scoring Commonwealth pilots of the war) 'Johnnie' Johnson—formed the core of the Canadian contingent. They were backed by a fighter-re-

83 German prisoners, taken during the early stages of the landing, carrying a wounded Canadian down to the beach. The Canadian clutches German boots and a helmet picked up as souvenirs. A Canadian corporal follows the stretcher; the sergeant and private on the left are British.

84 Canadian casualties wait to be taken off the D-Day beaches surrounded by British engineers and medics digging protective trenches to place them in, and with an abandoned German cannon looming ominously above them.

* He was sentenced to death, but despite a public outcry the sentence was commuted to life imprisonment by General Vokes, who was then commanding the Canadian occupation forces. Meyer was eventually released from Dorchester Penitentiary in September 1954.

85 Servicing a Spitfire at a forward airstrip in Normandy. This light-weight aircraft, with its comparatively wide and stable undercarriage, could land and take off from grass runways if necessary.

connaissance wing of Spitfires commanded by Group Captain E.H.G. Moncreiff (J.M. Godfrey became his 'Wingco (Flying)' on July 2) and by a wing of Typhoon fighter-bombers led by Wing Commander R.T.P. Davidson, RAF.

It was primarily the fighter-bombers—'Jabos' (for *Jagdbombern*), the Germans called them—that supplied 'the hell from the sky' that so impressed von Schweppenberg. Luftwaffe fighters appeared over the beaches on June 7, when Keefer's wing was credited with 12 destroyed, 1 probably destroyed, and 4 damaged; and again on June 15 when 127 Wing—whose first leader, Chadburn, had been killed in a mid-air collision two days earlier, to be succeeded by Bob Buckham—claimed another 9 destroyed and 2 damaged. Except for those two brief flurries there was little for the *Jabos* to worry about in the air. German planning had called for another 600 fighters to be brought from Germany in the event of an invasion of France, and these aircraft began to move on June 7 and 8. However, the weight of Allied bomber and fighter-bomber attacks on their assigned tactical airfields destroyed so many of the incoming machines before they could become operational and caused such havoc in the enemy's logistics system that, after June 12, no more than 250 German fighters were ever available for operations. The total was often much less.

In the absence of serious opposition the Tactical Air Force was able to play a major role in the land battle, slashing at the German supply lines as well as strafing and bombing in close support of the ground troops. Fighter-bomber attacks on road and rail bridges, locomotives, and trucks were very effective in slowing the rate at which the enemy's reinforcements reached Normandy. The 2nd S.S. Panzer Division, for example, which was stationed near Toulouse, was ordered forward in the early hours of June 6, but the last of its fighting units did not reach the battlefront until June 23, having taken seventeen nights to travel the 450 miles that could have been covered in a quarter of the time under normal conditions.

During the first four days of *Overlord* Allied fighters and fighter-bombers flew out of English bases, so that the duration of their missions over France and the weight of weaponry they could carry had to be balanced one against the other. Extra tanks of gasoline or additional bombs were alternatives that limited either flight time or the damage that each aircraft could inflict on the enemy. But on June 10 the first airstrip in the bridgehead was ready and that morning Johnson's wing of RCAF Spitfires became the first Allied aircraft to land there. As more airstrips were carved out of the countryside where aircraft could refuel and rearm, air support for the ground forces became both continuous and intense. Any reported movement of German tanks, any massing of his armour, brought an immediate and violent response from the fighter-bombers, so that the techniques of blitzkrieg and mobile warfare were useless to the Germans. Powerful Panther and Tiger tanks, the vaunted cutting-edge of the Wehrmacht, were compelled to adopt a largely static role as nothing more than armoured strong points during daylight. 'Branches and twigs were carefully cut out of a hedge and the tanks decorated with them until they seemed to have been spirited away,' wrote the historian of the élite Panzer Lehr Division. 'Next, the tank tracks in a field of oats had to be obliterated, or they would be a clear signpost for any fighter-bomber. Laboriously each blade was bent back again and made to stand upright.'[9]

The German attempts at sea to interfere with the development of *Overlord* were no more effective than their efforts in the air. On the evening of D-Day an anti-shipping strike wing of Coastal Command—consisting of 14 rocket-armed Beaufighters of 404 Squadron RCAF, and 17 from 144 Squadron RAF, with Mosquitos of the RAF's 235 Squadron providing fighter cover—surprised three German destroyers steaming north, about 30 miles south-west of St Nazaire on the French Atlantic coast, and attacked out of the setting sun. It was reported in the diary of the Canadian squadron that 'when the formation left, the centre destroyer was on fire and the leading destroyer was sinking.' Very early the following morning six of the Canadian Beaufighters found all three destroyers still afloat some distance to the north-west of their previous position. When they arrived, 'the centre destroyer was smoking slightly' and in the subsequent attack 'an explosion was observed in the 2nd or 3rd ship which lit up the ship ahead. The explosion burst to a height of 200 ft and when it subsided the ship was afire internally from stem to stern.'[10] Post-war studies show that no German destroyers were actually lost, despite this dramatic report. However, the prime aim of the Coastal Command strikes was achieved: these three warships played no further part in the prosecution of anti-invasion operations.

Four more German destroyers slipped out of Brest on the dark squally night of June 8 and started up-channel only to be picked up by the radar of a patrolling Allied destroyer flotilla whose eight ships included HMCS *Haida* and *Huron*. As soon as visual contact was established the Germans launched salvoes of torpedoes, then turned away to the west and north. Combing the enemy torpedo tracks, *Haida* and *Huron*, together with HMS *Tartar* and *Ashanti*, took up the chase. In the running fight that followed, *Tartar* was hit and her signalling and radar equipment were badly damaged; *Ashanti* sank one of the German ships; and *Haida* and *Huron*, although their guns scored some hits, were frustrated when their two adversaries escaped by cutting unwittingly across a British minefield without further damage.

While steaming back to their patrol stations, however, the Canadian ships raised another radar contact that proved to be the German vessel that had crippled *Tartar*. Again their enemy avoided them with a lucky dash across a minefield and the Canadians 'swung back northwards to skirt the barrier in an agony of suspense lest this destroyer should also elude them.' Twenty minutes later they found the enemy again and resumed their pursuit. Soon all three ships were bearing down upon the rock-bound French coast at high speed, with guns blazing. While the enemy's guns were still slightly off target, *Haida* and *Huron* were now hitting their quarry repeatedly. In the palest light of dawn the burning enemy destroyer was forced onto the jagged rocks of the Île de Bas. Later that day the Canadian-crewed Beaufighters of 404 Squadron completed its destruction.

On June 15 a heavy bombing attack on the docks of Le Havre disabled four more destroyers and ten motor torpedo boats. The only remaining German naval forces that might be brought into action were a number of light, high-speed gunboats (all of which found it

86 The wreck of a German destroyer that had been driven ashore on the Île de Bas by HMCS *Haida* and *Huron* on June 9, 1944. Its destruction was completed by rocket-firing Beaufighters of 404 Squadron RCAF.

37 HMCS *Haida* at speed, photographed from HMCS *Huron*.

virtually impossible to penetrate the Allied destroyer and MTB screens) and the submarine fleet. During the first week of the invasion, 43 U-boats left from bases in Norway and on the Atlantic coast. Of these, 12 had to return prematurely with mechanical defects or damage caused by Allied depth-charges, 18 were sunk, and only 13 succeeded in completing their patrols. During the first three months of *Overlord* the U-boats managed to sink between them only 7 small warships (from destroyer escorts to minesweepers), 3 landing craft, and 13 transports, totalling some 55,000 tons—an infinitesimal fraction of the invasion fleets.

On June 24, approximately 15 miles north-west of Ushant, U-971 was destroyed by the depth-charges and guns of *Haida*, working in conjunction with HMS *Eskimo*. After two hours of depth-charging, the submarine was forced to surface; gunfire from *Haida* blew open the base of its conning-tower and set it on fire. Two weeks later, on the eastern side of the invasion corridor, the Canadian destroyers *Ottawa* and *Kootenay* shared in the destruction of U-678.

Two of the seven Allied warships sunk by U-boats were Canadian. During June each of the Canadian corvettes made at least six return trips to the Normandy beaches. Despite attacks by the occasional enemy bomber, glider bomb or E-boat, they suffered no serious damage—though an American destroyer mistakenly put a shell through the engine room of the *Trentonian*. Fortunately there were no casualties.

Things were much the same in July—*Alberni* was credited with shooting down a Ju-88 bomber over the *Neptune* anchorage—but in August the Canadians' luck turned sour. On the 8th *Regina* went to the aid of a freighter that reported she had been mined off Trevose Head. In fact she had been hit by a torpedo and, while *Regina* stood by the crippled ship, she too was hit by a torpedo and sank in a matter of minutes with the loss of 28 men and the serious injury of 10 others, 2 of whom died before reaching shore. Two weeks later *Alberni* was torpedoed east of the Isle of Wight and rolled over and sank in seconds with the loss of 59 men. The corvettes were the hardest-hit category of all the Canadian naval forces involved in *Overlord*, losing altogether 90 killed and 30 wounded out of the total naval casualties of 120 killed and 159 wounded.

Early in July the desperate Germans resorted to somewhat ineffectual methods of attacking Allied shipping. Using one-man torpedoes, they succeeded only in sinking two minesweepers and damaging the obsolete old cruiser HMS *Dragon* seriously enough to warrant scuttling her as an additional breakwater for a 'Mulberry' harbour. Remote-controlled motor boats, loaded with explosive to the gunwales, were also employed rather fruitlessly and mine-laying in the invasion corridor by German night bombers gradually became more intense, but within its carefully layered air and sea defences the invasion build-up continued unabated. The result of the German efforts to interrupt it can best be summarized by pointing out that, in the first month after D-Day, only 261 vessels were destroyed or damaged by all kinds of enemy action, as against 606 lost by bad weather or human error. In the same time 875,000 men, half a million vehicles, and several hundred thousand tons of stores and equipment were landed in Normandy.

The area of the Allied toehold in France expanded much more slowly than expected. It took the Americans until June 26 to capture Cherbourg and on the eastern flank progress was even slower. The Canadians who had been in the environs of Carpiquet on June 6 did not succeed in occupying the village and the northern half of the airfield there until July 4, and even then the North Shore Regiment and the Régiment de la Chaudière suffered nearly 200 casualties in clearing a hamlet that was defended by only 50 Panzer Grenadiers. It had been planned that by the end of June the front line would run through Lisieux, Alençon, and Laval west of Rennes and then to the coast west of St Malo, but on that day the Allied forces found themselves still confined to a bridgehead, less than a quarter of the planned size, that did not include either Caen or St Lô.

In fact the logistics build-up was causing very real problems as more and more equipment and facilities were being crammed into a limited space. Men and matériel were trussed together in such a fashion that lateral mobility on any scale was virtually impossible, and even movement along the various axes of advance from the beaches was frustratingly slow and difficult. The rate of reinforcement had to be deliberately restricted and among those formations that were held back temporarily were the headquarters and a major part of First Canadian Army. Even though General Crerar had arrived in France on June 18 and set up a small tactical headquarters, his 3rd Division remained, for the time being, under the operational control of Second British Army. So too did the headquarters of II Canadian Corps, under General Simonds, and Major-General Charles Foulkes's 2nd Division (including the veterans of Dieppe), which began to move to France on July 7 and first entered the line on the 11th.

If the Germans had been able to employ their armoured divisions en masse against this solid but shallow wedge, they might well have cut their way through the bridgehead to the coast and then destroyed the Allied forces piecemeal. Although Montgomery enjoyed an overall superiority of ten or twenty to one, even he could never have manoeuvred his troops or deployed reinforcements quickly and effectively in such a press. However, time after time German tank concentrations were broken up by the dreaded fighter-bombers before they could be launched against the Allies. Meanwhile Montgomery was pushing forward at a snail's pace, trying to do with mass what he could not do by manoeuvre. Eventually heavy bombers based in England were brought in to supplement the immense weight of artillery, armour, and infantry in Normandy. On July 9 the

88 Men of the Queen's Own Rifles on the road to Caen.

British and Canadians finally took Caen, the hinge of the whole bridgehead.

The Americans also started to chew their way forward in the western sector. To stop them the Germans began reinforcing that part of their front with some of the armour that had previously been engaged against the British and Canadians in the east. However, Allied strategy called for holding the weight of German forces around Caen so that the Third U.S. Army on the other flank of the bridgehead could break out to the south in due course, and then sweep round to take the enemy in the rear. Pressure must therefore be maintained on the Germans in the vicinity of Caen, and in mid-July a series of attacks was launched that gained little ground but cost Montgomery's forces dearly. The Canadians—who had lost 1,194 men in two days while taking Caen—lost another 1,965 in four days' fighting, between July 18 and 22.

The intense pressure was weakening the Germans. On July 20 Field Marshal von Kluge predicted that 'the moment is fast approaching when this over-taxed front line is bound to break up' and events were soon to prove him right. Five days later co-ordinated attacks were begun all along the front by Americans, Canadians, and British as a week-long battle of attrition began, with HQ First Canadian Army easing slowly into a command role: it took under command I British Corps on July 23 and II Canadian Corps on July 31. By the end of the month the Americans had taken Avranches, the springboard for their intended breakout into open country, and on August 1 the Third U.S. Army, under the mercurial General Patton, began its dramatic exploitation of the hole that was opening up on the extreme left flank of the German front. Von Kluge's worst fears were about to be realized.

After driving 30 miles south from Avranches, Patton swung north-westwards towards Argentan and Falaise, enveloping the German Seventh Army and part of Panzer Group West in an enormous pocket. The opening of the pocket lay along the Caen–Le Mans highway, from Verrières through Falaise to Sées. The troops best sited to close it from the northern side were the Canadians.

The whole of the Canadian combat force in Northwest Europe was in Normandy by this time, Major-General George Kitching's 4th Armoured Division having begun to move to France in mid-July. A subaltern of the British Columbia Regiment wrote on July 29:

> Here I am a veteran of two days and though I have not seen any action I have had the opportunity to see most of the battlefields that the Canadians have fought in. I have seen towns in utter ruin where not a building is standing; I have seen trenches abandoned by the enemy in their hasty withdrawal inland; trenches, dug-outs and fox holes littered with equipment ... and big stuff like knocked-out tanks with their dead crews still in them; machine guns and artillery with

89 Canadian armour moves up to the 'start line' for Operation *Totalize*. The tank in the foreground is equipped with a 'Flail'—chains fastened to a revolving drum in order to explode anti-tank mines before the tank can be disabled by them. Another flail tank can be seen immediately behind the jeep.

shells still in the breach and indicating the crew were killed before they could fire.[11]

Not all of this debris of battle was German.

On July 31 the 4th Division entered the line under command of General Simonds' II Canadian Corps, now a part of General Crerar's First Canadian Army which was less than half Canadian in its total content because as well as I British Corps, a Polish Armoured Division had also been placed under Crerar's control. On the evening of August 3 General Montgomery instructed Crerar to 'break through the enemy positions to the south and south-east of Caen' as soon as possible. It could not have been an unexpected assignment because planning was already well in hand. Operation *Totalize* was launched within four days. The first phase was keyed to a preliminary bombardment by a thousand heavy bombers of the RAF and a night attack by the 2nd Division and 2nd Armoured Brigade, whose infantry were mounted on improvised armoured personnel carriers (soon to be known as 'Kangaroos' since each carried ten men in its 'pouch')—an innovation of General Simonds designed to add speed and weight to the assault. Initially things went well enough. The first of two major defensive lines was overrun, even though the darkness brought some confusion and several units lost direction and strayed from their proper axes of advance. By 7:00 a.m. on August 8 the Canadians had pushed 4 miles down the road towards Falaise. The 4th Canadian and 1st Polish Armoured Divisions were marshalling their forces for a second phase that would carry them right through the German defences, and the Canadian 3rd Infantry Division was moving up to support them.

The attack was scheduled for 2:00 p.m. and was to be preceded by an hour and a half of 'carpet' bombing by the U.S. Eighth Air Force. Most of the 1,500 tons of bombs they dropped landed in the right places, but in the cold jargon of the official American history, 'in one case faulty identification of the target by the lead bombardier led him to drop near Caen. ... In the second instance a badly hit lead bomber salvoed short and the rest of the formation followed in regular routine.' These bombing errors inflicted more than 300 casualties on the Poles and Canadians, including the 3rd Division's General Keller, who was wounded and had to be evacuated.

Nothing hurts morale more than losses inflicted by one's own side. In the ensuing depression and confusion the pace of the advance was unexpectedly slow and by dusk the Canadians had pushed forward only another 2 miles. Trying to build up momentum, General Simonds ordered his troops to press on, but most units suspended operations for the night. Momentum was entirely lost and the Germans were enabled to bolster their defences as the armoured units laagered where they were, or even withdrew to convenient defensive positions, harbouring in the manner to which they had all become accustomed during years of training in England. Two squadrons of the Canadian Grenadier Guards, for instance, fell back more than a mile to find themselves a suitable berth for the night. The next morning German resistance was predictably stiffer.

Moreover, during the first day of *Totalize* poor navigation and careless map reading had brought the virtual destruction of one Canadian battle group. Swinging left from their proper axis of advance, two squadrons of the 28th (British Columbia) Armoured Regiment—going into action for the first time—and two companies of the Algonquin Regiment ended up on a patch of high ground on the wrong side of the Falaise road and some 6,500 yards north-east of their true objective. They then reported their believed position by radio to HQ, 4th Armoured Brigade, but by some error in transmission the map reference figures were transposed from 0946—where they should have been but were not—to 0964, a position several miles to the rear of both their actual and believed positions. They waited patiently for reinforcements that in the circumstances could never come, and early the next morning they were discovered by an S.S. Panzer Group. Throughout the day they were subjected to an intermittent but devastating fire. Eight undamaged tanks escaped and a number of wounded were taken out in half-tracks; at dusk the surviving Canadians who could do so made their way back on foot to the Polish lines. The British Columbians had lost 47 tanks and over 100 men in their first days' fighting, while the two companies of the Algonquins had incurred about 50 per cent casualties.

90 Massed tanks of the 4th Canadian Armoured Division line up for Operation *Tractable*.

'Such losses would have been deeply regrettable even had they been the price of success,' wrote C.P. Stacey in his official history of the campaign. 'Unfortunately they were suffered in the course of a tactical reverse which did much to prevent us from seizing a strategical opportunity of the first magnitude.' But perhaps the best epitaph on the many contradictions of *Totalize* came from the pen of a North Shore officer who was there. 'Fighting heavy,' he noted in his diary for August 8. 'Bumped into quite a hornet's nest. Large signs up: "It is a Court Martial Offence to Dig Potatoes in the Fields and Gardens".[12]

General Simonds promptly ordered another attempt to close the gap, called Operation *Tractable*. (It was *Tractable* to the planners, but to the troops who carried it through it would ever afterwards be known as 'the mad charge'.) This was to be a daylight version of *Totalize*, hooking slightly to the left, with smoke providing the cover that darkness had given to the first phase of *Totalize*. Because a Canadian officer with a copy of the plan accidentally drove into their lines (where he was killed) the night before the attack, the Germans not only expected it but also knew precisely how it would develop and adjusted their defences accordingly. In the event, this knowledge did them little good, for the sheer pace of *Tractable* proved to be too much for them.

On the morning of August 14 the 3rd Infantry—temporarily commanded by Brigadier K.G. Blackader—and 4th Armoured Divisions formed up in two dense, close-packed columns just out of the enemy's sight. It was a perfect summer morning and the atmosphere on the start-line was reminiscent of a small-town carnival with men sitting atop their vehicles, whooping, hollering, and waving their helmets at friends and neighbours. At 11:42 a.m. the massive columns began to roll forward.

From time to time the infantry had to leave their vehicles in order to clear the enemy from wooded areas or buildings, but the overall impression—especially on the tank crews—was of a headlong chaotic rush towards Falaise.

> The smokescreen supposed to blind the enemy turned out to be a thick dense mist in the path of our advance, soon supplemented by the dust clouds created by the terrific bombing; the area was 'Vision Zero!' Very little could be done to keep direction, except by aiming the tank 'at the sun'. Speed, nothing but speed, and on we went, crashing through obstacles at 20 to 25 m.p.h., very rough inside a tank going across country. . . . We just barged ahead, some of the tanks appeared to be going on at crazy angles, and in the confusion I did not know who was right and who was wrong; I just kept charging 'at the sun', blasting everything large enough to hide a field gun, and taking a terrible whipping in the turret of the bucking 32-ton monster.[13]

Behind them came the infantry, in their 'Kangaroos' and Troop Carrying Vehicles (heavy trucks with a cross-country capability).

> As the speed of the movement increased, a cloud of dust rose that outdid the efforts of the artillery's smoke-screen. The parade-ground formation was broken and a careening mass of vehicles herded southwards across-country, completely disregarding roads, ditches, fences, or any other obstacle except hedges. Each time the vehicles approached a hedge, they pressed together to pass through the narrow gaps made earlier by the tanks. Many a TCV driver's heart was in his mouth as he competed with half-tracks, anti-tank guns, tanks and flails to reach the opening before his neighbour. . . . In the direction from which the column had come was a huge air fleet systematically bombing our own troops in the rear areas.[14]

91 Racing across a partly harvested grainfield, each vehicle in Operation *Tractable* raised its own small cloud of dust, which soon contributed to one vast fog of battle. In the foreground are 6-pounder anti-tank guns of the 3rd Canadian Anti-Tank Regiment; behind them are some of the new 'kangaroos' —the first armoured personnel carriers.

Many heavy bombers of the British and American air forces were attacking German defences in the path of *Tractable*, but 77 aircraft of Bomber Command, including 44 from Six (RCAF) Group, had failed to time their runs from the coast accurately and bombed short, causing nearly 400 casualties and the usual confusion and depression among the survivors. Nevertheless General Crerar, noting that far more bombs had fallen on the enemy than on Canadians, reported that the bombing 'contributed greatly to the great success' of Operation *Tractable.* As the afternoon wore on, however, the rate of progress slowed down in the face of fanatical resistance, although by nightfall the Canadians had broken the German line and taken nearly 1,300 prisoners in an advance of some 5 miles.

The fall of Falaise two days later deprived the Germans of their best line of retreat. However, they still held one main road running north-east from Argentan to Trun and a number of secondary routes. (The Americans had foolishly stopped just south and east of Argentan, along the line of their formal boundary with Montgomery's 21st Army Group.) Along these roads the Germans were now escaping from the pocket in great numbers as the Allied tactical air forces gave their main attention to targets further east, including the crossings of the Risle and Seine Rivers. On August 18 the bulk of the German forces were reported on the east bank of the Orne River, already more than halfway out of the pocket. However, under the pressure of events the Germans were compelled to re-adopt a policy they had abandoned in the first few days of the invasion: large-scale road movement in daylight.

The fighter-bombers fell upon them like wolves upon sheep. The 2nd (British) Tactical Air Force alone claimed 124 tanks destroyed and 96 damaged and nearly 3,000 transport vehicles destroyed or damaged. On June 19, 52 tanks were destroyed, 92 damaged, and 1,500 other vehicles destroyed or damaged. One squadron among many—the RCAF's 439 Squadron, which was flying Typhoons —recorded that 'any pilot engaged in attacking the 3000 M[otorized] E[nemy] T[ransport] in the area was more in danger from air collision than from enemy resistance. The congestion necessitated the maintenance of a left hand circuit. . . . A grand harvest was reaped by the squadron.'[15] But on June 20 the weather worsened and low-level operations became too restricted to have a large-scale effect.

The pocket was loosely closed at Chambois on August 19. A mile to the north-west, at St-Lambert-sur-Dives, Major D.V. Currie, with a squadron of the 29th Armoured (South Alberta) Regiment and three companies of infantry, was blocking a German attempt to break towards Camembert, where the 2nd S.S. Panzer Corps was waiting for them across the thinly stretched Canadian axis. Currie and his men held back many times their own number of Germans for the best part of three days before they were relieved. Currie's personal gallantry in this action brought him the first Canadian Victoria Cross of the Northwest Europe campaign. Despite his efforts, however, a desperate German assault briefly re-opened a corridor to the east on the 20th and some 40 per cent of the encircled enemy fought

92 Perhaps the most famous Canadian war picture: Major D.V. Currie at St Lambert-sur-Dives supervising the collection of German prisoners. When this picture was taken, Currie (on the left, with a pistol in his hand) had been fighting for three days to close and hold closed the German escape route from Falaise. No other VC winner has been photographed so soon after the events that won him his Cross.

their way out of the pocket. The scene they left behind was one to awe the most combat-hardened veterans. 'The road, as were all the roads in the area, was lined and in places blocked by destroyed German vehicles of every description. Horses and men lay rotting in every ditch and hedge and the air was rank with the odour of putrefaction.'[16] But even though their material losses were enormous and their organization shattered, the Germans had got the bulk of their fighting forces out before the pocket was firmly sealed.

Since June they had lost some 400,000 men, 1,300 tanks, 500 assault guns, 1,500 field guns, and 20,000 vehicles. The Allies had lost 206,000 men altogether—124,000 Americans, 64,000 British, and 18,500 Canadians—of whom nearly a third had been killed. The 3rd Canadian Division had suffered more casualties than any other division in 21st Army Group and the 2nd Canadian Division was next—regrettable distinctions that reflected their tactical limitations as well as their courage and tenacity in battle.

8
THE WAR IN THE AIR

In spite of the moderate expansion program begun in 1936 as war clouds gathered over Europe, the Royal Canadian Air Force could accommodate very few of the hundreds of young Canadians who saw in themselves the successors of the Canadian air aces of the preceding generation. They crossed the Atlantic to join the British Royal Air Force in such numbers that by the fall of 1939 there were far more Canadians flying with the RAF than with the RCAF. The ranks of Fighter Command contained so many Canadians that the British recognized the fact nominally by forming an 'all-Canadian' fighter squadron from a small proportion of them. At the end of November, 242 (Canadian) Squadron RAF, equipped with Hawker Hurricanes, mustered 21 Canadian pilots and nearly 200 British ground staff under the command of Squadron Leader F.M. Gobeil, an RCAF officer who had been on an exchange posting with the RAF when war broke out.

In April 1940 orders were issued for the Canadians to join the Air Component of the British Expeditionary Force in France, but their move was postponed owing to the German attack on Scandinavia, so that when the blitzkrieg subsequently struck France in May, 242 Squadron was still stationed in Yorkshire. The RAF units in France were providing air cover for the British ground forces as well as vainly attempting to slow the German advance by destroying key bridges behind the Panzer spearheads. Their losses were heavy and in the last two weeks of May, as the Luftwaffe mauled both air and ground forces, a number of pilots were detached to reinforce Hurricane squadrons already in France. Some went to 85 Squadron, where another Canadian, Flying Officer A.B. Angus, had already been credited with five victories and awarded a Distinguished Flying Cross before being killed in action. Others were split between 607 and 615 Squadrons, and it was while serving with the latter that Pilot Officer W.L. McKnight claimed 242's first victory on May 19; this initiated a personal score that totalled 16½ before his death in January 1941 during one of the early fighter sweeps over occupied France. In eleven days in May, Flight Lieutenant Mark Henry ('Hilly') Brown, a Manitoban serving in 1 Squadron RAF, registered 8½ victories. (Before he was killed over Sicily in November 1941, Brown was credited with the fourth-highest Canadian score of the war—18.)

As the Germans closed in on Dunkirk, the balance of 242 Squad-

93 Hurricanes of 242 Squadron RAF, the 'all-Canadian' squadron, turn for home at the end of a patrol over northern France.

ron, still based in England, moved south to Biggin Hill in Kent and began flying patrols across the Channel to protect the evacuation. On May 23, Fowler Gobeil became the first RCAF pilot (as opposed to Canadians in the RAF) ever to meet an enemy in aerial combat. The engagement proved indecisive, since the Messerschmitt 109 smartly evaded him, but two days later an Me 110 was less fortunate and Gobeil claimed the RCAF's first victory.

After the fall of France in June 1940, Britain's position seemed perilous indeed. Now the Germans held air bases along the entire Continental semi-circle to the south and east that stretched for 1,300 miles from Brest to Bergen. Stopping enemy bombers in the Battle of Britain, which lasted from July to October, was going to require every man and machine that could be found—even with the aid of radar (it was originally called Radio Direction Finding or RDF) and the sophisticated ground-based fighter control the RAF had developed.

Two RCAF squadrons were already at hand, but only one of them was equipped and trained for air-to-air combat. 110 Squadron had arrived in England during February and begun specialized training in army co-operation duties with the intention of accompanying the 1st Canadian Division to France. Its pilots were not trained in fighter tactics and, even if they had been, its Westland Lysanders—two-seater general-purpose machines, lightly armed, with a top speed of 220

94 Twenty years of peace had brought an unacceptable rigidity to the tactical formations and
combat theory of Fighter Command. Tactics had
needed to be more flexible in the light of experience against the Luftwaffe. Here, pilots of 1
Squadron RCAF discuss a new manoeuvre in August 1940. Flying Officer W.C. Connell (left) survived two operational tours and left the air force
in 1946; Flying Officer Ken Boomer (centre) became a squadron leader before being killed in
action in October 1944 during his third operational tour; and Flight Lieutenant Ed 'Pappy'
Reyno (right) went on to become Vice Chief of
the Defence Staff and Deputy Commander-in-
Chief of the North American Defence command
(NORAD). General Reyno retired in 1972.

m.p.h.—were totally unsuited to the role. (After 1941, re-numbered as 400 and flying successively Tomahawks, Mustangs, Mosquitos, and Spitfires, the squadron was to make its mark in air combat even though its mission was still primarily army co-operation.) 1 (later 401) Squadron RCAF, on the other hand, was equipped with a modern eight-gun fighter. It had been sent overseas in June 1940 under the command of Squadron Leader E.A. McNabb. On August 26 it became the first RCAF unit to meet an enemy in battle when its Hurricanes encountered a formation of Dornier bombers, shot down three of them, and damaged four more. The first fell to McNabb, who was subsequently forced down unhurt by damage resulting from his victim's return fire. Flying Officer R.L. Edwards was not so lucky. He destroyed a Dornier but was hit by his opponent, driven into an uncontrollable spin, and killed in the ensuing crash. The third victory was credited to Flight Lieutenant G.R. McGregor.

One pilot for three was a barely satisfactory ratio of losses in the cold logic of the Battle of Britain, but in fact the Canadians had been lucky, for they were still novices in combat. The next time they saw action, on the last day of August, their inexperience cost them dearly. While patrolling the Dover coast at 22,000 feet they were attacked out of the sun by high-flying Messerschmitts and three of them were shot down without loss to the enemy. Thus they learned painfully and expensively the truth of the old First World War adage: 'Beware of the Hun in the sun!'

Just the day before, 242 Squadron RAF had rejoined the battle, their 'Canadian content' now down to 75 per cent and with a new commander, the legless British ace Douglas Bader. Bader and the veterans of the French campaign supplied a leavening of battle experience in the squadron that stood it in good stead when, on August 30, nine of its pilots met more than a hundred enemy planes over Essex. 'I detailed the pilot from Calgary to take his section of three Hurricanes up to keep the thirty Messerschmitts busy . . . ' wrote Bader. 'The remaining six of us tackled the bombers. . . . With the sun at our backs and the advantage of greater height . . . we went straight down on them . . . the Canadian pilot who followed immediately behind took the one that broke away to the left while I took the one that broke away to the right. . . . '[1] When the sky had cleared, the squadron claimed twelve victories—and their Hurricanes were all unscathed.

The Battle of Britain was building to its climax. On September 15 the British exultantly claimed a total of 185 German aircraft shot down, with the loss of only 27 British machines and 11 pilots. Another 11 pilots, wounded or injured in crash landings, would live to fight again. Post-war research has settled on a figure of 54 German aircraft actually brought down; but the Luftwaffe had lost twice as many planes and nearly five times as many pilots as the RAF. This was not an acceptable loss ratio for the enemy, and although the tide of

5 The first class of observers graduated by the BCATP journeyed from their Canadian training school to bomber squadrons of the RAF in the UK in November 1940. One year later half the men in this picture were dead and several of the rest were prisoners of war.

battle would not begin to ebb visibly for another two weeks, September 15 marked the decisive turning-point of the Battle of Britain. The claims of the RCAF squadron were more conservative (and more realistic) than those of many other squadrons during that crucial month: in the eight weeks following August 26 it was credited with the destruction of 30 enemy aircraft, the probable destruction of 8, and with damaging 35 more. Its Hurricanes were not really a match for the Messerschmitt 109s and most of the success and glory went to the Spitfire squadrons of Fighter Command, but the Canadians played their part as best they could. McGregor and his fellow flight commander, B.D. ('Dal') Russel, in particular had begun to build themselves solid reputations. Otherwise the record of the squadron was unremarkable until September 27.

On that day the Luftwaffe's last major daylight attack was launched and the Poles of 303 Squadron RAF and the Canadians of 1 Squadron RCAF attacked the first wave of enemy bombers together. Flight Lieutenant John Kent, a Canadian in the British service who was leading the Polish squadron, remembers how

> we saw the hordes of German bombers and escorting fighters coming in. ... As the RAF fighters got stuck into them, we could see them falling away, plunging down with smoke pouring from them. It almost seemed that there was an invisible barrier over a certain point and that as soon as the bombers reached it large numbers of them suddenly began pouring smoke and going down.[2]

Thirteen pilots flew 26 sorties, during which they claimed 7 enemy aircraft destroyed, 1 probably destroyed, and another 7 damaged.

96   RCAF ground crew in England lived in Nissen huts made from corrugated iron sheets fastened to a semi-circular wooden frame and heated by a small stove (centre foreground). The airman laying his shirts to dry behind the stove wears a T-shirt that originated with the Central Navigation School at Rivers, Man.

The squadron was still to see some hard fighting before it was withdrawn to Scotland for rest and re-training late in October, but after September 27 there was a noticeable reduction in the weight of the Luftwaffe's air attack. It could not beat the British fighters from the skies to gain the air superiority that would be necessary to land and re-supply German soldiers on English beaches. Nor was there much future in trying to cripple British war industry in the face of an improving British air defence, which by now could shoot down one in ten enemy aircraft that appeared over England during daylight.

By mid-November daytime attacks had virtually ceased and the Luftwaffe had turned to night raiding. Against this type of action, Fighter Command was relatively ineffective. Ground-based radar could not guide night fighters on to the enemy with the pin-point precision needed in the dark if the fighter crews were to pick up their targets visually: airborne radar was still too undeveloped for aircraft to 'home' on the enemy with any degree of consistency, even when ground radar brought British planes within 2 or 3 miles of a potential victim. However, the Luftwaffe was also unable to locate targets precisely at night and its policy of aimed bombing—the only practicable one for the limited force of light and medium bombers, which were all the Germans had—soon degenerated into a sporadic and necessarily indiscriminate campaign that caused very little concern when measured against the totality of British industrial or moral resources. London, Coventry, Liverpool, Manchester, Plymouth, and Glasgow were all raided heavily during the winter of 1940-1, but with the coming of the shorter summer nights the attacks tailed off. London, hit by some 700 bombers on the night of April 19-20, 1941, was not assailed seriously again until the coming of the V-1 'flying bombs' in the summer of 1944.

But while the air assault against Britain was slowly fading out, another air offensive had been growing in intensity. In March 1941 the Luftwaffe moved into Sicily and North Africa to support the Afrika Korps' initial drive over the Egyptian border; in April Hitler pushed his troops into the Balkans; in May Crete fell. By June only the now-isolated island fortress of Malta, blocking the enemy's supply routes to North Africa with its aircraft and submarines, kept the central Mediterranean from becoming an Axis lake. The Germans hoped to force Malta's surrender by air attack and sea blockade without resorting to an opposed landing by their troops.

In the course of the air battles that accompanied these operations, four more Canadian airmen in the RAF played a notable part. Flying a Gloster Gladiator the RAF's last operational biplane fighter, Flight Lieutenant Vernon Woodward—'the imperturbable Woody'—was credited with 11 Italian aircraft destroyed in the Western Desert before flying to Greece. Switching to a Hurricane, he claimed 3 more Italian and 6 German planes there, and then—back in the desert—brought his total score up to 22, a record that made him by September 1941 the second-highest scoring Canadian fighter pilot of the war.

In the spring and summer of 1942, as the Germans vainly tried to match the British logistics build-up in North Africa, the strategic focus of the Mediterranean theatre was still the air battle for Malta, which commanded the German supply route. The British pushed what reinforcements they could into their island outpost and among them were two more notable Canadian flyers. Pilot Officer R.W. ('Buck') McNair, who had already claimed one Me 109 and damaged another while flying with the RCAF's 401 Squadron in England, arrived on Malta in March 1942. In his subsequent three-month tour he claimed 9 enemy aircraft. (Later he went on to command 126 (Canadian) Wing of the RAF's Second Tactical Air Force in 1944, and to become the sixth-highest scoring Canadian, with 16 victories.) His time in Malta overlapped with that of 'Wally' McLeod, who arrived in May and was credited with 12 'kills' during his tour. McLeod became the highest-scoring RCAF pilot of all, with 21 victories before his death in action during September 1944.

The exploits of Woodward, McNair, and McLeod have been largely overshadowed by those of a moody, solitary, cantankerous prodigy from Verdun, Que., George Frederick Beurling. Learning to fly at sixteen, Beurling tried to join the pre-war RCAF but was rejected because he lacked the necessary educational requirements. He was eventually accepted by the British in September 1940, but his early career in the RAF was stormy. Long-range sweeps over France by large, tightly disciplined formations were just coming into vogue when Beurling embarked on his operational flying career, and this was a style of fighting that he either could not or would not adapt to. Often to the anger of his superiors, and especially of the other mem-

97 'All over North America kids by the tens of thousands are whittling flying models,' wrote Flying Officer George Beurling, DSO, DFC, DFM, and Bar, in his autobiography, *Malta Spitfire*. While recuperating from the wound that ended his tour on Malta in October 1942, Beurling gives his youngest brother a few whittling tips.

bers of his flight, he broke away to chase the enemy on his own. Although this approach brought him his first two victories, it did nothing to endear him to his fellow pilots in an era when subordination of self and close team work were becoming the accepted essentials of air combat. Beurling spent more and more time alone, training his eyes to scan the sky with unerring speed, developing his reflexes, and working out his theories of deflection shooting. He was only an adequate pilot, but nothing escaped his roving eyes and his gunnery was 'unbelievable', according to his squadron gunnery officer.

In May 1942 Beurling got himself posted to Malta. Flying off an aircraft carrier in a Spitfire, at the very limit of its range, he arrived on the island with other reinforcements in early June. His new colleagues found him an odd, uncouth character. One of his pastimes was to throw morsels of meat on the ground, wait until they were covered with flies, and then stamp both meat and flies into the earth with the reflex epithet, 'Goddamn screwballs!', which he applied to anything or anybody that irritated him (there were many of both) and which soon gave him his air-force sobriquet of 'Screwball'. Three and a half weeks passed before he registered his first victory over Malta, but then his score began to mount with fantastic speed. By July 14, when he was slightly wounded, he had claimed 7 enemy machines; by October 14, when he was wounded again—more seriously, this time—and shot down into the sea, Beurling had 29 'kills' to his credit and had become the top-scoring Canadian of the war, collecting a commission he didn't want and four gallantry awards in the process. When he was posted back to Canada he found himself a national hero. To the media and the public at least, he was now Flying Officer 'Buzz' Beurling—'Buzz' sounded better than 'Screwball'.

Beurling transferred to the RCAF, which made no more fuss about his lack of educational qualifications. With the rank of flight lieutenant he returned to England and joined 403 Squadron RCAF, but he scored only two more victories before being taken off operations because it was generally felt that he would continue to take chances until he was killed. Beurling's propaganda value as a war hero was now more important than his skill as a fighter pilot. His British wing commander, 'Johnnie' Johnson, reports the following conversation:

> 'You know anything about this Mustang, Wingco?'
> 'Not much,' I said. 'I hear one of the 83 Group wings is going to get them and they have a tremendous radius of action. I hear they can easily fly to Berlin and back.'
> 'Can they now?' exclaimed the Canadian. I could read his thoughts. Give him a long-range Mustang, fill it up with petrol each day and he'd either get himself killed or would finish up with more Huns than the rest of us put together.'[3]

Beurling was taken off operations in January 1944. There were complaints that he went about the base throwing his hat in the air and shooting at it with his service revolver. Then there were threats of a court martial for low flying over the station headquarters during a senior officers' conference. In May Beurling was posted back to Canada and in August he was released from the RCAF at his own request. After the war, lost and lonely in a world without air combat—'It's the only thing I can do well; it's the only thing I ever did I really liked'—he joined the fledgling Israeli Air Force. But he saw no more of what he really liked. On May 20, 1948, he was killed in a crash near Rome while ferrying an aircraft to Israel.

By October 1942 the British attempt at a strategic air offensive had been under way for almost three years and for the first two of them it had been no more successful than the German air offensive. The RAF efforts had begun in the winter of 1939-40 with four comparatively small-scale daylight raids—never more than 50 twin-engined aircraft—against the German fleet and naval bases. They resulted in virtually no damage to the enemy, while the attackers incurred losses of up to 50 per cent—an unacceptable figure. The failure of this day-bombing concept, with all its concurrent implications of precision strikes on factories and military facilities, had led the RAF—like the Luftwaffe—to adopt a desultory, capricious, and often wasteful tech-

nique of ill-coordinated night attacks. A Canadian pilot who participated in some of them recalls that

> during the one month [August 1941] we advanced from the junior
> crew [on the squadron] to the most senior. ... I think one crew com-
> pleted their tour and the rest were shot down. ... Most of the time
> we were flying with no moon and it was difficult or impossible to rec-
> ognize cities. ... In those early days we could follow our own sched-
> ule and we would cross the Dutch coast after dark and try to cross
> back before daylight. That was the only restriction we had. We were
> given our target, we could pick our own route in.[4]

Because of the limited number of aircraft and the generally inaccu-
rate navigation, these raids did little significant damage. In mid-1941
the introduction of airborne cameras to photograph the actual target
when the bombs were dropped revealed that only one in five crews
bombed within 5 miles of the assigned aiming point. Over the Ruhr,
the most important target area, the ratio dropped to one in ten. Bomb
loads were small, their high-explosive content was not really very
'high', and a large proportion of them failed to explode at all.

As the RCAF could accommodate only a fraction of the men now
being trained in the British Commonwealth Air Training Plan, many
more RCAF aircrew were being posted to RAF squadrons. Though Canadians serving in the RAF's Bomber Command during 1939-40 were
probably outnumbered by their compatriots in the more glamorous
Fighter Command, the ratio was soon reversed. The Canadian content of Bomber Command, which would become by far the largest of
the operational commands, rose to more than a fifth of its total
strength in 1944—no other Dominion would even approach that proportion. When the RCAF formed its first operational bombing squadron, 405, in early June 1941, the initial aircrews were drawn entirely
from Canadians in the RAF. They were led by Wing Commander Pat
Gilchrist, who had joined the RAF in 1935, completed an operational
tour, and been awarded a Distinguished Service Order before he
took over the command.

The first operational flight of an RCAF bomber came on June 12 at
11:16 p.m. when a twin-engined Vickers Wellington—the first of
four, one of which returned early—rolled down an English runway.
The next morning the three crews that completed their missions
claimed to have dropped 4½ tons of high explosive and another ton
of incendiaries on railway marshalling yards at Schwerte, near Dortmund, 'though results were difficult to assess owing to ground haze'.
In the light of later findings regarding the RAF's bombing accuracy, it
seems statistically unlikely that they actually bombed Schwerte.
However, by the end of the month 30 operational sorties had been
flown for the loss of one aircraft and its crew.

In July the number of sorties more than doubled—to 79, of which
67 were considered 'successful'—for the loss of 6 aircraft. One of the

8 'Bombing up' a
Lancaster at an RCAF
base in Yorkshire. The
4,000-pound 'cannister'
bomb of high explosive
is accompanied by
racks of small incen-
diaries—a typical
bomb load once the
policy of area bombing
had been established.

missing machines was Gilchrist's. Shot down over France, he para-
chuted to safety, evaded the Germans, returned to England via Switzerland, and commanded RAF Coastal Command squadrons before
transferring to the RCAF in 1945. He was promptly succeeded as
squadron commander by another Canadian in the RAF, Wing Commander R.M. Fenwick-Williams. Not until February 1942, when
Wing Commander J.E. Fauquier took over the squadron, was an RCAF
officer considered sufficiently experienced to be given command. By
the end of 1941 three additional RCAF bomber squadrons had been
formed, each commanded by a Canadian from the RAF but with the
majority of their personnel drawn from the RCAF.

In 1942, which saw the formation of seven more RCAF bomber
squadrons, the technology of the bombing war was greatly altered.
Bomber Command introduced four-engined 'heavies', capable of lifting bomb loads of up to 10 tons each; the intricate concentration of
the first '1,000 bomber raid' on Cologne; an electronic navigation system called *Gee*; and élite Pathfinder crews to guide the main bombing force on to the target. When Bomber Command was assigned
an innovative, single-minded commander, Sir Arthur Harris, who
was dogmatically devoted to the idea of the 'strategic' bomber as a
war-winning instrument, the tempo of bombing operations was stepped up and the objective of all this effort was clarified. Since it was

still impossible to bomb precise targets such as factories at night, the aim would be to break German morale: what was euphemistically called 'area bombing' was formally approved. The proportion of high explosive used went down and that of incendiary materials went up, as Harris, with the enthusiastic backing of the Chief of Air Staff, Sir Charles Portal, and of Prime Minister Winston Churchill, set about scientifically trying to raze German cities to the ground. Harris's new policy led to heavy bombers' being loaded with one 4,000-pound high-explosive bomb—a drum-type canister, lacking any aerodynamic qualities, that simply tumbled through the air, since the precise location of the subsequent explosion was no longer important—and a mass of small incendiary bombs. The blast from the 4,000-pounder blew in doors, windows, and roofs over a wide area, creating effective drafts for the rain of incendiaries that accompanied and followed it.

Perhaps the point should be made here that, although the Canadian government, the RCAF staff, and public opinion in Canada accepted the propriety of this 'terror bombing'—Hitler's phrase for it—it was the British government and the RAF staff that were ultimately responsible. The RAF exercised operational control over all Canadian air formations outside Canada throughout the war, and the RCAF, says Colonel Stacey in his *Arms, Men and Governments*, merely endeavoured to 'hit the targets that were given it'.

In 1941 the damage done to Germany by British bombing had been negligible. A year later 3 per cent of the built-up areas attacked had been devastated. The raids were focussed on city centres, although factories were usually well outside those areas, and by the end of 1943 the estimate of destruction had risen to 38 per cent. In December 1944 the claimed figure was 42 per cent. At the time this bombing seemed a major contribution towards winning the war. One school of thought even held that bombing alone could bring victory, but hindsight tells us that British politicians and service chiefs consistently overestimated the economic damage of the night-bomber offensive. Germany's industrial production continued to rise more or less steadily until late 1944, when American precision daylight bombing (made practicable by the introduction of long-range fighter escorts) caused it to plunge irrevocably downwards.

John Fauquier had dropped the first 4,000-pounder to be delivered by the Canadians on Bremen in January, and 'saw it burst with terrific results in the middle of town'. Four nights later he and Fenwick-Williams each dropped another on the same target with very similar results. But the bomber offensive was still far from one-sided. Many crews never made the return trip at all, and among those that did there were many more that paid a heavy price. In the words of one Canadian combat report:

Five bursts of cannon fire hit the plane. The pilot managed to evade the attackers and at 6,000 ft with the starboard engine coughing called on the crew to bale out but got no reply from them. ... He decided to try and carry on to base . . . and arriving over England ... crash-landed. All the crew were found to be on board, though wounded. Sgt. (pilot) Farrow had a slight wound in the ankle. ... Sgt. Millward had a cannon shell wound in the leg but it is hoped that it will not be necessary to amputate. Sgt. May and Sgt. Baker were so badly wounded that they died within 48 hours.[5]

Among one group of about 50 navigators who trained together in the early days of the BCATP, only 5 completed a first tour (usually thirty missions over Germany). Ten were shot down and became prisoners of war. The rest were killed.

The first German city to be virtually destroyed was Lubeck, a port that handled the bulk of Red Cross shipments into and out of Germany. A medieval monument with a tightly knit core of largely wooden houses, it appeared to the Air Staff to offer an ideal opportunity for testing the new technique of area bombing, and its position on the coast made it comparatively easy to find from the air. In March 1942 the experiment was made by nearly 400 aircraft. A Canadian rear-gunner counted at least 95 major fires burning below as his Halifax turned for home, and the loom of them could still be seen when the bombers were 75 miles away. This attack resulted in German reprisals. Reinforced by two squadrons of bombers withdrawn from Sicily—an irrational move at the height of the campaign against Malta—a puny Luftwaffe bombing force launched a series of so-called 'Baedeker' raids against Exeter, Bath, Norwich, and York. The first two raids caught the British by surprise, but on the last two the Germans lost heavily as Fighter Command adjusted its defences. British airborne radar had improved greatly since the early days and the first RCAF night-fighter squadron, 406, had a particularly successful time, destroying three and claiming four more damaged. The Germans then abandoned the retaliatory aspect of a competition they now knew they could not win.

The Germans had used only 25 twin-engined medium bombers for their attack on Exeter. But a month later, mustering every serviceable machine he could cobble together and combing the Operational Training Units for additional aircraft and crews, Harris launched 1,047 aircraft—many of them the new, heavy, four-engined machines—against Cologne and swamped the German defences. Years later a Canadian pilot recalled the scene over the target:

We can see the black bursts of heavy flak, momentarily still, then whipping past the cabin as we leave them behind us at 180 mph. We can smell the cordite; if the burst is very close you can hear it; then it's time to move. For the most part, there is nothing to do amidst all the confusion but to hold Jake's course, grit the teeth, and sweat it out. ... There are other aircraft around us as Ole gives me directions until the moment when he shouts, 'Bombs gone!'... As I drop a wing to turn away, I get a full view of the target area. Immense fires are raging now, and bomb flashes are practically incessant.[6]

In 90 minutes 900 bombers dropped nearly 500 tons of high explosives and over 1,000 tons of incendiaries on the city centre. Only 39 aircraft were lost.

Two more 1,000-bomber raids (on Essen and Bremen) followed in the next month, but the Air Staff found that poor weather and the use of so many inexperienced crews from training units did not produce sufficient devastation to justify the effort required to organize and launch them. Furthermore they did not seriously damage German morale. Great comfort was taken, however, in the widespread enthusiasm for these gigantic raids that was expressed by the media and the public. (In Britain only the Bishop of Chichester and one parliamentary back-bencher tried to raise openly the moral issue and they were quickly put in their places by the Archbishop of Canterbury.)

For the rest of that year raids were continued on the old scale of less than 500 aircraft per strike, but even when the bombing was concentrated, the air offensive against Germany was not having the effect it was supposed to have. Between February and August 1942 German production increased by 27 per cent for guns, 25 per cent for tanks, and 97 per cent for ammunition. In the same period Bomber

99 This Lancaster of the RAF's 576 Squadron, whose crew included the usual quota of Canadians, staggered home from a raid so badly damaged that the rear turret fell off as the aircraft landed. The tail gunner's fate is not recorded.

Command flew 21,000 night sorties, dropped 28,000 tons of bombs, and lost 852 aircraft. The overall loss rate of nearly 4 per cent for 1942 was to be the highest of the air war. In human terms Bomber Command aircrews were enduring a greater proportion of casualties than any other category of servicemen, higher even than the rate of infantry losses during intense fighting.

Statistically less than a third of every 100 crews could expect to survive an operational tour of thirty missions, although pilots sometimes flew home machines that should surely have crashed. The official report of a Canadian crew assigned to attack Duisburg in August described one such aircraft:

> Whilst doing his bombing run on the target, this aircraft was attacked by an enemy fighter. ... There were three large holes in the elevators, one in the port aileron, one large hole in the port tail fin, one huge rent at the intersection of the tail boom and the fuselage, another large hole in the bottom of the port engine nacelle, the top gunner's cupola was smashed and the magazines shot away from his guns, all port [fuel] tanks were riddled, the hydraulics shot away and the side of the fuselage seamed and scored with bullets. ... Following the encounter the pilot attempted another run on the target and successfully unloaded his bombs.[7]

On the way back the port engine stopped and the plane staggered home on one engine to make a 'wheels-up' landing off the runway at the nearest English airfield.

NORTH SEA

IRELAND

SWEDEN

DENMARK

SIX GROUP BASES

ENGLAND

BALTIC

FRISIAN ISLANDS

Kiel

200 MILES

Wilhelmshaven

Hamburg

NETHERLANDS

Sterkrade
Gelsenkirchen
Wanne Eickel
Osnabruck

Munster

Hanover

Berlin

English Channel

Calais
Boulogne

BELGIUM

Duisburg
Dusseldorf
Cologne

Essen
Bochum
Castrop Rauxel
Dortmund
Hagan

POL

Mons

GERMANY

Caen

Biennais

Elbe

Brest

Falaise

Frankfurt

Chemnitz

Lorient

L'Isle Adam
(Bois de Cassan)

Mainz

Ludwigshaven

Mannheim

CZECHOSLOV

400 MILES

Stuttgart

Bay of

Biscay

FRANCE

Rhine

SWITZERLAND

AUSTRIA

600 MILES

YUGO

SIX (RCAF) GROUP
& 331 WING OPERATIONS
1939 - 1945

ADRIATIC

ITALY

CORSICA

400 MILES

Formia

LEGEND

Bombing sorties over 1000 . . . . . ■

Bombing sorties 500-1000 . . . . . . ●

Bombing sorties 250-500 . . . . . . ▲

Bombing sorties 100-250
(Mediterranean only) . . . . ·

Mining sorties 350-400 . . . . . . ▦

Mining sorties 200-250 . . . . . . ⠿

Naples
Torre Annunziata

Salerno
Battipagli

SARDINIA

200 MILES

Messin

ALGERIA

**331 WING
BASES**

SICILY
Gerbini

MEDITERRANEAN
SEA

101 A bomb-aimer's view of the target, taken at 18,000 feet over Duisburg in May 1943. The intricate patterns of light are formed by searchlight beams, flak, sky markers, exploding bombs, and the glow of ground fires.

Sir Arthur Harris was no more easily distracted from his objective than his crews were from theirs. (The media christened him 'Bomber' Harris, perhaps because the abbreviated nickname of 'Butch', by which his airmen affectionately referred to him, had more to do with his ostensible lack of concern for them than with his intentions towards the Germans.) By the end of the year two more sophisticated electronic navigation systems had been added to the Pathfinder technology—*Oboe*, a long-range direction-finding navigation aid, and *H2S*, a radar navigation and target-finding device—together with the first of a whole range of visual target-indicator equipment. Bomber Command now included more than 500 four-engined machines. Although the tactical contest with the German night-fighters and anti-aircraft guns saw first one side and then the other gaining a temporary advantage, the long-term balance was imperceptibly swinging in favour of the Allies by weight of numbers alone. The introduction of the 'bomber stream' (a carefully pre-arranged approach to the target area), the exploitation of diversionary tactics by other aircraft, and an ever-increasing concentration of the raiding force over the target in both time and space all helped to swamp the German defences where the closer targets were concerned. But

Harris's first attempt to destroy Berlin, a distant target, in the winter of 1942-3 had to be abandoned in the face of unacceptable losses.

Nearly every Bomber Command aircrew included at least one Canadian until the end of the war in Europe. In the famed 617 ('Dambusters') Squadron, for example, there were 29 Canadians among the 133 airmen who flew in the spectacular low-level mission that smashed the Mohne and Eder dams in May 1943. Eighteen months later, when a combined force from 617 and 9 Squadrons RAF crippled the German battleship *Tirpitz* in a Norwegian fiord, 26 of the 195 flyers involved were Canadians. But there were now enough RCAF bomber squadrons in operational service to justify the formation of a specifically Canadian group. On January 1, 1943, Six (RCAF) Group became operational under the command of Air Vice-Marshal G.E. Brookes. 'The move [to form a Canadian group] was very unpopular with Canadian airmen,' wrote a pilot who went to an RCAF squadron for his second tour. RCAF squadrons could accommodate less than 10 per cent of Canada's BCATP graduates, and most of those who went to the RAF seemed quite satisfied with the company of fellow graduates from other Commonwealth countries and the United Kingdom. After serving in both RAF and RCAF units, a navigator noted that he had been far more humanely treated in the former. In the RAF, 'if you were going to fly at night, someone would come in with a cup of tea and wake you up. On the Canadian squadron the way they woke you up was to put the sirens on.'[8]

On the other hand there seemed little chance for Canadians to gain higher command experience without their own group. The principle of posting senior RCAF officers to operational formations was accepted by the Air Ministry but resisted in the various commands, and Canadians posted into formations at senior levels were sometimes kept supernumerary for months. Only the creation of a Canadian group could ensure that Canadian airmen obtained some staff and command experience at group level, although it also meant that the new group usually could expect to get the worst of the available equipment. Naturally enough, the British favoured their own groups when the latest technology was put into operational use and the Canadians got what was left.

102, 103 Before and after the raid on Hildesheim. 100 Lancasters of Six Group were among the 220 Bomber Command aircraft, led by the Pathfinders of 405 Squadron RCAF, which destroyed most of this medieval city in fourteen minutes. The resulting cloud of dust and smoke, rising 15,-000 feet, was visible 200 miles away.

On the operational level the assertion of national identity at first proved a poor substitute for professional expertise, and inevitably many mistakes were made in the early months of Six Group's existence. Moreover, the group flew Wellingtons and Halifaxes: the former were obsolescent and the latter had a low ceiling that left them particularly susceptible to flak. The first Lancaster was not to be taken on strength until August 1943. Although the older aircraft were slowly replaced, many Halifaxes, somewhat improved by extensive modifications, were to remain in service with the group until the end of the war in Europe.

Finally, despite their common national origin, it took a long time to

eliminate a lack of cohesion in the group as a whole, which represented various levels of experience. In mid-May three of the group's most experienced squadrons moved to North Africa, where they formed a Canadian wing under Group Captain C.R. Dunlap. From bases in Tunisia they participated in the interdiction bombing of Italy, attacking ports and railway facilities in support of Allied ground forces, before returning to Six Group in November 1943. When the last RCAF bomber squadron to be formed overseas was added to Six Group in September 1943, an excellent example of the difficulties of forming an effective Canadian group was provided. Five experienced crews, most of whom had been in disciplinary trouble in their previous units—blamed mainly on high spirits and low flying—were posted in to form a nucleus, but three of the five very soon went missing on operations and the senior man left with operational experience was a lowly pilot officer.

During its first year Six Group was distinguished by its high percentage of both operational losses and training accidents, and by its low percentages of aircraft serviceability and of aircraft actually attacking the target. Losses in April 1943 reached the 5-per-cent figure at which the RAF's Director of Bomber Operations felt operational effectiveness might become 'unacceptably low' if it were maintained over three months. In May the Group's loss rate touched 7 per cent and in June it passed 7.2 per cent, figures at which the operations research scientists were proclaiming that any bomber force must certainly become 'relatively ineffective'. Between March 5 and June 24, 1943, the fledgling Canadian group lost over 100 aircraft; a loss rate of over 7 per cent, as in June, meant that only 12 out of every 100 crews commencing a 30-mission tour could expect to survive it. But in spite of its losses the Group was still able to make a substantial contribution to the Allied air attacks on Hamburg in July.

Seventy-two Canadian aircraft were among the 791 bombers that struck the city on July 24-5, when the target area 'was left a mass of raging fires with dense black smoke rising to over 19,000 feet', although of the 728 crews who claimed to have attacked the target only 306 had in fact dropped their bombs within 3 miles of the aiming point. Two nights later 81 Six Group machines were among the 787 that returned to Hamburg to create the world's first 'firestorm'. An eyewitness in the city reported officially what happened:

> As the many fires broke through the roofs of the burning buildings, a column of heated air rose more than two and a half miles high and one and a half miles in diameter. ... The column was turbulent, and it was fed from its base by in-rushing cooler ground-surface air. One and one and a half miles from the fires the draught increased the wind velocity from eleven to thirty-three miles per hour. At the edge of the area the velocities must have been appreciably greater, as trees three feet in diameter were uprooted. In a short time the temperature reached ignition point for all combustibles, and the entire

area was ablaze. In such fires complete burn out occurred; that is, no trace of combustible material remained, and only after two days were the areas cool enough to approach.[9]

(In the last two years of the war such firestorms were to wreak far more havoc on Japan than the two atomic bombs that would dramatically end it, at Hiroshima and Nagasaki.)

In August 1943 came an attack on Peenemünde, the research and experimental station on the Baltic where the enemy was developing rocket-powered 'V-weapons'—Bomber Command's first attempt at something like precision bombing by other than specially selected and trained crews since early 1942. Pathfinders—including the RCAF's 405 Squadron, which had joined them in April 1943—played a major role, using *H2S* to find the target and then dropping coloured visual markers to guide the main force on to it. Six hundred bombers were used, including 63 from Six Group. The Pathfinders' exploits were highlighted by the work of Wing Commander Fauquier, the associate Master Bomber, who controlled the aircraft streaming over the target for the full forty-five minutes the raid lasted before dropping his own bombs. Extensive damage was inflicted and several important German scientists were killed. The development of the 'V-weapons' project was set back severely, but the price was high. Overall Command losses were nearly 7 per cent and Six Group lost nearly 16 per cent of its aircraft.

During the next three months the Canadians flew mostly against targets in the Ruhr and Rhineland where the 'flak' was heavy and night fighters numerous, but the comparatively short time spent over German territory reduced the chances of being shot down. 'Our aircraft all reported in early this morning . . . ', one squadron diarist reported jubilantly, 'as no losses on two consecutive nights is almost a record.' Nevertheless the Canadian losses never dropped below 4½ per cent per month and in October were close to 6 per cent.

Despite the resolution shown by the great majority of bomber crews, when particularly dangerous targets were assigned some crew members disabled equipment or reported imaginary faults in order to justify not taking off or making an 'early return'. Although the percentage of Canadian machines designated serviceable each day rose substantially during 1943, the number of crews failing to take off after manning their aircraft and the number of early returns also increased. When 115 Six Group machines were assigned to Berlin, 5 failed to take off and 11 returned early. On another occasion at the end of December, when 135 crews were ordered to the same very dangerous target, 6 failed to take off and 15 returned early. Even back in June, 75 per cent of the early returns had had their alleged malfunctions subsequently found to be 'OK on test' and by September the number of failures attributed to 'faulty crew manipulation' or subsequently found 'OK on test' was alleged to be 'just as high as ever, if not higher' in Six Group's engineering reports.[10]

Air Vice-Marshal C.M. ('Black Mike') McEwen took command of the Group in January 1944 when its fortunes were at their lowest ebb. On January 20, 147 Canadian aircraft were assigned to attack Berlin but 3 failed to take off, 17 returned early, and 9 were lost. The next night a raid on Magdeburg, in north-central Germany, was scheduled. Eleven out of 125 aircraft failed to take off, 12 returned early, and a horrendous 24 went missing. Moreover, many crews who did press on apparently did not go where they were supposed to. Aircraft carried cameras triggered by the bomb release gear in order to photograph the targets they attacked and confirm their bombing accuracy, but during January there was 'a large increase in the number of [camera] failures which could not definitely be explained', reported the Group's photographic equipment staff. 'The camera operated perfectly before take-off and afterwards.'[11]

Discussing the morale problems of the Command as a whole, Air Vice-Marshal Bennett, the Pathfinder leader, observed that 'a very large number of crews failed to carry out their attacks ... in their cus-

105 Survivors of the bombing of Mannheim.

tomary determined manner.' It is hardly surprising that morale in Six Group seemed to be slipping. During the second Battle of Berlin, Bomber Command's loss rate averaged 5.4 per cent, but the Canadians were enduring a rate of more than 6 per cent and in January their losses reached 7.3 per cent. In such circumstances only ten crews in a hundred would survive a tour. However, the omens of January were not fulfilled for Six Group. In February 1944 the loss rate was down by two percentage points; in March it fell dramatically again; and during April, when Bomber Command flew entirely under the operational control of General Eisenhower in support of the forthcoming invasion of France and far fewer missions were flown into Germany, it was down to 2 per cent, while the scale of operations continued to increase sharply. All the RCAF squadrons were now equipped with Lancasters or Halifaxes and a new unit, 415 Squadron, was added to the Group from Coastal Command, giving it a total of 14 squadrons.

From March to September Bomber Command's chief object was to

106 Flight-Lieutenant Dick Audet, DFC and Bar, established an RAF/RCAF record that still stands—and is unlikely ever to fall—when he destroyed five enemy machines in five minutes. In less than a month of combat Audet was credited with 11½ German aircraft. He was killed on March 3, 1945, when his Spitfire was hit by flak during a low-level sweep over northern Germany.

interdict the Normandy battlefield, a mission that involved striking at targets in France. The 4,000-pound canister-type 'blockbusters' and the large proportion of incendiaries disappeared from the bomb-bays, to be replaced with aerodynamically designed 8,000- and 2,000-pound bombs. It soon became clear that Harris's men had the technical capability to engage successfully in precision bombing at night, for it was politically expedient to do as little injury as possible to the French population. Canals, railway marshalling yards, and repair facilities were the primary targets and they were totally destroyed one by one, while the towns and cities that bordered or surrounded them were left virtually untouched.

After Allied troops landed in Normandy on June 6, the weight of Bomber Command was diverted from time to time to give immediate tactical support to ground forces engaged in 'set-piece' assaults. Some of these attacks were successful, some were not, and occasionally Allied troops were hit by their own bombers, but the armies—the Canadian army in particular—could never get too much of this heavy-bomber tactical support. Another part of the bombing effort was turned against the launching sites of the V-1 'flying bombs' that began to fall on London and southeastern England in June 1944.

These sites, scattered along the Channel coast, were hard targets to hit and harder still to damage and the nearly 5,000 tons of high-explosive bombs that were aimed at them had little effect. However, the sites were overrun by Canadian ground forces before the Germans were able to develop a maximum effort from them.

Throughout Bomber Command loss rates dropped steeply, but in the Canadian case the drop was extreme. From sharing (with Four Group) by far the worst record in the Command in January, they became, in May, the Group with the lowest percentage of losses. (Why this should have happened is not yet clear and much research remains to be done on this fascinating historical problem.)

Losses were down to 1.6 per cent in June, the invasion month, when Pilot Officer A.C. Mynarski of 419 Squadron posthumously brought Six Group its only Victoria Cross of the war. He was the mid-upper gunner of a Lancaster sent to bomb the railway marshalling yards at Cambrai, in northern France, a week after D-Day. When his aircraft was attacked by a German night fighter and set on fire, the pilot ordered his crew to bail out and then jumped himself, but Mynarski, realizing that the rear gunner was trapped in his turret, struggled back to help him. As the blazing Lancaster spiralled down, Mynarski fought to free his fellow gunner until his own clothing and parachute were also on fire. Only then, at the urging of the trapped man he was trying to save, did he make his way back up the flaming fuselage to an escape hatch and jump himself. He reached the ground safely but died from his burns soon afterwards. The man he had endeavoured to free miraculously survived the crash and was able to tell the story of Mynarski's valour.

In October Bomber Command was returned to the operational control of the Air Staff and Air Marshal Harris promptly reverted to the area bombing of German cities. Loss rates, which had fallen to .3 per cent in September, began to climb again, but the six-month breathing space they had been vouchsafed had worked wonders with Six Group. It had been able to build up a cadre of experienced crews large enough to effect, by example and transmitted doctrine, the performance of the whole. At the end of 1944 McEwen was able to point out, in a summary of his tenure in command, that not only had the Canadians 'sustained the lowest losses . . . in the whole of Bomber Command' but also that 'a study of the bomb plots shows the standard [of accuracy] to be well in the van of the command.'[12] After wrestling successfully with the various problems that had beset it during its first twelve months, the Group began its third year in triumph.

In the early spring of 1945 the pace again quickened for the final all-out offensive against Germany. American daylight (and pin-point) attacks on synthetic fuel plants, which had begun during the previous summer, were playing havoc with the Luftwaffe's fuel supplies; the German fighter defences were being overwhelmed as their com-

munication networks were destroyed; and Bomber Command, its aircraft now escorted by long-range fighters, turned increasingly to daylight attacks, reinforcing the American success. Night attacks and area bombing were not abandoned, however, and Six Group contributed 66 aircraft to the notorious destruction of Dresden on a February night when the bulk of the Canadian planes were attacking the synthetic oil plant at Böhlen. Two Canadian aircraft were lost out of 183 that flew that night; between 30,000 and 50,000 Dresdeners—the exact number will never be known—were burnt or asphyxiated in the firestorm that engulfed the city.

By March 1945 it was clear that the end of the war in Europe could not be long delayed. Yet in the last two months of the war a large part of the cultural heritage of Europe was destroyed in order 'to intensify the chaos behind the lines'. On March 17-18 the beautiful Baroque city of Würzburg was wiped out; on March 22 the medieval centre of Hildesheim was gutted; on April 3-4 the thousand-year-old town of Nordhausen suffered the same fate; and on April 14 Potsdam was devastated. There was, perhaps, more justification for the attack on Hitler's Bavarian retreat at Berchtesgaden on April 25, when the Pathfinders of 405 Squadron led an attack by 300 bombers. That same day the Canadian Pathfinders flew a second mission to mark two coastal defence batteries in the Frisian Islands for 192 Six Group bombers. Four of the aircraft did not return, but when the last Lancaster of 428 Squadron touched down at 8:30 p.m., Six Group's last bombing operation of the war was over.

Bomber Command's strategic air offensive was intended to win the war, or at the very least to shorten it significantly. The price paid in human lives was enormous, but it failed to achieve its objectives. When the war in Europe came to an end, Bomber Command had dropped—in round figures—nearly a million tons of bombs in the course of 365,000 sorties. Six Group's contribution to that total included 126,000 tons in 41,000 sorties. The Command's casualties numbered 47,000 aircrew killed (over 8,200 of them Canadians) and 4,000 wounded. Ironically, perhaps, many Canadians who had volunteered for aircrew duties in the belief that it offered a more individualized, more human environment than either the army or the navy had found themselves committed to a malevolent, technological, impersonal battle waged primarily against women and children. German casualties resulting directly from the Allied bombing offensives totalled more than 560,000 dead and 675,000 wounded, the majority being woman and nearly 20 per cent children under sixteen. The British official historians have estimated that the loss of German war production that resulted from all this may have amounted to 1.2 per cent![13]

107   The charred corpses of two children, Hamburg.

9

NORTHERN ITALY AND NORTHWEST EUROPE 1944-1945

Rome was the first European capital to be taken by the Allies on their march to Berlin. Its capture on June 4, 1943, freed the Vatican from the direct pressures of Fascist diplomacy and propaganda and heartened Catholics throughout the world. But with Rome in their hands the American strategists very soon lost what little interest they had ever had in the Italian campaign. They transferred their attention to the largely Franco-American landings (the Canadian-American First Special Service Force was also involved), which took place in the south of France on August 15. However, the British were committed to their Italian strategy and dreamed of a breakout into Austria and the Balkans through the Ljubljana Gap in the eastern Alps. All through the long, hot summer of 1944 the Allied forces in Italy pushed doggedly north.

After the fall of Rome most of the Canadians in Italy went into army reserve for a well-earned rest and a re-structuring of the 5th Armoured Division, which had proved tactically unbalanced in the stress of mobile war. Only the 1st Canadian Armoured Brigade accompanied the British spearheads in their advance from Rome to Florence. (According to General Leese, the Eighth Army's commander, it was 'the most experienced armoured brigade in Italy and therefore in great demand.') However, the Canadian Corps headquarters was not in demand: quietly overlooking his own responsibility for some of the problems that had beset the Canadians in the battle for Rome, Leese now argued that they were not really competent to handle a fluid battle at the corps level and suggested that the Corps 'be broken up and the divisions placed under command of a British corps'. When his views were transmitted to England, both General Crerar and General Stuart, the Canadian Chief of Staff there, objected to further fragmentation of the Army Overseas. Several command and staff changes were made, but discussions between Stuart (who flew out from England) and Leese, together with a reluctant vote of confidence that Stuart wrung from General Burns's two divisional commanders, Vokes and Hoffmeister, enabled Burns to keep his job for the time being.

For the men of the 1st and 5th Divisions, encamped in the Volturno valley north of Naples, life was pleasant enough. Training in the foothills and on the sun-baked Volturno flats was interspersed with short leaves in Rome and nearby coastal resorts. Ball games were played, teeth were fixed, and minds and bodies rested. At the end of July an inspection by 'General Collingwood'—who turned out to be King George VI travelling incognito—brought their idyll to an end and the next day the Corps set off north to play its part in breaking the Gothic Line.*

In the last week of August the Canadians found themselves back on the Adriatic coast, with the little town of Cattolica, some 20 miles ahead, as their objective. The lessons of the Hitler Line had been well learned and, with the 1st Division leading as far as the Foglia River, where the 5th Armoured drew alongside so that the Corps could attack on a two-division front, 'the Canadians broke through the Gothic Line by finding a soft spot and going through,' wrote Martha Gellhorn, the American war correspondent.

> It makes me ashamed to write that sentence because there is no soft place where there are mines and no soft places where there are Spandaus and no soft place where there are long 88mm guns, and if you have seen one tank burn with its crew shut inside it you will never believe that anything is soft again.[1]

The German Tenth Army's defences included 2,375 machine-gun posts, 479 anti-tank guns, mortar- and assault-gun positions, and 22 panzerturm—tank turrets set in concrete—protected by 100,000 anti-tank and anti-personnel mines, 117,000 metres of wire obstacles, and 9,000 metres of anti-tank ditches. An evening attack by the West Nova Scotia Regiment led them into one large minefield where the battalion reeled under a storm of fire from the enemy's automatic weapons, mortars, and artillery, trapped in exactly the sort of killing-ground the designers of the German defences had aimed to create. Next morning, in the pre-dawn twilight, the 'Van Doos' made an attempt to take the same German position. 'The advance across the minefield was slow and laborious,' wrote one of their company commanders.

> We had to follow a white tape which the engineers had unwound to mark where they had swept the path. Now and then, in the semi-darkness, we nearly stepped on a mine which they had lifted and left beside the tape in their anxiety to finish before daylight. Here and there mutilated bodies still twitched in a final spasm. They were men of the other regiment who had attempted the assault the previous evening. Some wounded were lying in the middle of the minefield after several stretcher-bearers had got themselves killed or wounded in trying to help them.[2]

Once through the minefield the French Canadians burst into the

---

* For this campaign, see the map of Italy on page 126.

108   A bulldozer was needed to drag this 3/4-ton truck, and the 37-mm Bofors anti-aircraft gun it was towing, up the muddy bank of an Italian stream.

machine-gun posts that covered it and that had wreaked such havoc among the West Novas the night before. 'Firing from the hip, throwing grenades and howling like demons delivered from hell we charged the position, giving no quarter and asking none.'

There were, however, some strong points that were less adamant than others—some of them softened-up by 417 Squadron RCAF, which had been converted from a fighter to a fighter-bomber squadron on June 22. The change had not proved to be a major chore: their Spitfires were fitted with a 500-pound bomb rack under each wing, the pilots were given two days to practise their new art over a nearby lake, and operational flying resumed with a dive-bombing role added to their other responsibilities. The paucity of specialized training may have contributed to the loss of three pilots in five days at the beginning of July. By the end of August they were flying as many as 40 sorties a day from airstrips just behind the front. Day after day, at the request of 'Rover' radio nets (forward air liaison officers operating on the ground from armoured cars, working in close co-operation with the front-line troops), they attacked gun emplacements, enemy headquarters, transport, and mortar pits with bombs and machine-gun fire. On September 3 one mission saw:

> Eight aircraft airborne to carry out close support with Rover Jimmy. They were directed on to the Regimental HQ . . . which they attacked at 17.15 hours scoring two hits beside house and 25 yds

from small woods in which two small green tents were identified. Both sections then strafed the tented area. Intense light ack-ack from northeast and southwest of target.[3]

By September 3 the Gothic Line was broken, the leading Canadians were north of Cattolica, and the enemy was in such disarray that a company of the motorized Westminster Regiment found a German truck, loaded with the first hot food it had seen in two days, driving right into their positions. They soon reported, with some satisfaction, that Wehrmacht cooking 'was not a damn bit better than ours', but had more trouble convincing regimental headquarters that the German beer accompanying it tasted like 'low grade spring water'.

The Germans very quickly recovered their balance, however. The road northwards, through the Romagna, crossed a dozen rivers before debouching into the wide Lombardy plain, and they skilfully took advantage of the ground while Kesselring switched reserves from his western flank, where the Fifth Army had not yet closed with the formidable fragment of the Gothic Line that faced it across the lower Arno. Digging in on each river line in turn, the Germans put up a fierce resistance before slipping away—from the Conca to the Marano, from the Marano to the Ausa (it was mid-September and the weather was deteriorating now), from the Ausa to the Marecchia, the Marecchia to the Fiumichino, the Fiumichino to the Savio. Here, on the north bank of the river, Private E.A. 'Smoky' Smith of the Seaforth Highlanders won Canada's third and last Victoria Cross of the Mediterranean campaign before the winter rains settled in, the rivers rose, the roads turned to bogs, and the Eighth Army's momentum once again began to peter out. In a month the Canadians had endured nearly 4,000 battle casualties, while a further 1,500 men had gone down sick or suffering from battle fatigue.

The Corps went into reserve at the end of October amid rumours—strengthened by the appointment of General McNaughton as Minister of National Defence on November 2—that they were soon to be reunited with First Canadian Army. General Burns relinquished his appointment on November 5. He had exercised only an adequate control of the Corps since the summer and too many of his command relationships were still poisoned by earlier criticisms of his handling of operations on the road to Rome. 'No one can be an impartial judge in his own case,' General Burns observed, but 'during the period of my command the corps had taken all objectives assigned to it, inflicting heavy losses on the enemy. ... Though progress was not always as rapid as desirable, nevertheless, during our period of action we went further and faster than any other Corps [in Italy].'[4] However, there seems little doubt that Burns was essentially a staff officer rather than a battlefield commander and that much of the Corps' progress was due to his hard-driving divisional commanders, Vokes and Hoffmeister.

General Foulkes came from Holland to take command of the Canadian Corps and General Vokes left Italy to exchange commands with Major-General H.W. Foster of the 4th Armoured Division in Holland.

From a professional point of view the Canadians had come of age. Sicily had been a haphazard affair, southern Italy a chase. Ortona and the Hitler Line had been marred by technical failures in several respects. On the Gothic Line and in the Romagna, however, the Canadians were recognized as master craftsmen and, had they known of it at the time, they might have appreciated most of all the tribute of one of their most notable opponents, General von Vietinghoff, the commander of the German Tenth Army: 'I am told that the 5th Canadian Armoured Division was excellent,' he reported to Field Marshal Kesselring;' ... though not strong in numbers, the Canadians are excellent soldiers.'[5]

In December the Eighth Army—against the better judgement of its new commander, General Sir Richard McCreery—made one last try at a breakthrough into the Lombardy plain. The Canadians, in the lead again, ploughed forward to the Senio River, compelling Kesselring to draw more forces from his western flank. Now the Germans were really desperate in their resistance. Another step backwards would have taken them beyond the river lines into open country where Allied armour might be deployed en masse to charge the Ljubljana Gap or to surround their Fourteenth Army facing the Americans on the other side of the Apennines. The Germans on the river were aided by the weather and topography—the Senio's wide floodbanks stood 40 feet above the plain, the outer slopes were steep, the inner slopes were stepped, and the winter current was fast—and they stopped the Eighth Army in its muddy, exhausted tracks. North-west of Ravenna elements of the Canadian Corps, holding the northernmost outpost of the entire Italian front, settled into winter quarters.

More dramatic events were occurring in Northwest Europe* as the disabled German armies fell back across France. Bypassing Paris, Patton's Third U.S. Army spearheads were across the Meuse on the last day of August, while General Hodges' First U.S. Army, crossing the Seine north-west of the French capital, was also driving east at top speed. In front of Montgomery's 21st Army Group the Seine ran deeper and wider between very steep banks and fresh German forces from the Pas de Calais were able to fight an effective rear-guard action. But the British were in Amiens by the end of the month and their momentum carried them to Brussels on September 2 and to Antwerp the following day. There the advance guards were allowed to stop and rest.

---

* For this campaign, see the map of Northwest Europe on page 149.

109 Winter in northern Italy. Battle-wise soldiers, like those of the Ontario Regiment, chose not to live in buildings, which were automatic targets for enemy mortar fire. Instead from sandbags and tarpaulins they built 'hoochies' against the back of their tanks and slept under the tanks themselves. This picture was taken on January 21, 1945.

If Field Marshal Montgomery (as he now was) had spurred them on to Bergen op Zoom, only 20 miles to the north, he would have trapped the German Fifteenth Army on the South Beveland peninsula, ensured the early clearance of the Scheldt estuary, and opened the approaches to Antwerp by the end of the month. Pre-eminently a general of mass and matériel rather than manoeuvre, Montgomery of all people should have seen the importance of opening the greatest port of Europe when a million and a half men were having to be supplied through the now-distant port of Cherbourg. But he failed to press the pursuit over those last few miles, the Germans smartly reorganized their defences, and Antwerp's vital facilities were thereby denied to the invading armies until the end of November.

On the Channel end of the Allied line, First Canadian Army had been left far behind. Their problems in crossing the Seine were greatest, their formations had suffered most in the Falaise battle, and they were left to deal with the German garrisons of the Channel fortresses—Le Havre, Dieppe, Boulogne, Calais, and Dunkirk—that punctuated their axis of advance. Nor, perhaps, were they driven as hard as they should have been. On September 2 Montgomery had signalled General Crerar to 'push on quickly', but Crerar's response

110 The race across France: a Canadian artillery regiment rolls through the ruins of Falaise in August 1944.

was cautious to say the least. Le Havre fell to a combined assault by his I British Corps and the RAF's Bomber Command on September 12, and the Canadian commander then wrote to Montgomery that, 'while the rapid fall of Le Havre has favourable potential influences, it is most important that the effect so gained should not be more than lost by an unsuccessful attack on the next objective, Boulogne. I therefore want Simonds to button things up properly, taking a little more time if necessary, in order to ensure a decisive assault.' If Crerar had been a British rather than a Canadian general, he might not have lasted much longer in command of one of the Field Marshal's armies.

The 2nd Division had triumphantly re-entered Dieppe—from the landward side, this time—without much opposition on September 8. Boulogne, the most important port between Le Havre and Antwerp, was defended more resolutely. Its capture was assigned to the 3rd Division (now commanded by Major-General Dan Spry, who had been promoted from a brigade in Italy), together with nine artillery regiments borrowed from neighbouring British formations, 750 heavy bombers of Bomber Command, and a substantial part of the 2nd Tactical Air Force. In ninety minutes on the morning of September 17 the aircraft dumped 3,232 tons of high explosive exactly on target and the artillery added every round they could fire to the bombardment. Then the armour moved in, although the extensive cratering impeded armoured vehicles, and over the next four days the German defences were battered down yard by yard.

The high point of the Boulogne battle proved to be the capture of the so-called 'citadel', a walled fortification perched on a limestone hill in the centre of the town that dates back to the thirteenth century. It fell to a singular combination of bizarre storybook tactics and modern technology, after a French civilian had shown an officer of the Stormont, Dundas and Glengarry Highlanders a secret tunnel leading into the fortress. The SDGs soon had a platoon in the tunnel and at the same time 'the Engineers in their armoured vehicles began to place petards against the portcullis. As the gate was blown in the Company Commander and his platoon deal the *coup de grâce* to the morale of the defenders by suddenly appearing in their midst out of the tunnel. Scores of dirty white things immediately were seen fluttering from the walls in token of surrender.'[7] Only a beauteous and suitably grateful princess was needed to provide all the elements of a Hollywood epic!

Meanwhile Montgomery had belatedly realized the importance of the Scheldt estuary and had again ordered General Crerar to move his army up as quickly as possible. Calais fell, on October 1, to an assault that lacked only the romantic aspects of the attack on Boulogne. The planned attack on Dunkirk was abandoned,* and First Canadian Army began to concentrate on the banks of the Scheldt.

Though the British were already in Antwerp, their hold on the port

* Dunkirk remained under siege until the end of the war in Europe and the garrison did not capitulate until two days after the signing of the final German surrender.

11 When the Canadians re-entered Dieppe in September 1944, one of the first tasks assigned was the painting of the plain wooden crosses that marked the 355 graves in the Canadian cemetery.

112 A seemingly endless line of Sherman tanks of the Fort Garry Horse advancing across the South Beveland isthmus in October 1944 with flooded *polders* on one side and an embankment on the other.

was far from complete. The Royal Hamilton Light Infantry, relieving a British battalion in the harbour area, were assigned to guard the locks that controlled the harbour water level. They found that remnants of the German garrison were still holding out in the vicinity and for a few days they engaged in a weird kind of skirmishing as the enemy tried to take and hold the locks long enough to blow them up. One Hamiltonian has recalled:

> The troops were billeted in hotels or quarters with many of the amenities of home. When duty called they took a street car to the waterfront and used all available cover to crawl to their positions. At 'lunch-break' some of the drier souls risked sniping for a sip of heavy ale at the nearest pub. [In some taverns] we would usually be there in the day time. The Germans were generally there at night. . . . The innkeeper thought it was a great joke, but the Germans crossed us up one day and came in when we weren't exactly looking and we were driven out for a while.'[8]

In order to retain control of the estuary, the enemy held a pocket on the south shore, around Breskens, which was largely supplied from the island of Walcheren at the tip of the South Beveland peninsula. The Canadians' first priority was therefore to cut the Beveland isthmus and thus drastically reduce the German Fifteenth Army's flow of supplies. While the 3rd and 4th Divisions—Major-General H.W. Foster had replaced General Kitching in command of the 4th Armoured on August 22—began to crush the Breskens pocket in Operation *Switchback*, the 2nd Division started to push, painfully slowly, across the base of the Beveland isthmus on October 2. By that time General Crerar, suffering from persistent dysentery that had not responded to the usual medical treatments, had returned to England. The clearing of the Scheldt was left in the hands of General Simonds, as acting army commander, while General Foulkes temporarily led II Canadian Corps and Brigadier R. H. Keefler commanded the 2nd Division.

Under an umbrella of artillery fire and direct air support the Canadians could only inch forward and it took them three full weeks of vicious, bitter fighting to advance some 7 miles and isolate the defenders of the Scheldt from landward re-supply. Much of the area consisted of flooded *polders*—sections of reclaimed land lying below sea level between breached dykes running more or less at right angles to each other. The Germans could burrow into a lateral dyke from the back, **break**ing only a small hole in the forward face through which **to poke** their automatic weapons, or in the top in order to align their mortars. The Canadians, on the other hand, were limited to narrow, exposed, and frequently mined lines of advance along the dykes, swept by German fire from a broad front. Mostly they stumbled and crawled along the sides of the dykes, between wind and water, eating, sleeping, fighting, and dying in sodden uniforms and squelching boots. This pattern was typical of much of the Scheldt fighting and more than neutralized any advantage of air support and vastly superior logistics the Canadians enjoyed.

The Black Watch of Canada, for example, experienced the most terrible day in its history—on Friday, October 13—as it tried desperately to close a gap that was now little more than a mile wide. Their attack was launched early in the morning, but 'by 1000 hours the leading company [still] lay on the start line, their ranks cruelly decimated by the withering fire,' wrote the historian of the Toronto Scottish, some of whose machine-guns and mortars had been assigned to provide fire support.

> The next company lined up and began to pass through. For two hours they too tried vainly to advance and a very small gain was made. The remaining companies then took their turn, each advancing a short distance at alarming cost. The gruelling battle carried on throughout the day and as evening fell the reformed companies were still pushing on yard by bloody yard. Every conceivable form of support was ordered up. Tanks were available but could not negotiate the flooded fields nor the narrow roads [along the top of the dykes] .... Shortly before midnight the survivors reached their objective but were too few to hold it against a counter-attack.[9]

All four of the Watch's rifle company commanders had been killed during the day. Between the 8th and the 10th the battalion had suffered 81 casualties. After two days' rest they had gone back into the line and in two more days of envenomed fighting lost another 183 men—more than a third of the unit and nearly all of its rifle companies gone in less than a week!

In the Breskens pocket, operations were equally difficult, although more use was made of close ground support by aircraft than on the north shore of the estuary. It was provided by 2nd Tactical Air Force's 84 Group, which had rocket-firing Typhoons, the most devastating airborne close-support weapons system of the war.*

Just south of Biervliet a company of the North Shores, which had already been accidentally shot up by Spitfires that morning, was being heavily mortared by the Germans when along came a flight of Typhoons. One of the North Shores recalled:

> The flight leader came down to about twenty feet from ground level to see who we were. I stood up and used pantomime to tell him about the enemy mortars back of the orchard and he was a bright lad. Away he went to look at the place and went back and picked up his flight and the mess they made of Jerry's mortar position was beautiful to behold.[10]

From time to time, inevitably, there were accidents in which airmen strafed their own side, but in the battlefield balance of human lives (no more delicate scale exists) close air support was worth much more than it cost. The historian of the North Nova Scotia Regiment, recording an attack in the pocket during which one of its companies took 50 prisoners, wrote that 'this attack might have been costly had it not been for an assault on the enemy by our aircraft—rocket firing Typhoons—immediately before the assault started .... [They] let go their rockets right on top of the artillery concentration and the enemy taken prisoners were obviously quite shaken by it all.'[11]

Not until November 2 was the Breskens pocket finally eliminated and an entry made in the 3rd Division log to that effect. Beside it somebody wrote 'Thank God!' The Division had suffered over 2,000 casualties, something close to a quarter of them being fatal.

Practically every Allied aircraft in Northwest Europe was now involved, to some extent or other, in the direct support of ground forces, which meant that the bulk of their casualties were a result of ground fire. In their air-superiority role the Allied fighters had very little to worry about, although the advent of enemy jet aircraft in the early fall must have given them a few moments' pause. However, on October 5, Spitfire pilots of the RCAF's 401 Squadron showed that the new jets were not invulnerable as they claimed the RAF/RCAF's first victory over a jet fighter—a Messerschmitt 262. 401's eventual total of 195 enemy aircraft destroyed was to make it the top-scoring RCAF squadron of the war.

---

* 84 Group contained no Canadian squadrons, while 83 Group, which flew fighter-bombers and worked with Second British Army, was very heavily Canadian in its content. Early pre-invasion planning had reversed these assignments, but that arrangement, which seems through Canadian eyes to have been both sensible and appropriate, had been unaccountably altered shortly after the departure of General McNaughton from the Canadian command in December 1943.

84 Group, with its rocket-equipped Typhoons, was made responsible for the whole of 21st Army Group's front *west* of the Rhine (i.e. close support), while 83 Group concerned itself primarily with the enemy's lines of communication *east* of the Rhine. Thus the Canadian fighter-bombers in 83 Group, now commanded by Group Captain Paul Davoud and flying out of Eindhoven, were usually striking deep into Germany but did provide some close support from time to time, notably during the ill-fated Arnhem operation, in which Canadian ground forces were not directly involved. The majority of its missions were flown against transportation targets across the Rhine, however, with such success that the Germans even resorted to camouflaging their railway locomotives. But there was no way they could camouflage the smoke from their furnaces and steam from their boilers, or the lines and bridges that the trains ran on. By the end of October, when winter weather began to restrict flying operations, rail traffic over the Rhine had been virtually stopped and road traffic was being hammered unmercifully during the daylight hours.

The South Beveland peninsula was secured by October 31, but there remained the island of Walcheren at the end of the peninsula, garrisoned by 3,000 Germans well stocked with food and ammunition. Its batteries of heavy guns still commanded the mouth of the Scheldt.

The capture of Walcheren was directed by First Canadian Army, but only the first stage of it was launched by Canadian troops. During the last day of October and the first of November the 2nd Division, together with elements of the British 52nd Division, fought desperately to cross the 1,200-yard-long perfectly flat causeway that joined the island to the Beveland peninsula. The eventual honour of being 'first across' fell to 'B' Company of the Calgary Highlanders, although they were forced back on to the causeway again and the final lodgement on Walcheren was established by Le Régiment de Maisonneuve. So desperate was the close-quarter fighting that the Germans were using 81-mm mortars at less than 50 yards' range. With the other companies of the battalion strung out along the narrow causeway behind them, the Highlanders' 'B' Company commander recalled later, 'it was here that George Hees contacted us in search of 'A' Company, which presumably he was to command [since it] ... had lost all of its officers ... wounded.' 'A' Company must have been back behind Major Hees, huddled somewhere on that bleak, fire-torn, and interminably long causeway over which he had come.

On November 3 the 2nd Division was withdrawn from the battle, having lost 207 officers and 3,443 other ranks in a little over a month. Walcheren, its perimeter dykes breached and its centre flooded as a result of massive raids by the Lancasters and Halifaxes of Bomber Command, was subsequently captured by British Commandos and the 52nd Division. Their two amphibious assaults, although costly in human lives, were not nearly as wasteful as the drive down the

113

CHRISTMAS PREPARATIONS—A LA MODE.

causeway had been and were much more productive, for the British troops who took over the Canadian lodgement from the Maisonneuves were unable to expand it until German resistance began to collapse as a result of the amphibious landings. With the fall of Walcheren on November 8 and the subsequent opening of Antwerp, General Simonds received the enthusiastic congratulations of both Crerar and Montgomery, but in retrospect one may wonder whether the assault on the causeway was in the finest traditions of generalship. The amphibious attacks showed that there had been an easier and less expensive way to take the island.

In November the Canadian ground forces in Northwest Europe found themselves manning a line along the Waal and Maas Rivers. They fought no major battle during the three winter months, but there was much nasty fighting in a minor key. The damp, penetrating cold, the mud, and the flooded ground also played their part in making the combat soldier's life miserable even when nobody was shooting at him.

A subaltern in the North Nova Scotia Highlanders found himself

> living in caves and dugouts scooped out of the wooded hills ... There is a telephone in my dugout, ... hooked up so I can communicate

with company headquarters, a half mile back, or with our artillery 'forward observation post', a quarter of a mile on ahead of me. I often pick up the phone and listen in. The difference in voices. The people at HQ relaxed, unworried, loud (they shout over the phone), whistling, singing, joking, playing cards. The men at the observation post overlooking the enemy position whisper into the phone. . . . They try to end conversations as soon as possible, and seem to be talking with their heads pulled down into their greatcoats. This strange dialogue goes on intermittently all night.

Two weeks later he was

back again in trenches, the December rain and hail, one day clear in four, two hours of windy sunshine a week, mud to the ankles. Some days we lie in the mud. . . . We eat twice a day, morning and night. Food is brought down a slippery path, mined along the fringes, under darkness and between scattered bursts of enemy fire, for they know our habits.[13]

In Italy more significant and dramatic events were taking place. Eight months earlier a tentative suggestion by Ottawa that I Canadian Corps might be reunited with their comrades in Northwest Europe when circumstances permitted had failed to arouse any kind of positive response from the British. A more direct approach, made only ten days after General McNaughton assumed the portfolio of National Defence, proved no more successful at first, but over the turn of the year the Canadian pressure on London became steadily firmer and more persistent. At the end of January 1945 the Combined Chiefs of Staff, meeting in Malta, finally decided to seek an immediate decision against Germany in Northwest Europe and ordered the transfer of some forces from Italy. Field Marshal Alexander, the Mediterranean commander, pointed out that 'the Canadian divisions were the easiest to move quickly'. The Canadians were chosen and the first of the two divisions was in Holland by early March. General Foulkes's Corps HQ became operational again on March 15 and by April 3 the last of the Canadians from Italy had rejoined First Canadian Army. The largest Canadian combat force ever assembled now held the left flank of an Allied line that stretched from the Swiss mountains to the North Sea.

Before their arrival in Northwest Europe, the German counterattack in the Ardennes, which culminated in the 'Battle of the Bulge' at Christmas 1944, had little effect on the Canadian ground forces' holding the extreme left of the Allied line. But the enemy's last great aerial gamble, which followed a few days later, did leave its mark on the RCAF. On New Year's morning, when the Luftwaffe calculated that most of the Allied aircraft in Northwest Europe would be grounded with their crews nursing hangovers, 800 fighters and fighter-bombers were launched against tactical airfields in a last-ditch attempt to inflict a major defeat on Allied air power. The Ger-

114 Wreckage left on the airfield at Eindhoven, Holland, after the Luftwaffe's 'forlorn hope' attack on New Year's Day 1945.

mans put every possible machine in the air, including their new jets and even some captured Mustangs and a Spitfire with Luftwaffe markings—an indication of their desperate straits.

One hundred and forty-four Allied aircraft were destroyed and 84 damaged in the space of an hour and a half, but German losses turned out to be just about as high and the remnants of the Luftwaffe were far less capable of absorbing such punishment. 2nd Tactical Air Force alone claimed 47 enemy aircraft destroyed and nearly half of that total fell to the RCAF's 126 Wing, now commanded by Group Captain G.R. McGregor with Wing Commander 'Dal' Russel as his Wingco (Flying).

Eindhoven, where the Canadian Typhoon fighter-bomber and Spitfire reconnaissance wings were stationed, was hit particularly hard. A few planes had already taken off when the first wave of enemy aircraft came in, but eight of the Canadian Typhoons were on the runway and five of them, together with a considerable number of other machines that were parked in the vicinity, were destroyed and a great many more damaged. When the Germans arrived at Evère, where Group Captain 'Iron Bill' MacBrien's 127 Wing was based, four Spitfires were already in the air and claimed six of the attackers, but eleven Canadian machines were destroyed on the ground and a dozen more damaged. Johnnie Johnson, the Wingco (Flying), was watching 416 Squadron turn from the perimeter track to the runway when the Germans arrived.

> From our reasonably safe position on the ground Bill [MacBrien] and I took stock of the attack. The enemy fighters strafed singly and in pairs. Our few light ack-ack guns had already ceased firing; later we found that the gunners had run out of ammunition. The enemy

completely dominated the scene, and there was little we could do except shout with rage as our Spitfires burst into flames before our eyes.[14]

At the third Canadian base, Heesch, the story was very different. A large part of the McGregor–Russel wing, which was stationed there, was already airborne when the first Germans arrived to bomb and strafe the runways without inflicting either casualties or damage. Then the Canadians already in the air pounced on them and in the ensuing combat claimed 24 enemy destroyed, 3 'probables', and 7 damaged for the loss of only 2 Spitfires. Two of the Germans were claimed by Flight Lieutenant Dick Audet of 411 Squadron, but in a sense his victories were anti-climactic. Only two days earlier Audet had been credited with his first five enemy aircraft, two Me 109s and three F-W 190s, in a fight that lasted less than five minutes—and established an RAF/RCAF record that still stands.

Operations *Veritable* and *Blockbuster*, designed to clear the land between the Maas and the Rhine, began on February 8 with an attack by XXX British Corps (placed under First Canadian Army's command) that drove the enemy back some 10 miles through the Reichwald forest. Initially Canadian participation was largely limited to General Spry's 3rd Division, sailing (in amphibious armoured vehicles) up the flooded Waal/Rhine flats until the widening of the front made it possible for General Simonds to deploy his other infantry division. The 2nd Division, now commanded by Major-General A.B. Matthews, was inserted into the line on February 14.

Two weeks later the weight of the whole operation was shifted to the left flank as the Canadians moved on to higher ground. The two infantry divisions now slogged their way forward into the heart of another forest, the Hochwald, while General Vokes's 4th Armoured Division first cleared the northern end of the vital Calcar-Uden ridge

115 Amphibian 'Alligators' of the 3rd Canadian Infantry Division ploughing up the flooded Rhine near Nijmegen, Holland, in February 1945.

116 Kranenberg, Germany, was flooded when the Germans broke the dykes along the lower Rhine. The town was shelled and bombed, but the church spire remained standing.

and then swung south, across the infantry's rear, to drive through the 'railway gap' that separated the Hochwald from the smaller Tuschenwald and Balbergerwald to the west. Now that they were fighting on German soil the opposition became quite fanatical and the Canadians were faced by hard-fighting paratroopers of General Alfred Schlemm's First German Parachute Army. They formed a core around which gathered 'old men and young boys who had hand grenades and old rifles and hearts full of hate'.[15]

The Germans had concentrated an unusual amount of supporting fire-power, which had been pre-registered on every key crossroad or forest ridge where, in the mist-shrouded woods, many German shells exploded on impact with the tree-tops, creating 'air bursts' whose shrapnel often inflicted heavy casualties. The enemy's fire could not be neutralized to the usual extent by tactical air power since the low cloud ceilings and very poor visibility inhibited close air support. During the whole course of this Battle of the Rhineland, close air support was impossible on 19 of the 31 days' fighting.

118 Closing the Rhine. Canadian trucks and armour struggle over a muddy track through the Hochwald in February 1945.

The infantry's task was not made any easier by the occasional lack of adequate direction. 'It was late afternoon before we finally got word to start ... and no one had given us any compass bearing to use,' complained a company commander of the North Shore. 'We simply had to enter a forest that contained many enemy strongpoints and blunder through as best we could.'[16] When they had thus

TOURISTS IN THE HOCHWALD.

119 German refugees and prisoners of war move back through the Canadian lines, south of Calcar, Germany, at the end of February 1945.

finished blundering through the forest, two Canadian infantrymen had won Victoria Crosses. Sergeant Aubrey Cosens of the Queen's Own Rifles, whose battalion had lost 100 men, won his posthumously. Major F.A. Tilston of the Essex Scottish, which took 130 casualties, lost both his legs in winning his.

The armour also had its troubles, with their Sherman tanks bogging down in the shell-pocked, water-logged ground or stalling on steep slopes. Moving up in preparation for driving out of the eastern end of the railway gap on February 28, two squadrons of the Canadian Grenadier Guards lost half their tanks before they even reached the start-line, and of those that crossed it three out of ten 'were almost immediately put out of action by five or six anti-tank guns firing from the right front.'[17] Six hundred yards further on, four of the remaining seven were also disabled by German 88s. On the 27th and 28th, 4th Armoured Division lost more than a hundred tanks.

While the Canadians were storming the Hochwald and pushing southwards up the west bank of the Rhine, the Ninth U.S. Army was driving north against rather less formidable opposition. On March 10, opposite Wesel, the last German resistance west of the river was finally pinched out. Further south the Americans already had a toe-hold on the east bank, having captured a bridge at Remagen, halfway between Düsseldorf and Mainz, three days earlier. But the Remagen lodgement (and the one that General Patton established even further south on March 22) led only to the rolling, wooded hills of Hesse and Thuringia and the certainty of more of the close, brutal infantry fighting that overwhelmingly favoured the defence. Allied strategy demanded that the point of main effort be located further north, where there was the prospect of a break-out into the great North German plain and armoured columns would be able to make proper use of their speed, flexibility, and hitting power.

An amphibious crossing of the Rhine, between Emmerich and Wesel, took place on the night of March 23-4, preceded by the heaviest artillery bombardment of the war and a massive air bombardment. The Germans had been seriously weakened by their efforts to hold the west bank, a struggle that had cost them approximately 90,000 men on the First Canadian and Ninth U.S. Army fronts alone. Moreover, the continuing bombardment stunned their forward defences and sealed off the selected zones, so that the actual crossing proved to be comparatively easy.

This assault on the Rhine was directed by Second British Army and carried out by XII and XXX Corps, the latter with the 3rd Canadian Infantry Division under its command for the occasion. Canadian involvement was supposed to be largely nominal—a graceful tribute to their doughty work in clearing the west bank—until a solid bridgehead had been established. The 3rd Division had landed with the British on D-Day and now its 9th (Highland) Brigade would cross the Rhine with them too. It was attached to XXX Corps' 51st (Highland)

120 In a railway yard in northern Germany a Canadian soldier waits for transport to take his prisoner away.

Division and the first Canadians across the Rhine were the men of the Highland Light Infantry of Canada. They arrived in front of Spel-drop, a mile and a half away, just as a battalion of British highlanders had been forced out of it by a German counter-attack. However, remnants of the Scottish regiment were fighting on, cut off and surrounded though they were.

The Canadians attacked in the late afternoon, supported by the fire of six field and two medium artillery regiments and two 7.2-inch siege batteries from the other bank of the Rhine. Still, it took two days to clear the village of its garrison of German paratroops. 'We began the house and barn clearing on the edge of the town,' wrote one veteran infantryman. 'Not many prisoners were taken, as, if they did not surrender before we started on a house, they never had the opportunity afterwards.'[18]

With a bridgehead well established, XXX Corps began to develop its attack on a three-division front. The Canadians took the left wing so that, having fought their way upstream along the west bank of the Rhine, they were now fighting their way downstream along the east bank. The Highland Light Infantry had been followed across the river by the North Nova Scotians and they too drew a particularly unpleasant ticket in the lottery of battle. On March 25 they came up against elements of a Panzer Grenadier division that had been ordered to hold the key road junction at Bienen.

> My platoon assaulted in a single extended wave. Ten tumbled down, nailed on the instant by fire from two or maybe three machine-guns. . . . The rest of us rolled or dropped into a shallow ditch, hardly more than a trough six inches deep, at the bottom of the dyke. The Bren-gunners put their weapons to their shoulders but never got a shot away. (I saw them after the battle, both dead, one still holding the aiming position) . . . A rifleman on my left took aim at a German weapon pit, and with a spasm collapsed on my arm. His face turned almost instantly a faint green and bore a simple smile.[19]

By nightfall the Maritimers held the southern part of the village. The battalion had lost 114 men—43 killed—in taking it, however, and the following morning the Highland Light Infantry came back into the line to capture the northern half. As for the author of the quotation above, he, like many another brave soldier, had reached the limits of psychological endurance after seven months of more or less continuous front-line duty. Still unwounded after the battle, he made an effort to report to his commanding officer. 'I hadn't any idea, apparently, of how far gone I was emotionally. Instead of furnishing a coherent account, I simply stood in front of him weeping inarticulately, unable to construct a sentence, even to force a single word out of my mouth.' Two days later he was on his way back to England.

The initial amphibious crossing had been quickly followed by an airborne landing of the British 6th and American 17th Airborne Divi-

121   Troops of the Black Watch of Canada crossing a makeshift bridge over the Regge River near Ommen, Holland, April 10, 1945.

122 A Sherman tank of the Fort Garry Horse surrounded by civilians in Rijssen, Holland, April 9, 1945.

sions, the British force including the 1st Canadian Parachute Battalion. The Canadians encountered severe machine-gun and rifle fire but, like other airborne units, took their objectives without delay or heavy casualties. During the fighting, however, one of the battalion's medical orderlies, Corporal F.G. Topham, won the fourth and last Victoria Cross to be awarded to a Canadian during the campaign for his courage and persistence in attending the wounded despite being wounded himself. Three of the four Crosses had been won on the banks of the Rhine within a month as the Germans fought for their own soil with a courage borne of desperation.

By the end of March 1945 the 2nd Infantry and 4th Armoured Divisions had joined the 3rd Division on the east bank of the Rhine and all three formations were re-united under the command of II Canadian Corps. Storming north along the river, the Canadians had taken the Hoch Elten, a wooded ridge some 3 miles north of Emmbich, and in the shattered town itself Canadian engineers were constructing and floating across the Rhine a 1,400-foot-long pontoon bridge. The completion of this bridge, on April 1, gave Simonds' men their own lifeline to the west bank and a more or less exclusive share of the torrent of equipment and matériel that was now pouring out of Antwerp.

I British Corps, which had been under General Crerar's command since the Normandy days of *Overlord*, now reverted to British control and Crerar was left with the two Canadian corps and a Polish armoured division. He launched the Italian veterans of General Foulkes's I Corps against the German Twenty-Fifth Army in western Holland, between the Rhine/Waal and Ijssel Rivers, and II Corps, together with the Polish armour, into the rich, open farmland between the Ijsselmeer and the Weser River. There was still some hard fighting to be endured, but German resistance was now rapidly collapsing and the sporadic opposition increasingly ill-coordinated On April 11 the Americans reached the Elbe, by the 21st the British were in Hamburg, and three days later the Russians completed their encirclement of Berlin.

In his steel-and-concrete bunker deep under the heart of Berlin, just before 3:30 p.m. on the last day of April 1945, Adolf Hitler put a pistol barrel in his mouth and pulled the trigger. Four days later, at a few minutes to eight in the morning, a sharp-shooting rifleman of the Lake Superior Regiment, riding on a tank of the Canadian Grenadier Guards along a road just north of Oldenburg, 'drilled the bicuspids of a German posed with a bazooka ready to fire.'[20] It was, so far as can be ascertained, the last Canadian bullet of the war against Germany, for at eight o'clock exactly the cease-fire sounded in Europe.

By the end of the war in Europe, Canadian ground forces had been fighting continuously for more than two years. The ratio of battle casualties to the total numbers who became prisoners of war is a rough indicator of soldiers' morale over a period of time, and the Canadian ratio was the highest of all the Allied armies in the European campaigns. Their killed and wounded in Italy totalled 24,885; in Northwest Europe, 44,735. In Italy only 1,004 were taken prisoner; in Northwest Europe, 1,864. Canadian soldiers showed themselves to be as brave and tenacious as those of any nation and, in the case of other ranks and junior officers, as skilful as most.*

* Man for man, the Germans were probably the most skilful troops at the end of the war, as they had been at the beginning.

123   General Foulkes accepting from General Reichilt the surrender of German forces at Wageningen, Holland, May 8, 1945.

The Canadian weakness lay in the paucity of talent at the higher levels of command, which was a reflection of the small number of professional officers in the pre-war service. Success at those levels normally requires both long and careful training and natural talent, but the small budget and low profile of the Canadian forces in pre-war days meant that young officers had little opportunity to get the necessary training. General Maurice Pope (who was one of them) has since commented that 'the Canadian military were not soldiers, although we had many experts on the King's Dress Regulations.'[21] Among Canadian divisional commanders and above, only Simonds, Vokes, and Hoffmeister could possibly be ranked as first-rate. McNaughton was barred from operational command, and Salmon, who had shown the most promise of them all, was accidentally killed before he could take his division into action. Many of the others were better staff officers than combat commanders. General Vokes had the truth of it when he said that 'Command is often not *what* you do but the *way* you do it.'

Nevertheless, despite their faults and their comparatively small numbers, the Canadians left a distinct imprint on the record of the war in Europe. Not perhaps as deep a one as their fathers had left a generation earlier, but one to justify the adjective applied to them more than once by Field Marshal Montgomery—'magnificent'.

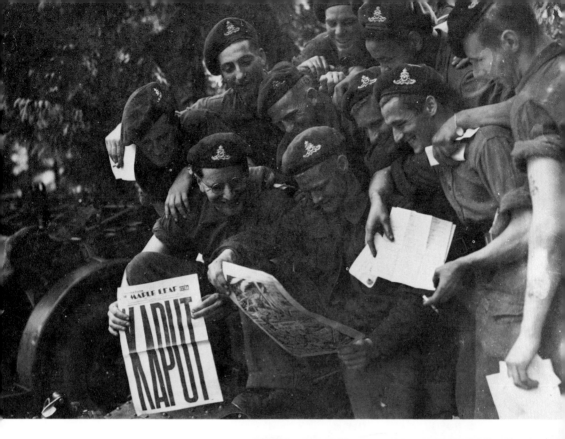

125 (ABOVE) Canadian gunners display a copy of the *Maple Leaf*, the Canadian army newspaper, announcing Germany's surrender.

124 (LEFT) A Canadian corporal supervises two German prisoners stacking helmets and shell cases somewhere in northern Germany.

126 (RIGHT) Dutch civilians celebrate the end of the fighting in Europe by climbing aboard Canadian carriers in the suburbs of Rotterdam.

10

THE WAR AGAINST JAPAN

Victory in Europe (VE-Day) came on May 5, 1945. The exuberance of the celebrations that marked the end of the war in Europe seems to have been, generally speaking, inversely proportional to the physical distance of the celebrants from the actual fighting. The great day was spent quietly by Canadians in Germany, gaily by those in Holland, boisterously in England and Canada—with the riotous exception of Halifax (described in the next chapter). The Queen's Own Rifles, still in action in front of Aurich until the last minutes of the war, noted in their diary that 'there is no celebration but everybody is happy'. In western Holland, where military operations had virtually ceased two weeks earlier, units of the 1st Division pressing into Rotterdam to take the surrender of the German garrison found themselves swamped with schnapps and pretty girls until their formations lost all coherence. In London, Canadians sang sentimental songs in Piccadilly Circus and stood on their heads atop the great stone lions that guard Nelson's Column in Trafalgar Square.

In one sense all these celebrations were premature, for Japan had not surrendered. But Japan had never been the threat that Germany had been. Despite the economic potential of its territorial acquisitions in South East Asia, its defeat had always been inevitable. The Japanese industrial base—the foundation of success in modern warfare—was very weak. In 1938, for example, Japan produced only seven million tons of crude steel and the United States, its prime enemy, more than ten times as much. By 1944 Japanese production had actually decreased, while American production had risen by another five million tons. And Japan had no oil of its own. It had captured all the oilfields and rubber plantations of South East Asia, yet in 1942 only 40 per cent of the output of the Dutch East Indies oilfields reached Japan; in 1943 only 15 per cent; in 1944 a mere 5 per cent; and in the last eight months of the war, none at all had evaded the United States Navy submarines blockading the Japanese islands.

Canada played no part in weakening Japan's war potential and was required to do very little in combatting the Japanese before the end of the war in Europe. In March 1942, when the British needed another coastal reconnaissance squadron in South East Asia, the RCAF's 413 Squadron, equipped with Catalina flying boats, was sent to Ceylon from the United Kingdom, where it had been formed the previous July. It started its Far Eastern tour spectacularly a week after

127 Canadian troops (wearing American helmets) file aboard an American transport at Nanaimo, B.C., bound for the invasion of Kiska.

the arrival of the first aircraft in Ceylon. A Catalina searching for a Japanese fleet known to be prowling the Indian Ocean found it some 350 miles south of the island. 'We immediately coded a message and started transmission,' the pilot has recorded. 'We were halfway through our required third transmission when a shell destroyed our wireless equipment ... Shells set fire to our internal tanks. We managed to get the fire out, and then another started and the aircraft began to break up. Due to our low altitude it was impossible to bail out, but I got the aircraft down on the water before the tail fell off.'[1] An RAF air gunner whose leg was severed went down with the aircraft. The rest of the crewmen swam clear of burning gasoline, pulling with them two of their comrades who were injured and unconscious but wearing life-jackets. Japanese aircraft strafed them continuously and the two men wearing 'Mae Wests', who could not dive under the surface, were killed. The six swimmers—all of them wounded and three seriously hurt—were recovered by a Japanese destroyer and spent the rest of the war in prison camps.

But their warning had been picked up in Ceylon, and when aircraft

128 Conditions were cramped aboard the troop transports that carried the 13th Canadian Infantry Brigade to Kiska.

from the Japanese carriers attacked Colombo next morning they were met by every fighter the British could put into the air. There were about 19 Canadian Hurricane pilots serving with the RAF on the island and at least eight of them flew against the Japanese that day. They claimed two of the seven aircraft lost by the enemy. One of the Canadians was shot down without injury.

In June 1942 Canada contributed two fighter and one light-bomber squadrons for defensive air patrols on the Alaska mainland when a Japanese strike force occupied Attu and Kiska, the westernmost islands of the 1,000-mile-long American-owned chain that loops out into the Pacific from the southern shores of Alaska. The Japanese, who were attempting to divert American resources from the south-central Pacific, were now occupying North American territory, but the problem they posed was not serious. In the cold, foggy, poorly charted island fortresses of the Aleutians it was extraordinarily difficult to mount continuous operations even on a minor scale. Some of the Canadian fighter pilots flew with their American allies on operational missions over the islands and five of them died when an entire formation flew into the side of a fog-shrouded mountain on July 13, 1942.

In May 1943 the Americans retook Attu, using a division with massive air and naval fire support to subdue the brigade of Japanese infantry that garrisoned it. In a short, small-scale, and exceptionally bloody campaign it took the Americans twenty days and nearly 4,000 casualties—half as many again as the total number of Japanese on Attu—to destroy the Japanese force. The assault on Kiska followed. The 13th Canadian Infantry Brigade from General George Pearkes's Western Command and partly composed of NRMA men,* together with the élite Canadian-American Special Force—which later fought in Italy and the south of France—joined some 30,000 American combat troops scheduled to attack the island on August 15, 1943. Aircraft and ships pounded the barren muskeg and rock with bombs and gunfire for three weeks before the troops swarmed ashore, but there was nobody there. 'You are dancing the foolische order of Rousebelt,' proclaimed a message scrawled on an abandoned barrack wall. 'We shall come again and kill Yank-joker.'

The invaders then inflicted a fair amount of damage on themselves without any assistance from the enemy. Twenty Americans were killed by their own comrades as over-nervous patrols prowled the island in search of Japanese soldiers who might have been dedicated to a suicidal last stand. Booby traps and mines left behind by the Japenese garrison killed four others. Fifty Americans were wounded —blown up or shot—and 130 went down with trenchfoot during the first two months of Allied occupation. Among the Canadians, two were killed by booby traps and two in accidental explosions.

The islands were garrisoned until the end of the war. The Canadians stayed on Kiska exactly six months, filling in the time with fatigues, complaints about the lack of mail, and a protracted legal wrangle with National Defence Headquarters in Ottawa. Early in the war troops serving outside the western hemisphere had been exempted from paying income tax. Now the Canadians on Kiska, who had become geography conscious, were quick to point out that longitude 177 degrees 30 minutes East—the hemispheric boundary—lay a mile or so east of their camp. They appealed for a rebate of all taxes while they were thus serving outside the western hemisphere. Canadian bureaucrats at Pacific Command headquarters in Vancouver responded by noting that the International Date Line, which generally followed the hemispheric boundary, jogged slightly in order to place the whole island in the western hemisphere for purposes of time—legally a dubious argument. The authorities in Ottawa argued more decisively that 'the United States say the island is in the Western Hemisphere. There is no overriding authority to say that it is not, therefore Kiska must of necessity be where its owners say it is—in the Western Hemisphere.'

The first direct attack on Canadian soil since the 1871 Fenian raid

* See pp. 237, 245-6.

129 On a British Columbia hillside an officer of the Royal Canadian Engineers, a sergeant, and the forest worker who discovered it inspect a Japanese 'balloon bomb' from a safe distance.

in Manitoba occurred on June 20, 1942, only days after the Japanese occupation of Attu and Kiska. A Japanese submarine that had been patrolling off Seattle was ordered north to support the Aleutian assault and, in passing, chose to lob a few shells at the isolated lighthouse and radio station at Estevan Point on Vancouver Island. There were no casualties and very little damage was done. In the late fall of 1944, however, a potentially much more serious attack on North American territory was initiated by the Japanese. During the following winter 9,000 balloons—their gasbags made of mulberry bark paper—were launched from Japan. They carried high-explosive or incendiary bombloads of approximately 50 pounds each—usually four incendiary devices accounting for about two-thirds of the payload, together with an explosive 'core' designed to ignite and distribute the incendiaries over a 20-metre radius. They were carried across the Pacific at a height of 20,000 to 30,000 feet by the prevailing winds. Their makers hoped they would cause widespread forest fires as well as panic and confusion in western Canada and in the United States. However, their main value may have been to provide an offensive element to Japanese strategy on which Japanese public opinion —developing a defeatist tinge by 1944—could focus.

Japanese sources have estimated that 10 per cent of the 9,000 balloons actually released should have reached North America, but in fact there are only 296 balloon incidents on record, 80 of them in Canada. The first to be reported in this country arrived on January 12, 1945, at Minton, Sask., with all but one of its bombs failing to function. British Columbia received more than half the Canadian total. The most easterly landing in Canada came near Nelson House, Man., the most northerly at Canol Road in the Northwest Territories. Three of the balloons included in the Canadian total were shot down by the RCAF.

The initial reaction of both American and Canadian authorities was to impose a total security blanket on the presence of the balloon bombs, but a report from Alberta of schoolboys using a red hot poker to unsolder the connections from a bomb container soon necessitated restricted publicity. Police and servicemen were authorized to pass warnings by word of mouth to 'any members of the public whom the authorities consider it desirable to be told of the balloon occurrences . . . dependence must be placed on ranchers, trappers, H.B. Posts, etc., passing word along of findings.' After a woman and five children were killed by a balloon device near Bly, Oregon, on May 5, the security net was further modified and newspapers were encouraged to publicize the existence of the balloons without mentioning either the total numbers reported or the government's fears that bacteriological warfare might be resorted to by this means. One DND official wrote, 'At this stage it is definitely considered that reference should not be made to the possibility of contaminated substance being carried . . . and it is sufficient if information is given to the effect that persons should be kept away from balloon material because of possible danger from explosive missiles.'[2] Fears of anthrax in the Alberta cattle country or typhoid on the Pacific watershed proved groundless, however, and in April 1945 the Japanese abandoned the campaign, apparently assessing it (quite correctly) as an operational failure.

In contrast with this ineffectual undertaking against North America, an American strategic bombing assault on Japan created enormous havoc. In November 1944, B-29 Superfortresses operating from the Marianas—Saipan, Tinian, and Guam—began to raid Japan in force, using the same tactics that the United States Eighth Air Force had previously employed against Germany. The bombers were unsupported by long-range fighter escorts and made high-level attacks using primarily high-explosive bombs. These attacks inflicted considerable but not vital damage on the Japanese war potential and were accompanied by an unacceptable overall loss rate of 6 per cent, so that enthusiasm quickly began to flag. There was a dramatic change, however, in February 1945 when General Curtis LeMay took over control of the American bombing force. Applying the experience he had gained in the air war against Germany, LeMay decided to try low-level (7,000-foot) incendiary attacks by night. The first such raid, flown against Tokyo in early March 1945, resulted in the destruction by fire of 15 square miles of the city, with an estimated 83,000 dead and 97,000 injured. LeMay's bombers then began the systematic destruction of urban Japan. Benefitting from the fact that Japanese radar was comparatively unsophisticated and severely limited the effectiveness of Japanese night fighters, the American loss rate dipped to 1.4 per cent. In April P-47 fighters began to provide fighter cover and the Superfortresses could fly by day *and* night, their task being made even easier by the grave shortage of gasoline that increasingly handicapped the Japanese defences. Then, on August 6, 1945, came the atomic bomb. Suddenly the enormous, complex, and intricate accumulation of men and material being assembled by the Allies for the invasion of Japan was no longer needed.

Planning for the assault on Japan had been under way for a long time. Even before the United States had entered the war, in the course of Anglo-American 'conversations' held during March 1941 in Washington, Great Britain and the United States had agreed that the defeat of Germany was their paramount concern. But once Germany was defeated, Phase II of the war would begin and the full weight of the Allies would be applied against the Japanese. The formulation of this strategy—and the ensuing debates over it—did not involve Canadians; grand strategy never did, unless Canadian territoriality was involved. But Mackenzie King accepted that Canada had an obligation to fight in the Pacific too, although he cautiously argued that it would be 'reasonable to take into account our four years of war to the Americans' two. Also we may be sure we will get little credit for anything we do, either on the part of the United States or Great Britain.'

Early in 1944 Ottawa informed London and Washington that Canada's position as a Pacific power, as a member of the Commonwealth, and as an American nation, made necessary its participation in the defeat of Japan. However, it was not made clear whether Ottawa felt Canada should work with the Americans or the British. Chubby Power, King's Minister of National Defence for Air, later claimed that during the first eight months of 1944 'we were unable to formulate any definite plan of campaign against Japan'. This was not entirely the Cabinet's fault, although King's obvious reluctance to enter into any kind of 'imperial' commitment was partly to blame. Fearful of being labelled a tool of British imperialism, King refused to pledge Canadian resources to their campaign in South East Asia—the only decision that could have been made quickly—and Canadian planning for Pacific operations could hardly begin until the Anglo-American relationship in that theatre had been settled. Meanwhile King told Churchill that if operations were to take place in the North Pacific, then Canadian forces should serve there.

The British acknowledged that this would be acceptable on strategic, political, and administrative grounds. They still hoped, however, that Canada would join them in South East Asia, as 'British manpower will be severely strained.' In July 1944 the British chiefs of staff put forward proposals for each of the Canadian services. The RCN might reinforce the British fleet, probably in the Bay of Bengal or the Southwest Pacific, with the possibility of a later switch to the north, since the Royal Navy still did not know whether or not the United States would accept a British fleet in the central Pacific. The RCAF could operate with the RAF, also in South East Asia or the Southwest Pacific, and the chiefs of staff suggested that the army be held ready in Canada for employment wherever required by the Americans.

King was not yet prepared to make any firm commitment, however, arguing that Allied strategy should be determined first. He was also insistent that financial considerations be given priority. He suspected that 'the Defence Ministers were pretty much set to make a very large contribution', but he himself was not, and as usual he got his way. The Cabinet decided that only one division would be offered, while the navy proposals would be cut by 50 per cent and the air-force contribution substantially reduced. It was formally agreed that Canadian forces should 'participate ... in operational theatres of direct interest to Canada as a North American nation, for example in the North or Central Pacific, rather than in more remote areas such as South-East Asia.'[3] The exact contribution would be decided after the Quebec Conference of September 1944, code-named *Octagon*.

At *Octagon* the outlines of the British role in the Pacific were determined. It was also agreed that Canadian participation in the main operations against Japan would be acceptable 'in principle', but no attempt was made to discuss the nature of the contribution. Although Mackenzie King wanted a Canadian presence in the Pacific, he remained totally opposed to operations by Canadians in South East Asia. He claimed, probably quite rightly, that 'no government in Canada once the European war was over could send its men to India, Burma and Singapore to fight with any forces and hope to get through a general election successfully.' Convinced that the services and the defence ministers were scheming to commit Canadians to an 'imperial' war, he noted in his diary on September 13, 1944, that in Cabinet he had had to 'do most of the fighting myself to maintain what I would call the only tenable position which means keeping our forces for North or Central Pacific areas.' The British influence in these areas was and would be negligible, the American influence overwhelming. With this purely political decision King unwittingly committed Canada and Canadians to the American way of war.

The dogmatic attitude of the Prime Minister makes it particularly hard to understand how the RAF in the South East Asia theatre came to be reinforced by two RCAF transport squadrons in October and November 1944. In June, Power—apparently without reference to the Cabinet—had accepted an agreement between Air Marshal L.S. Breadner, now commanding the RCAF Overseas, and the British Air Ministry for the formation of three RCAF medium-range transport squadrons, two in India as soon as possible and the third in the United Kingdom during 1945. Meanwhile a Canadian Air Liaison Mission to India, after examining the situation of the Canadians already there, had suggested that 'the RCAF not participate in the war in South-East Asia'. The Air Staff's subsequent decision to organize the two squadrons in India suggests that the RCAF's top management did not always know exactly what it was doing. They began to form in Gujrat, north of Lahore in what was then northwest India, in October 1944.

Whether at this stage Mackenzie King became aware of the RCAF's commitment is not clear, but in September Power cabled Breadner to arrange the posting or the withdrawal of 413 (Coastal Reconnaissance) Squadron to 'offset' their retention in India. Two months later 413 Squadron was informed that it would shortly return to the United Kingdom for conversion to a bomber role, and in mid-January 1945 it embarked for England. The two transport squadrons remained in South East Asia until the end of the war. Before they left Burma, in September 1945, 435 and 436 Squadrons had accumulated over 50,000 operational flying hours and delivered 46,000 tons of cargo and nearly 28,000 passengers to their various destinations.

Meanwhile, Canadian planning for Phase II was going ahead in Ottawa. In November 1944 the Cabinet approved a force of one division and ancillary troops for the Pacific. The United States rejected a Canadian suggestion that would have substituted an armoured for an infantry division (the armoured division would be smaller and easier to man) and the final agreement called for an infantry division, possibly reinforced with armour and some support troops. The Canadians would be organized on American lines and train in the United States to use American equipment and tactics—in short, to be treated as an American unit. They would be used 'as a follow-up in the main operation'—the invasion of Japan—and eventually be returned to Canada 'in a priority consistent with that applied to other forces engaged in the Pacific war'; in other words Canada's control of its troops would be significantly reduced.

Two months after the end of the war in Europe nearly 10,000 officers and 70,000 men had volunteered to join the Pacific Force. Of these only 2,796 officers and 36,386 men were found suitable in terms of service record, health, and age, but there were more than enough for immediate requirements and three months' reinforcements. The force began concentrating at nine stations across Canada in July 1945. American training teams came to Canada and Canadian instructors were sent south to be introduced to American methods and organization, while plans were put in hand to send the whole force to Camp Breckenridge, Kentucky, for further individual and unit training along American lines.

The RCN's major aim was to acquire more of the 'big ships' that would make them a balanced fleet instead of one that left them essentially a convoy escort force. The Pacific war seemed to provide a strong justification for doing so, but King was having none of it and the navy's Pacific planning was eventually reduced to encompass two cruisers, *Uganda* and *Ontario*, the *Prince Robert* (an anti-aircraft cruiser), two light fleet carriers (still under construction when the war ended), 16 destroyers, 36 frigates, and 8 corvettes. However, only one of the cruisers, HMCS *Uganda*, saw combat service in the Pacific. Commissioned into the RCN in October 1944, *Uganda* joined a British Task Force that was operating with the U.S. Third Fleet's Fast Carrier Force in March 1945. This formation was supporting the American assault on Okinawa, and *Uganda*'s main task was as anti-aircraft guard for the carriers, but at the end of July—just a couple of weeks before the war ended—she left the theatre because of a Cabinet policy decision that only volunteers would serve in the Pacific. Not enough of the crew was prepared to volunteer and *Uganda* thus established the unique but dubious distinction of being the only Canadian unit that ever voted itself out of combat.

The RCAF also had ambitious plans for Phase II. There was a strong desire to field an integrated force under full Canadian command and control, but a combination of Cabinet reluctance to make major commitments and American pressure to make the RAF/RCAF contingents entirely self-supporting reduced their proposal, step by step, from a balanced force of 12 bomber, 6 fighter, 3 transport squadrons and one air-sea rescue squadron to 8 bomber and 3 transport squadrons. Eight squadrons of Six Group flew from the United Kingdom to Canada in June 1945 for re-training and the thirty days' leave granted to all volunteers for the Pacific.

They were to return to Britain for conversion to Avro Lincoln aircraft in September, and the first two bomber squadrons were scheduled to arrive in Okinawa in December 1945. When the other six squadrons arrived, a Canadian group was to be formed and eventually the contingent would total 15,000 men. However, these plans were abruptly halted by the two atomic bombs dropped on Hiroshima and Nagasaki on August 6 and 9, 1945. On August 10, 1945, an Imperial Conference in Tokyo decided to sue for peace; on August 14 all hostilities ended; and on September 2 the Japanese formally surrendered.

On August 9—at almost the same moment that the second atomic bomb was falling on Nagasaki—a Canadian pilot in the Royal Navy's Fleet Air Arm, Lieutenant Robert Hampton Gray, led a flight of Corsair fighter-bombers from HMS *Formidable* against a number of Japanese ships at Onagawa Wan on the northern island of Honshu. Having already led very similar strikes against five Narvik class destroyers in a Norwegian fiord a year before, and against a Japanese destroyer in the Inland Sea just a few days earlier (an attack that won him the Distinguished Service Cross), 'Ham' Gray knew what to do and did it unflinchingly. Flyers astern of Gray saw him go into a run aimed at one of the destroyers. As his plane swung onto an attacking course a cone of fire from ships and shore batteries centred upon it. A first hit registered; then a second. A moment later streamers of flame began to bleed out astern of the aircraft. It still held steadily to its course. Weaving and ablaze it bore down to within fifty yards of the destroyer before its bombs were seen to fall. One struck directly amidships; a second fell on or near alongside the target. The ship sank almost immediately, but before it disappeared Gray's riddled plane had dived into the waters of the bay.

Three months later, as Canada settled to the calmer routines and more uncertain problems of peace, the *London Gazette* announced the posthumous award of a Victoria Cross to Gray for his 'brilliant fighting spirit and most inspiring leadership'.

Canadians played only a minor part in the design and production of the atomic bombs that ended the war against Japan. In the summer of 1939 experiments at Columbia University—the culmination of thirty years of theorizing and experimentation in Europe and America—indicated the possibility that uranium might be used to liberate a million times as much energy as any known chemical explosive. The war seemed imminent in Europe, and Albert Einstein, probably the best-known scientist in the world at that time, wrote his now-famous letter to President Roosevelt, reporting that ' . . . it may become possible to set up a nuclear chain reaction in a large mass of uranium by which vast amounts of power . . . would be generated. . . . This new phenomenon would also lead to the construction of bombs.'

From that moment the race was on to unlock the secrets of nuclear fission, and uranium acquired unusual importance. It was not a common element but, in the form of uranium oxide, it was a by-product of radium extraction. Radium, the basis of cancer therapy in the 1930s, came from pitchblende, and a rich deposit of pitchblende had been worked by Eldorado Gold Mines on the eastern shore of Great Bear Lake in the Northwest Territories since 1933. The ore was transported to Port Hope, on Lake Ontario, where the largest refinery of its kind in North America (and probably the largest in the world) was turning out radium at $30,000 a gram—and uranium oxide for nothing.

In 1940 economic difficulties connected with the expansion of Canada's war industry had led Eldorado to close down its mining operations in the North, although the Port Hope refinery was still extracting radium from accumulated stocks of ore. Suddenly, how-

130 The Eldorado Mine camp at Port Radium, N.W.T., on the eastern shore of Great Bear Lake. This photograph was taken in 1937 when radium was extracted from pitchblende for use in cancer therapy and uranium was an unimportant by-product of the refining process.

ever, a new market appeared in the early spring of 1942 when the possibility of atomic bombs began to acquire practical military significance. Vast quantities of uranium were needed. With the prospect of a large American contract in sight, Eldorado began to re-open the mine, which was in production again by August 1942. However, before that time control of it had been taken from Eldorado. On June 15 Mackenzie King recorded in his diary 'an interview with Malcolm MacDonald [British High Commissioner in Ottawa] and two scientists from England about the acquisition of some property in Canada, so as to prevent competition in price on a mineral much needed in connection with the manufacture of explosives.' The Canadian government promptly bought a majority interest in Eldorado.

One product of uranium fission is a number of relatively fast-moving neutrons. In order for an uncontrolled chain reaction (i.e. a nuclear explosion) to occur, these neutrons must initiate fission of other atoms by 'bombarding' them in turn. Since such fission is brought about most readily through the impact of comparatively slow-moving neutrons, it is necessary to introduce some medium that will moderate the speed of the emitted neutrons. In 1942 two possibilities seemed to offer promise as moderators: graphite and 'heavy water' (deuterium oxide). It was not yet clear which was the better prospect. Heavy water had theoretical advantages but it was as uncommon as radium, and although it was noticeably cheaper at 50 cents a gram, estimates of the quantity needed ran between 30 and 100 tons—at $500,000 a ton.

Graphite was much cheaper and seemed quite practical. Experiments continued using both graphite and heavy water. For the large-scale production of heavy water, heavy hydrogen offered a convenient starting-point. Again Canada had a built-in advantage, for heavy hydrogen was a by-product of the production process employed in the manufacture of ammonia, and the largest ammonia producer on the continent was the Consolidated Mining and Smelting Company in Trail, B.C. During the summer of 1942 the United States contracted for additional facilities at Trail as well as at three other plants in West Virginia, Indiana, and Alabama. The Trail plant was first into production by six months, but heavy water in the required quantities did not become available until the middle of 1944.

Long before that time, however, Canada had been eased out of the apparent mainstream of American research directed towards the production of an atomic bomb. As the probability of atomic weapons became more and more definite during 1942, the American military had taken an increasingly protective approach to the atomic project. In January 1943 the Americans decided unilaterally to 'restrict our interchange [of all scientific information] by the application of the principle that we are to have complete interchange on design and construction of new equipment *only* if the recipient of the information is in a position to take advantage of it in this war.'[4] This ruling effectively barred both Britain and Canada from all American nuclear know-how, including that related to post-war applications, since neither claimed the economic and industrial potential that would have permitted them to manufacture atomic bombs in the foreseeable future.*

Using the extant Canadian resource capability, a small Anglo-Canadian program of research into the use of heavy water as a neutron moderator in the fission of uranium had begun in Montreal during 1942 and the scientists there continued to provide some input into the American project. Canadian research expanded to Chalk River, Ont., in the summer of 1944, where the facilities required for the operation of a nuclear pile were conveniently available. By that time American research had confirmed the adequacy of much cheaper graphite as a moderator for wartime purposes, but the work in Montreal and Chalk River had paradoxically laid a basis for Canadian eminence in that post-war field of nuclear industrialization in which the Americans had hoped to reign supreme.

Meanwhile Canadian uranium continued to fuel laboratories and workshops of atomic bomb technology in the United States, and individual Canadian and British scientists were employed in the highly compartmentalized and strictly censored project the Americans code-named *Manhattan District*. One of the Canadians was

* Bearing in mind the relative magnitude of the Commonwealth commitment against international aggression both before and after the United States entered the war, the American attitude towards post-war applications of nuclear knowledge can hardly be described as generous. On the other hand the post-war Gouzenko revelations in Canada and the convictions for espionage of Allan Nunn May, Klaus Fuchs, and Bruno Ponticorvo (all of whom had worked on British atomic research teams) suggest that, from a security point of view, these precautions had considerable justification.

131 Louis Slotin working on the University of Chicago's cyclotron.

Walter Zinn, who assisted Enrico Fermi in establishing the world's first nuclear chain reaction at the University of Chicago on December 2, 1942. Another was Louis Slotin, a wiry young man from Winnipeg who had helped to build the University of Chicago's cyclotron ('atom-smasher') in 1938. After working with Fermi and Zinn at Chicago, Slotin went to Oak Ridge, Tennessee, to help build the first plutonium reactor. When that project was accomplished he moved to Los Alamos to play a major part in the construction of the first bomb.

Although he had a Ph.D. in bio-chemistry and a mind quite capable of appreciating the esoteric principles of nuclear physics, Slotin worked on the practical application of atomic theory rather than in the realm of theory itself. The creation of a 'critical' mass of uranium that might result in a nuclear explosion could only be roughly determined by theoretical calculation. But precision and certainty were essential in building the bomb, and Louis Slotin and Luis W. Alvarez, a Californian, were the scientists who ascertained, by practical experiments, the exact circumstances that would make the uranium critical. Slotin's approach was pragmatic to an extreme. Carrying out adjustments with an ordinary screwdriver, he allowed two hemispheres of uranium or plutonium to slide together along a rod while, with his ear cocked to the ticking of a Geiger counter, he measured the rising neutron count. His object was to just reach the 'critical point' at which a chain reaction would begin and then quickly ease the hemispheres apart again. If he passed that point—measured in fractions of a millimetre—or was not quite quick enough in parting the hemispheres, then the mass might become 'super critical' and produce a nuclear explosion. Slotin called this process 'tickling the dragon's tail'.

American security regulations and Slotin's 'foreign' citizenship combined to prevent his being posted to the South Pacific to assemble the bombs that would be used against Japan. Alvarez went instead. The Canadian remained at Los Alamos and built the explosive mechanism of the experimental 'Trinity' bomb that exploded at Alamogordo at ten minutes past five on July 16, 1945, and altered the course of world history. People were transfixed with fright at the power of the explosion. Dr Robert Oppenheimer, a key figure in the bomb's design, clinging to an upright in the control room five and a half miles away and watching the sinister mushroom cloud form, was reminded of the words of Sri Krishna in the sacred Hindu epic, *The Bhagavadgita*, 'I am become Death, the shatterer of worlds.'[5]

On May 21, 1946, while working on the post-war testing program, Slotin 'tickled the dragon's tail' once too often. His screwdriver slipped, the hemispheres came too close, and the material became critical. The laboratory was instantly filled with a dazzling bluish glare and the neutron-counter 'blew' as the radiation level soared right off the scale. Instead of freezing or flinching, Slotin tore the hemispheres apart with his hands, told his colleagues to stand still, and sketched on a blackboard each man's position so that doctors would be able to calculate accurately the degree of radiation to which each of them had been exposed. For him, who had been closest and who had touched the hemispheres, there could be no hope. After nine days of agony Louis Slotin died. His body, packed in a lead-lined coffin, was brought back to Winnipeg by a USAAF airplane. The *Winnipeg Free Press* reported that 3,000 people attended his funeral. None of them knew the cause or circumstances of his death, for the techniques of manufacturing atomic bombs were still 'top secret'.

11

THE HOME FRONT

The population of Canada between 1939 and 1945 varied between eleven and twelve million. Well over two million made a direct contribution to the war in uniform and by working in industry, government, or on associated tasks. This amounted to total mobilization for war on the Home Front because virtually everyone else in the population was a dependant or unavailable for 'essential' war work. As in any belligerent nation, total mobilization was accompanied by arbitrary government. Propaganda and censorship became commonplace. The War Measures Act, originally brought in during the First World War, came into effect. 'These were the tools of totalitarianism,' two Canadian historians of warfare and society have remarked.[1] To avoid the permanent replacement of democratic with totalitarian government, which would be likely to follow a serious weakening of society caused by the strains of war, the government had to minimize the basic weaknesses and emphasize the strengths of that society, providing a solid foundation on which to build when the war was over.

The central concern was manpower. Mackenzie King's constant preoccupation was to keep the size of the armed forces within reasonable bounds because, as a cross-section of leaders in all parties perceived, compulsory military service overseas would arouse bitter opposition, particularly in Quebec. Isolationist sentiments expounded by Henri Bourassa and his followers in the First World War were renewed in Quebec by disciples of Bourassa who opposed participation in what they considered to be a British and imperial war.[2] Even for those who did not subscribe to the isolationist position, there were important differences in language and culture with the rest of the country that impeded active contributions to a war effort dominated by English Canadians. Though Allied defeats in Europe in 1940 provoked a surge of sympathy for France among Québécois, this was tempered by general indifference towards that country and was not exploited with any success.

In March 1939 and again on September 8, King promised that there would be no conscription for service overseas. In October 1939 the federal Liberals were able to take that message to Quebec during a provincial election. Premier Maurice Duplessis's attack on federal war policies, which he said would undermine provincial autonomy and bring about assimilation, would amount to a provincial rejection

132 An anti-conscrip-
tion rally in Montreal,
March 1939.

of these policies if he was re-elected. King's Quebec-based Cabinet
ministers—Chubby Power, P.J.A. Cardin, and Ernest Lapointe
—announced to the Quebec electorate that they would resign from
the Cabinet if Duplessis won, thus leaving King with a Cabinet
that—according to statements made by its English-speaking
members—would almost certainly become pro-conscriptionist.
Adélard Godbout's Liberals defeated Maurice Duplessis and the
Union Nationale party, however, and as a result there would be no
formal opposition to Canadian war policies. But the promise that
overseas conscription would not be implemented was resented by
many in the Cabinet, in Parliament, and in the country as a whole,
particularly in the armed forces.

A few months after King's great victory in the general election of
1940—the government was returned with 181 seats—the National
Resources Mobilization Act, which authorized conscription for home
defence, was passed by Parliament in June 1940. Single men and
childless widowers between 21 and 45 were required to register for
military service.* The first three groups of young men called up,
beginning in October 1940, had to spend thirty days in training—an
exercise that, as it produced no trained soldiers, occupied instructors
and equipment that could have been better used elsewhere. None-

* The mayor of Montreal, Camillien Houde—who had featured so prominently in the
Royal Visit and who had come to be a folk hero—publicly stated his intention not to
register and urged others to join him in disobeying the law. He was interned under the
War Measures Act until 1944.

133

theless it was the first step towards a more active involvement of the population in the war effort. In February 1941 the system was altered to require four-month periods of enlistment, and after April 1941 NRMA men were required to serve for the duration of the war. Later nicknamed 'Zombies' by the General Service men who volunteered for overseas service, these home-defence conscripts had an unenviable reputation in the armed forces and in most of the country. The fact remains, however, that the Zombies released volunteers for overseas and also provided military defence that sometimes—as at Kiska in 1943—was more than a token contribution. Moreover, NRMA service was no disgrace in many of the communities the men came from, not only in French Canada but in many other parts of the country as well.

By the summer of 1941 General McNaughton and staff officers of the three services had begun to worry that to maintain an army that now comprised four divisions and to continue the expansion of the navy, and most particuarly the RCAF, would require more men and women than the population could provide without full conscription. There was no doubt that hard fighting lay ahead. The question was to what extent Canada should be committed. Two divisions were now in England serving as a garrison and training for the invasion of Europe; two other divisions were preparing to join them overseas. At a time when the Canadian navy and air force were in active operations against the enemy, there was a growing feeling that Canadian soldiers should be getting a share of the fighting. With this in mind General McNaughton in July 1941 warned Chubby Power, the Associate Minister of National Defence, that 'before embarking on new adventures . . . we should be certain that we will be in a position to carry out . . . the military commitments already undertaken.' As these commitments would create a need for replacements, once the army was in combat, any additional military undertaking might bring about the very thing Mackenzie King feared: a reinforcement crisis.

For the moment the manpower question was more one of principle than of need. The Canadian army—except for the two battalions that went to Hong Kong—did not see action until the summer of 1942 at Dieppe. What worried many people—described by General Pope, soon to become vice-chief of General Staff, as 'over-zealous and impatient spirits, principally in Ontario'—was that, unlike Canadians, every British (and subsequently every American) serviceman could be sent to serve in any theatre. Why should Canada restrict its conscripted troops to service at home? For most French Canadians the question was beside the point. They showed their feelings in the national plebiscite of April 1942 on the question: 'Are you in favour of releasing the Government from any obligations arising out of any past commitments restricting the methods of raising men for military service?' Four-fifths of French-Canadian voters opposed any change to the National Resources Mobilization Act. On the other hand the national result—two to one in favour of overseas service for NRMA men—forced the government to introduce into Parliament an amendment to the act removing the prohibition on overseas service. Mackenzie King was attacked by both wings of his Cabinet. Public Works minister P.J.A. Cardin resigned because the government had gone too far. Defence Minister Ralston tendered his resignation (he was talked out of it) because the government would not go far enough: he objected because King insisted that overseas conscription could not be implemented without a vote of confidence in Parliament. The amendment was passed and in spite of King's compromise formula—'not necessarily conscription but conscription if necessary'—was nothing less than a violation of his 1939 pledge, particularly in the eyes of Quebec.

One can sympathize with both sides in this situation. King had to some extent painted himself into a corner by trying to cater to opposite opinions. Each decision he made, though apparently essential at the time, had moved the country inexorably towards 'conscription if necessary'. Yet the possibility always existed for meeting manpower demands with volunteer forces. However, this depended on a sympathetic understanding of French-Canadian attitudes and language requirements and on the co-ordination of recruiting programs in all three services.

In June 1941 an army staff analysis indicated that enlistment figures in Quebec were much higher than at a comparable period of the First World War. (There was no way of calculating exactly how many recruits were of French-speaking origin.) But the army concluded that French-Canadian response could still be improved upon, not only by a more imaginative approach to recruiting but by providing more appropriate conditions of service. Recruiting should take into account that when a French Canadian volunteered he might have to accept a certain loss of face in his own community. Gabrielle Roy captured the situation well in her 1947 novel *The Tin Flute*. A young soldier tries to explain to his family and friends why he joined the army:

> 'But Ma Philibert', he said trying to soothe her, 'if your neighbour's house was burning, you'd go and help him, wouldn't you?
> 'The devil I would.'
> Boisvert snorted. 'Ugh! We have our share of burning houses right here. And plenty of troubles of our own. You don't have to go so far away to find 'em.'
> 'I know', said Emmanuel. 'I didn't enlist to save Poland either, believe me.'

'Then why did you?', demanded Boisvert, nonplussed ....

'Has it never occurred to you', he asked, 'that sometimes a man helps himself when he helps others?'

The hell he does', resplied Boisvert. 'These days its every man for himself.'[3]

It was discouraging for a volunteer to find not only that his motives were likely to be misunderstood at home but that he did not stand an even chance of being accepted in a fighting capacity unless he spoke English. Of 55,000 French-Canadian volunteers in the army, more than half served in anglophone units. Only the 'Van Doos', Le Régiment de la Chaudière, Le Régiment de Maisonneuve, Les Fusiliers de Mont-Royal, Le 4e régiment de l'artillerie, and three medical units were entirely French speaking. Nine English-speaking units had from 30 to 65 per cent French-Canadian content; forty-four had from 5 to 25 per cent.

There were no francophone units in the navy. The addition of French-speaking ships to the Canadian fleet would have added a massive administrative and training burden to the undermanned and overwhelmingly anglophone staffs in naval bases and training schools. When a nation with an enormous coastline had seen fit to support a minute naval service prior to 1939, it is hardly surprising that its composition did not reflect the English-French make-up of the population. It was an unfortunate situation, but one for which no remedy existed when there was not even a small nucleus of fully trained French-speaking personnel to train ships' companies, let alone take ships to sea in the face of the enemy. (The navy had its hands full meeting these requirements for English-speaking ships' companies.) The RCN did institute special English-language training, but in spite of this, and in spite of the fact that numerous French-Canadian officers and men served with great distinction, it is true that owing to language problems a great many French Canadians were considered suitable only as stewards, or as seamen without technical specialization.

The air force was the most difficult service for a French Canadian to enter. It was more particular about documentation than the other services and the RCAF did not open a recruiting centre in Montreal until the summer of 1941. To join, a recruit had to produce birth and marriage certificates, diplomas, two letters of reference, and his full name. Men of rural origin ran into difficulty here because their Christian names took various forms, different documents gave different names, and the recruiters were thoroughly baffled. In 1942 the RCAF reluctantly formed 425 ('Alouette') Squadron, equipped with Halifax bombers and attached to Bomber Command of the RAF, as a French-Canadian unit. It was not easy to find a French-speaking squadron commander, but by 1942 there were 300 French-speaking Canadians in the unit, forming 50 per cent of the aircrew and 90 per cent of the ground crew. This, however, was still not enough to compensate for the obstacles to entry and advancement in the RCAF for most French Canadians.

In all three services, prejudice played its part in varying degrees. On some bases not only was English the working language, but the speaking of French was forbidden at all times. Quebec, then, was an obvious centre of resistance to the military manpower policy eventually settled upon. But it was not just resistance that led to shortcomings in the volunteer system. These were also caused by uncontrolled competition for recruits among the services.

The three services were able to recruit freely those Category 'A' men whose physiques, psyches, and mental abilities made them suitable for front-line duties, but the air force got the lion's share. There was a great demand for aircrew and this coincided with the spontaneous desire of a very large proportion of the country's youth to join the RCAF. Flying offered a much more acceptable way of fighting the war than clumping through the mud as an infantryman or riding through it in a tank. The cockpit of a Spitfire held more attractions than the bridge of a corvette. The romance of 'the wild blue yonder', and the prospect of an environment less inimical to the individual than the earthbound army and navy, brought patriotic youngsters flocking to enlist as aircrew. The ultimate result of this enthusiastic response was excessive recruiting by the RCAF at the expense of the army. However, the extraordinary success of the BCATP, which trained aircrew for the RCAF and provided a large-scale military commitment at home (while offering men of military age an alternative to compulsory military service overseas), made it easy for the Cabinet to allow this rather reckless use of manpower resources.

Because of the fluctuation in demand, the large proportion of men who had to drop out of training for various reasons, and the length of time it took to train aircrew to an operational standard (not less than nine months), the BCATP found it necessary to build up a very substantial pool of aircrew candidates who could be fed into the training stream as required. Both the ups and downs experienced by the RCAF in meeting its aircrew quotas are well illustrated by the revisions in age qualifications for pilot training. In April 1940 all aircrew candidates were required to have passed their 18th birthday and pilot applicants were not to have reached their 28th. By September 1941, as the strategic bombing offensive against Germany began to increase in tempo, a falling off in enlistments brought a lowering of the minimum age to 17½ and a raising of the maximum to 33 (35 with special permission). In August 1943 the minimum age for aircrew enlistment was lowered to 17 and the 17-year-olds were placed in a 'holding pattern'. They could not begin flying training until their 18th birthday and in the meantime were either sent on leave without pay or given pre-aircrew academic training. They returned to basic service training at 17½, and six months later were fed into the aircrew training stream. Their enlistment reflects the desperate manpower situation as the air war over Germany peaked and also emphasizes the attraction the air force held for Canadian youth. In the third quarter of 1943 boys of 18 or under accounted for 50 per cent of the total RCAF aircrew intake.

The constant need for replacing training failures was always a problem, particularly with pilots, and great efforts were made to keep the failure rates as low as possible. The first difficulty arose over selection procedures. How was aircrew potential to be assessed? Physical failings were easy to spot and it was possible to make fairly accurate judgements of mental stability, but intellectual capabilities were harder to pin down. At first, selection procedures relied on education levels—only junior matriculants or higher were eligible. Then an 'ability to learn' test was devised and in 1942 an improved version of it, known as the 'classification' test, was introduced. It supplied a much better assessment of flying potential, but failure rates remained high at elementary flying training schools: between June 1943 and March 1944 they were just over 30 per cent. One student pilot reported that at the start of the course

> my instructor mentioned that I would be given, like everybody else, eight—and only eight—hours of instruction, by which time I would be expected to go solo. ... One or two needed that extra hour denied by service regulations and this I thought was a great pity, for who knows what talent was likely to be relegated to lesser service [sic] by this very stringent rule.[4]

Another problem was created when men (especially potential pilots) were reluctant to apply for aircrew training for fear of failing. The Inspector-General of the RCAF noted in July 1943 that the selection and training of pilots 'has become so systemized and mechanical that the fact that we are dealing with human beings has been lost sight of.'[5]

Failures were replaced by recruits from the 'pool', which also included a number of ground crew who had volunteered for aircrew training. In the early days of the BCATP, the RCAF had made a deliberate policy of recruiting—in far greater numbers than necessary to meet aircrew requirements—tradesmen for ground crew who were medically fit for air training. In March 1943 the air force, although it refused to give up its skilled technicians, conceded that the army had been deprived of an important source of recruits. When the army agreed to refer to the air force all its recruits who were medically qualified for aircrew, the RCAF agreed to stop enlisting men for ground duty who were fit for overseas service for the army. It further promised to try to direct aircrew who failed to graduate into the army. By February 1945, however, only 38 rejected airmen had transferred—nearly 11,000 had been kept in the RCAF and assigned to ground duties.

Ironically, just as the two services reached agreement after eight-

135 Among the countless schools created by the BCATP was No. 1 RCAF Officers' Training School, set up as a 'finishing school' for officers. Chubby Power is taking the salute at the opening of the school at Domaine d'Estrel, Que., on July 31, 1943. The officer behind him on his right (at the end of the line) is Air Marshal L.S. Breadner, Chief of Air Staff.

een months of undignified scrambling for men, and just as the casualty rate in Bomber Command began to drop dramatically, the British suddenly discovered that instead of a shortage of aircrew they had an embarrassingly large surplus, especially of pilots, scattered in remote parts of the world and previously overlooked. A scaling down of the BCATP began in November 1943 and developed rapidly in the new year. The enlistment of 17-year-olds was discontinued and the upper age limit for all aircrew was lowered to 28. After February 1944 only a token number of new candidates were taken in because a large reserve of trainees had been built up over the previous two years—in September there were 5,400.

This surplus was in sharp contrast to the shortages that became apparent in the Canadian army at the same time. Although the army had been industriously trying to convert Home Defence conscripts to General Service status, and although it objected to the RCAF's competition for recruits, the General Staff was singularly slow in recognizing that a reinforcement crisis was in the making.

In December 1943, while the 1st Division was fighting its way into Ortona, Brigadier A.W. Beament, in charge of the Canadian reinforcement system in Italy, raised a danger signal: battle losses in the infantry were higher than expected. General Stuart at Canadian Military Headquarters in London did not believe casualties would continue at such a high rate. Rather he accepted the rates proposed by Army Headquarters in Ottawa—based on British figures from the Western Desert and Tunisia in 1942 and 1943—and sent reinforcements accordingly.

On March 14 Stuart issued instructions that no important communication on reinforcements was to be sent out from CMHQ in London without being approved by him. Although during the next three months a number of staff officers raised the spectre of infantry shortages in internal correspondence, CMHQ sent no reports to Ottawa that might suggest there was a reinforcement difficulty. Ralston's military advisers in Ottawa were therefore in no position to offer him conflicting advice. On June 7, the day after D-Day, the Adjutant-General told the Minister: 'I concur in Gen. Stuart's opinions. . . . I can state with confidence that from our present resources we will meet our commitment for 1944.'[6]

Their optimism was totally unjustified. Efforts to find replacements from artillery, engineer, and armoured corps units brought about 4,000 men to the infantry, but with the high casualty rates in Northwest Europe there was still a deficiency of nearly 2,000 infantry men in General Crerar's First Canadian Army in August 1944.

In mid-September, what had previously been a matter of internal urgency assumed the proportions of a full-scale crisis. Conn Smythe, the former hockey star turned Toronto sports promoter, now a major in the army and convalescing from a wound received in France, told the Toronto press on September 18 that the level of training of infantry replacements in Europe was unacceptably low. He claimed that 'large numbers of unnecessary casualties result from this greenness, both to the rookie and to the older soldiers who have the added task of trying to look after the newcomers as well as themselves', and suggested that 'the relatives of the lads in the fighting zone should ensure no further casualties are caused to their own flesh and blood by the failure to send overseas reinforcements now available in large numbers in Canada.'[7]

The furore that Smythe's statement aroused sent the Minister of National Defence scuttling off to Europe to see for himself. He found the training to be satisfactory in both Italy and Holland, but wherever he went the infantry was shorthanded. At CMHQ in London, staff officers doubted whether they could maintain even the present flow of reinforcements. Thus, even though the standard of training was adequate, the need for reinforcements was greater than Ralston had been told. He came back to Canada in mid-October. Reporting that Stuart 'had painted too rosy a picture' in August, he argued vehemently for conscripted service overseas. The ensuing Cabinet meetings considered every possible alternative. However, there was no consensus. A substantial minority that included Ralston's associate minister for naval services, Angus L. Macdonald, T.A. Crerar, J. L. Ilsley and, eventually, C.D. Howe, hewed resolutely to the conscriptionist line.

Discussions might have continued for ever when Mackenzie King suddenly began to interpret events in terms of a conspiracy to unseat him as Prime Minister of Canada. His reaction was dramatic. Early on the morning of November 1 he discussed the conscription issue with General McNaughton, whom he had previously been considering as the next governor general. McNaughton did not see conscription as inevitable and 'agreed that the Canadian Army was not needed for the winning of the war.'[8] That was enough for King: he promptly dismissed Ralston, and McNaughton was sworn in as Minister of National Defence the following day. The conscription crisis was still unsolved, but the circumstances in which it would now be considered appeared to have altered radically.

When General McNaughton had first discussed the problem with King he had been somewhat out of touch with military matters, having been on indefinite leave since his return from England. However, a quick survey of the manpower situation as presented by his new staff had convinced him that there was indeed an urgent need for some 15,000 additional General Service men. He had ordered a campaign to persuade the Zombies to volunteer for General Service—the NRMA men seemed the only source for sufficient trained infantry—but it was not pushed too enthusiastically by some of his pro-conscriptionist commanders, who had been pursuing this policy with only limited success. The widespread belief among General Service men that only conscription for overseas could meet national requirements, because NRMA men would respond to no other incentive, is well represented in reports on army morale in the Pacific Command. 'Zombies' there were frequently contrasted with 'REAL CANADIANS' who were doing the fighting. A staff officer summarized the situation in 1944:

> The general GS complaint is why people like these be allowed to live in this country and derive benefits from the efforts of Canadians, who are fighting and helping win the war so that this country may remain free. When the peace has been won this will be a great country, and why should these spineless jellyfish be allowed to progress with the country when they have not had the courage to help her in times of trouble?[9]

Attitudes like this no doubt had the effect of stiffening the resistance of Zombies to General Service. As the officer went on to say, the Zombies, when asked why they would not join the GS,

> state that they do not owe the country anything, that during the 'Depression Years' the country didn't care whether they were alive or not, but now it is at war they are wanted. When it is pointed out that they [sic] are plenty of men O/S [overseas] who were just as badly off as they were, they merely state, 'If they want to be suckers, we aren't.'[10]

The comparative failure of the campaign converted McNaughton, albeit reluctantly, to the conscriptionist view. His conversion was reinforced too by the resignation of the commander of the Winnipeg district, who considered it impossible to adhere to the Minister's policy. 'If the Commanders, one after the other, began to resign, the whole military machine would run down, begin to disintegrate and there would be no controlling the situation,' he told King by phone on the 22nd. For the Prime Minister this news came as a blow. The war was so close to being won. But as he groped for a course of action he suddenly recollected that he had always claimed that if conscription *was* necessary it would be enforced. Now conscription surely was essential, both to find the reinforcements for the front and to prevent the collapse of the military machine. Thoughts of a military revolt also crossed his mind. He decided to change his course and that night he told the Cabinet of his decision to introduce overseas conscription. Unknown to the Prime Minister, most of his key English-speaking ministers had been meeting that day and this group—including Howe, Ilsley, Crerar, and Macdonald—had decided to submit their resignations if conscription were not enforced. 'It was apparent to me,' King wrote in his diary, 'that it was only a matter of days before there would be no government in Canada.' Among the opponents of conscription only Chubby Power, the Minister of National Defence for Air, resigned. The King government had survived the crisis.

When conscription was brought in there were no civil disturbances like the riots of 1917, but among NRMA units there were incidents of mutiny and rioting in British Columbia. At Terrace, B.C., the situation became serious for a few days, but eventually the troops responded to the very moderate disciplinary measures imposed by General Pearkes's staff, who felt the trouble had been caused by a handful of men. 12,908 NRMA men eventually went overseas but only 2,463 ever served in field units in Europe. They suffered 313 battle casualties, of which 69 were fatal, and, in the words of the official historian, 'there were no complaints of their performance in action.'

The conscription issue was an artificial one. Even before large numbers of reinforcements were needed, Canadian military leaders consistently underestimated infantry replacement rates because they were relying on British figures even when Canadian casualty rates proved to be higher. Whether the Canadians fought harder, were assigned the most difficult tasks, were more careless or less well trained, their losses can hardly be atributed primarily to the 'greenness' of their reserves since their casualties had been peculiarly high all along. And the casualties alone are not enough to explain the reinforcement problem. It was also a result of inflexibility in the Canadian military organization.

The British in Italy and the Americans in Northwest Europe coped with their shortages much more effectively than the Canadians, not only by going to reserve forces at home but by reorganizing the forces available in the field. In the European theatre less than 4 per cent of American troops were assigned to headquarters duties compared to the Canadian 13.6 per cent. The Canadians might have emulated the example of General Patton, who in September 1944, finding that his army was 9,000 riflemen under strength, lopped an arbitrary 5 per cent off the establishments of his various headquarters organizations. 'This has produced loud wails from all the section chiefs, who declared they could not run their offices,' he recalled. 'As a matter of fact, even the 10 per cent cut which we subsequently made had no adverse effect.'

Energetic remustering, cuts in headquarters personnel, the combing out of 'lines of communication' establishments and, if necessary, a reduction in fighting strengths could surely have seen the Canadians through. In spite of high casualty rates only 15,000 reinforcements were needed and there were over 40,000 General Service men medically suitable for infantry (Canadian standards were uncommonly high) still in Canada, with perhaps 15,000 more in the United Kingdom. However, the failure to use these men may be explained in part by General Burns's comment to Ralston in Italy that 'the troops would not feel that the government and country was supporting them wholeheartedly ... if ... it allowed them [the NRMA men] to sit comfortably in Canada.'

For Canadians in every walk of life, in or out of the service, the reinforcement problem, which brought the conscription issue to a head, reflected emotional and cultural prejudices rather than military necessity. A combination of political paranoia, inept administration, and the widespread conviction of the volunteer servicemen and veterans of every age, rank, and description that the army could not carry out its mission without conscription, had created a mountain out of a molehill.

Conscription for military service overseas was not the only problem encountered in the use of manpower. Rapid industrialization and the modernization and expansion of existing industry created —especially after late 1941—an insatiable demand for workers. Anticipating future needs, the government formed the National Labour Supply Council in June 1940 and set up an Inter-Departmental Committee on Labour Co-ordination in October of that year. The Committee's report, twelve months later, revealed that competition existed 'between the armed forces and industry, between war and non-war industries and among industrial concerns generally'. So the Cabinet set up the Manpower Committee and brought in National Selective Service. King tabled the necessary Orders in Council on March 24, 1942, emphasizing measures to encourage women to join the labour force. In July 1941 the army had created the Canadian Women's Army Corps, and the air force formed the Canadian

Women's Auxiliary Air Force, later changed in name to the Royal Canadian Air Force (Women's Division). A year later the navy brought in the Women's Royal Canadian Naval Service.

By the end of the war these services had increased to a strength of 21,624, 17,018, and 6,781 women respectively. Another 4,518 women were in the medical services. They helped to release men for other duties, and performed some tasks that men could not have done so well. Similarly there was a rapid increase of women in industry. Although at the peak period there were 1,075,000 women in all kinds of employment compared with 638,000 in 1939, women could not provide the complete answer to manpower shortages in industry. It was necessary in January 1943 to impose new National Selective Service Civilian Regulations that resulted in the compulsory transfer of about 127,000 principally male workers from low- to high-priority industries over the following two and a half years. Men in the armed forces were given special leave to bring in the harvests—a severe disruption to both training and morale in many units—and some military personnel were released to work in the coal-mining and lumber industries. One way or another over a million Canadians eventually joined the industrial work force.

Nevertheless war was straining national resources to the limit and in the process was uncovering some of the weaknesses in the Canadian social structure. In wartime the pace of living speeds up, change occurs at a faster rate, and what in peacetime might be unacceptable behaviour becomes tolerated. Racism, for example, is usually frowned on in polite society, but a war against another race or nation almost fosters it. Not surprisingly in the circumstances, therefore, the nastiness of war made one segment of the Canadian population suffer some of the miseries shared by the millions of displaced persons who formed the human debris of the war in Europe.

Japanese immigrants had begun to arrive on the west coast of Canada more than half a century before Japan's attack on Pearl Harbor.[11] By 1942 people of Japanese descent living in British Columbia numbered 22,096, of which the majority—13,309—were Canadian born (Nisei) and therefore citizens of Canada, 3,223 were naturalized Canadians, and 5,564 were Japanese nationals (Issei), most of whom had resided in Canada for a generation and 2,006 of whom were women. A law-abiding, industrious people, the vast majority were successful fishermen or market gardeners, while a few of them had branched out into the business world and were running small shops or taxi services that for the most part served their own communities. They lived in Vancouver, in various communities along the southern British Columbia coast, and on farms in the Fraser and Okanagan Valleys.

The attitudes of the Caucasians who composed the majority of British Columbia's population in pre-war days were heavily influ-

136 Expropriated Japanese-Canadian fishing vessels, December 1941.

enced by rather widespread anti-Oriental feelings that were particularly strong in the Pacific province (and on the Pacific coast of the United States), where immigration from Asia of Chinese, Japanese, and Hindus had been opposed and feared for over half a century. The sinister image of the 'Yellow Peril', which conveyed a threatened extinction of the white race by Orientals, found its way into published diatribes in the early part of this century, and this kind of racism was not absent from the agitation against the Japanese—often stirred up by politicians as an easy crowd-pleaser—that came to a climax after the bombing of Pearl Harbor when war hysteria on the west coast gave a new meaning to the 'peril' of the Japanese presence.

The industry and efficiency of the Japanese had made them highly competitive in a depressed labour market and suggested to the business community that they might easily become serious rivals at higher economic levels. Attempts were made in the twenties to remove them from the fishing industry by reducing the number of licences issued; naturalized and native-born citizens were denied the vote (on the pretext that those who had Canadian citizenship but had retained their Japanese citizenship were untrustworthy); and for two decades after 1928 the possibility of 'repatriating' or expelling the Japanese was intermittently discussed. The few voices that were raised in protest against this treatment—among them those of the *Vancouver Province* and the CCF—were largely dismissed. In fact, in the federal election of 1935, anti-Japanese propaganda against the CCF was widely used by the Liberals. For example, the slogan 'Look behind the solicitor for a CCF candidate, and you will see an Oriental leering over his shoulder with an eye on you and your daughter' was heard on radio broadcasts in Vancouver.[12]

With Japan's attack on Pearl Harbor in December 1941 and Canada's declaration of war on Japan, anti-Japanese interests in British Columbia were finally provided with a golden opportunity to deal

137 Japanese-Canadians in Vancouver begin the journey to the interior of British Columbia and three years of internment.

with the 'problem' that obsessed them. Action against the Japanese began with the arrest and internment of 38 who were already on RCMP dossiers as potential subversives; some 1,200 fishing boats were impounded; and registration of all persons of Japanese origin, regardless of citizenship, was required. There was a groundless but firmly held belief that the attack on Pearl Harbor had been aided by a Japanese fifth column in Hawaii (where none of the large population of Japanese descent was ever interned, although the Americans did evacuate nearly all people of Japanese ancestry from their own west coast); there was talk of invasion—the possibility of which General Maurice Pope, Vice Chief of the General Staff, thought absurd—and of the need to protect national security from acts of treachery. At meetings in Ottawa with British Columbia politicians on January 8 and 9, 1942, the army point of view was expressed by Pope, who echoed the comment of General Stuart, then chief of General Staff: 'I cannot see that they constitute the slightest menace to national security.'[13] The RCMP was satisfied that it had interned the few Japanese who were possibly dangerous; and the navy saw no problem, since all Japanese fishermen had been removed from the sea. The politicians, who represented and largely shared their constituents' widespread fear and distrust of all people of Japanese

138 The community kitchen of the camp at Slocan City, B.C., about 1943.

origin, objected strongly to this attitude. General Pope has reported a conversation with one of them: 'Sadly he said that for years his people had been telling themselves that war with Japan would afford them a heaven-sent opportunity to rid themselves of the Japanese *economic* menace for evermore. And now after a period of some weeks nothing had been done. Not a word did they say about national security.'[14]

When the evacuation of all male Japanese nationals between 18 and 45 (some 1,700) was announced on January 14, British Columbia politicians, their political organizations, and regional pressure groups launched a campaign on Ottawa to have all resident Japanese Canadians interned. On February 26, 1942—bending to the pressures of the local majority that were either irrational or self-seeking and sometimes both, and to some expressed fears that riots might ensue if the Japanese Canadians were not all removed—the government announced a mass evacuation under the War Measures Act, which gave it sweeping powers that included 'arrest, detention, exclusion and deportation' and that could be enforced unchallenged.

Over the next eight months a clumsy and sometimes callous handling of the evacuation brought much hardship and degradation to some 19,000 hapless people. They were sent by special trains to the interior valleys of British Columbia, most of them being housed in hastily constructed shacks in the vicinity of Slocan Valley. Until these huts were put up, many of them were housed in tents or under the leaking roof of a dilapidated hockey rink. In addition, there were psychological hardships. The majority of these men and women were citizens and were being treated differently from all other citizens (those of German and Italian descent merely had to report regularly to the Registrar of Enemy Aliens). They were members of a tightly knit cultural community that was unexpectedly splintered by external forces totally beyond its control. Family groups had already been broken up by the initial evacuation of adult males. When some of the men, temporarily housed in the Vancouver Immigration Building, refused to board trains without their families, force had been used to bring them to order. 'We worried about what would happen to the women and children,' one evacuee has recorded.

> We said 'After we know that our families are safe and well looked-after then we will go anywhere.' . . . But when we resisted the police came and took us one by one. . . . My wife was sent to Slocan, to Lemon Creek, along with my daughter and my sister. My daughter was still small, less than a year old . . . they had to put up tents for temporary housing. Later they started building cabins—two families to each cabin. It was cold and they had no heat, they used to put the lantern underneath the bed for warmth.[15]

Those men who refused to accept passively the injustice of the evacuation, and in many cases of being separated from families, were sent to internment camps in northern Ontario, where the conditions were even worse.

> There was nothing we could do, so we gave up. I was in that camp for four years. When it got cold the temperature went down to as much as 60° below. We lived in huts with no insulation. Even if we had the stove burning the insides of the windows would all be frosted up, really white. I had to lie in bed with everything on that I had. . . . At one time there were 720 people there, all men, and a lot of them were old people. We were treated just like prisoners of war . . . We were allowed one card and one letter a week from our families, but those letters were all censored. . . . I used to wonder how my family was getting along, I only heard from them occasionally.[16]

In the spring of 1945 the federal government offered the Japanese a choice of settling 'east of the Rockies' or of being 'repatriated' to Japan. (By the end of the war some 7,000 Japanese had taken the opportunity offered to them of leaving the internment camps to perform various kinds of labour in other parts of Canada.) Over 10,000 initially chose repatriation, knowing they were expected to relinquish any claims of Canadian nationality. Their decision was based on fifty years of prejudice, the 1942 evacuation, and the current plan for post-war resettlement outside of British Columbia, which portended the same prejudicial treatment that had marked their life in Canada to the present. Some 4,700 later sought to change their decision and remain in Canada, but in 1946 nearly 4,000 of them returned to Japan. Those who remained spread across the land with memories that became less bitter as the years passed, in spite of the fact that reparations for property that had been sold without consent came only after each claimant was subjected to an elaborate government cross-examination and were often far less than the value of the property. Citizens of Japanese descent were finally granted the franchise federally in June 1948 and in British Columbia in March 1949.

Spawned out of the democratic process, the events in British Columbia and even aspects of the conscription problem represented the sorts of evils the democracies were fighting to destroy. Two kinds of military service put the equality of Canadians into question and led to potentially nation-splitting crises, yet they resulted from what the Prime Minister perceived as the necessities of the war situation and the requirements of national unity. Evacuation of the Japanese was a fundamental violation of individual freedom, but in the final analysis it was also the expression of the will of the politically influential in British Columbia. The times exposed the flaws of human nature more readily than usual. Mackenzie King, his ministers, and many leading personalities in the country deserved criticism for failing to anticipate and cope appropriately with both problems. The Cabinet, on the other hand, compensated for its mistakes in these areas by an excellent pragmatic grasp of social and economic requirements. Under its direction, war-nourished industrial and economic growth brought desperately needed improvements in the Canadian standard of living.

From the very beginning of hostilities, social and economic matters were seen as an aspect, not just of the war effort but also of reconstruction after the war. Armed with the bitter experience of twenty years, Canadian leaders were determined to prevent a repetition of the high prices and inflation of the First World War, the post-war rehabilitation problems of the twenties, and the Depression of the thirties. On December 8, 1939, Ian Mackenzie, Minister of Pensions and National Health, became chairman of the Cabinet Committee on Demobilization and Re-establishment. It slowly started the machinery for what became an excellent rehabilitation program, and Mackenzie took advantage of the Prime Minister's obvious interest in social reform by proposing the introduction of unemployment and health insurance without delay. The principal obstacle to such reforms in the past had been the difficulty of obtaining the approval of the provinces for enacting such federal legislation. The time was ripe, Mackenzie argued, to receive such agreement, and in the case of unemployment insurance King agreed.[17] Eight of the nine provinces had Liberal governments, and as the Prime Minister pointed out, the current prospect of economic gain afforded precisely the conditions needed to start building up financial reserves for an unemployment insurance program. Ralston, Ilsley, and Howe—who then held the Finance, National Revenue, and Transport portfolios—opposed the measure vigorously because the money would be needed to support the war,[18] but they were unable to overcome King's advocacy of the reform in Cabinet. Thus in August 1940 unemployment insurance became law—the first step in introducing a national social-security program.

Mackenzie, encouraged by his victory, expanded his interests beyond rehabilitation to reconstruction and persuaded King to approve the establishment of a Committee on Reconstruction in February 1941. Chaired by Principal F. Cyril James of McGill University, it was designed to chart a course in line with Mackenzie's own interpretation of social security based on the Prime Minister's 1918 book *Industry and Humanity* and, as he told a House of Commons Committee, the inspiration of the young Lloyd George. Out of the James Committee's work came the Marsh Report. Entitled *Report on Social Security for Canada* and published in March 1943, it was prepared in less than a month by Leonard C. Marsh, a young British-born economist who held social-welfare views similar to those being espoused by the CCF, as Canada's response to the famous *Beveridge Report* (the blueprint for Britain's post-war welfare society) of December 1942. The British plan was for individual security from the cradle to the grave, achieved by careful economic planning and a highly centralized administration. The Marsh Report was more sweeping. Like Beveridge, Marsh advocated family allowances, health insurance, and funeral benefits. He went beyond Beveridge in recommending a post-war employment program that would cost one billion dollars. Marsh in fact was advocating a social-security scheme that involved protection against unemployment, sickness, and old age. It was seen by many in the press and in Ottawa as wild-eyed radicalism. Nonetheless the social-security expenditures would prime the pump and help avoid a post-war depression.

Even before the Marsh Report, the James Committee had come out in favour of a Ministry of Economic Planning and in support of a national health-insurance scheme that had been maturing for years. The government's Economic Advisory Committee—consisting of the Deputy Minister of Finance Clifford Clark, W.A. Mackintosh, an economist from Queen's University, Graham Towers, Governor of the Bank of Canada, Donald Gordon, and Norman Robertson —opposed these recommendations and advised the Prime Minister to restore the responsibility for reconstruction planning to the existing departments of government. King had by this time developed grave reservations about James and his committee and withdrew his earlier support. In September 1943 he told his Liberal caucus—nervous about CCF gains in the polls and in the Ontario pro-

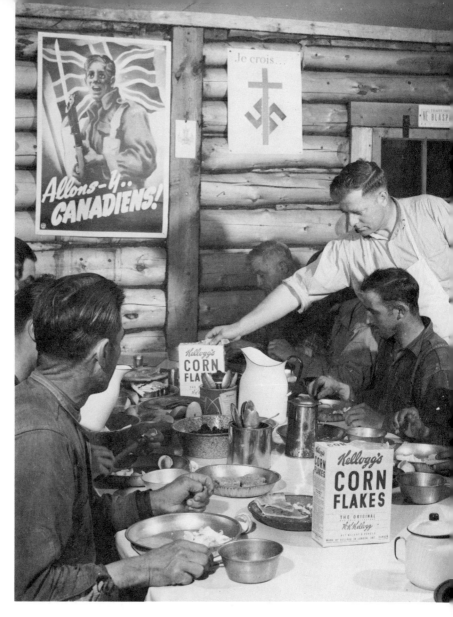

139 Propaganda is only one of the purposes of the graphics in this scene at a Quebec lumber camp, May 1942.

vincial election of August 1943 when it had become the official Opposition—that it was appropriate 'to have everything in readiness for the moment the war was over, to improve conditions, but we should not forget until that moment came that the supreme duty of the Government and everyone in the country was for the men at the front and the winning of the war.'[19]

King's doubts about the commitment of public funds to social security were alleviated in subsequent months; particularly when his secretary, J.W. Pickersgill, Ian Mackenzie, and his new Quebec lieutenant, Louis St Laurent (who joined the Cabinet after the death of Ernest Lapointe in November 1941), persuaded him of the political

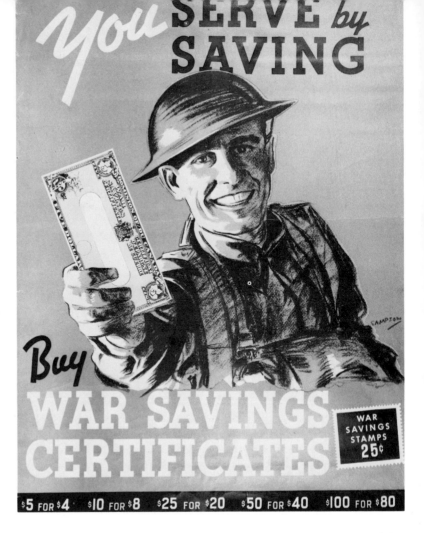

YOU SERVE by SAVING

Buy
WAR SAVINGS
CERTIFICATES

WAR SAVINGS STAMPS 25¢

$5 FOR $4 $10 FOR $8 $25 FOR $20 $50 FOR $40 $100 FOR $80

140 This poster was widely used and had several texts.

and economic advantages of the program. They reminded him of the impressive swing towards the CCF, the strength of labour as a political force, and the likelihood that it would have to be appeased by offering security to workers. C.D. Howe emphasized the need to maintain full production after the war and supported a pension system for workers as well as health insurance, although he opposed family allowances. The need to maintain production, of course, meant continuing exports—a need already expressed in Mutual Aid and one that demanded energetic measures for preserving the industrial capacity that had been built up by the war. St Laurent and Howe differed over family allowances. The latter claimed they encouraged idleness. St Laurent's justification suggested, on the contrary, that there was a link between family allowances and industrial capacity:

> There can be no doubt that the father of a large family has burdens that are more onerous than those of a single man or even the head of a small family; he requires more but there can be no system

under which an employer could be required to pay him more, because that would make it more difficult, if not impossible, for him to get any work at all.[20]

In 1944 and 1945, therefore, the Cabinet, overcoming the opposition of some ministers to certain aspects of the reconstruction program, brought in legislation for farm-improvement loans, an agricultural and fisheries support program, the Industrial Development Bank, the National Housing Act, the Veteran's Insurance Act, the Export Credit Insurance Act, and that most potent of political weapons, family allowances. These measures would help re-elect the Liberal government in June 1945.

At the same time the government was engaged in a vigorous battle against inflation. In the previous war costs had increased with great speed, leading to demands for increased wages and long, costly strikes. The King government was determined to avoid the same mistake in this war and it created the Wartime Prices and Trade Board on September 3, 1939. The WPTB was given sweeping powers to control the price, supply, and distribution of the necessities of life, but in its first two years it played a limited role. The Cabinet intervened in the economy in December 1940, imposing a form of wage control on war industries, while the WPTB imposed partial price controls on rents, coal, sugar, timber, steel, milk, and other essentials. But by the fall of 1941 stronger measures were necessary to deal with a sudden, sustained spurt in the cost of living, and the government imposed a total freeze on wages and prices.

Announced in a radio address by Mackenzie King in October 1941, the freeze was the most radical measure of its kind employed by any of the belligerent powers. The WPTB, under Donald Gordon, became at a stroke one of the most powerful agencies in the land, intruding into every aspect of life. Rules and regulations abounded, and Canadians at home were at last faced with the reality of total war. Permission was required to change jobs, to be promoted, to get gasoline for an automobile, and coupons were necessary to purchase meat.

Yet despite the controls and the bureaucracy, the policy was a success. The consumer price index increased by less than a point between 1943 and 1945. The national cost of living index rose from 101.5 in 1939 to 120.4 in 1945, and most of that increase took place before the wage and price controls of October 1941. By contrast, the average annual income of Canadians rose from $975 at the beginning of the war to $1,538 in 1945. People were generally better off than they had been for years, with more real income in their pockets, with unemployment insurance as a cushion against lay-offs, and, by the end of the war, with family allowances.

Above all, war-induced prosperity brought jobs. In 1939 more than 10 per cent of the labour force were out of work. By mid-1941 this rate had been cut in half and by 1943 Canada reached full

141

employment. As a result, labour unrest was not a major source of social disruption during the war. There were strikes—serious ones on occasion—but even in vital war industries the disturbances were seldom serious enough to warrant unusual precautions for maintaining public order. At the Aluminum Company of Canada in Arvida and Shawinigan Falls, troops were called out to protect the plants from possible sabotage, once in July 1941 and once in November 1943. The trouble on the second occasion seems to have stemmed as much from the efforts of the American Federation of Labour to move in on the National Catholic Syndicate as from the desire to imitate steel workers and coal-miners, who had been striking throughout Quebec, by going out to win concessions. There were no riots and no untoward behaviour reported by the military. Most of those incidents that did occur took place in pleasant summer weather: 'Thirty or forty below zero seems a little too much to face,' reported an observer at Arvida, Quebec, in 1943. ' . . . trouble will occur as soon as the weather turns for the better.'[21]

The unions grumbled that controls on wages stopped them from making headway at a time when their role was vital. But in fact the war gave Canadian unionism an extraordinary boost and total membership almost doubled from 359,000 in 1939 to 711,000 in 1945. Many labour leaders remained grateful to the Liberal government and showed their support at election time, something that had the effect of weakening the CCF, itself desperately trying to forge firm alliances with the labour movement.

Full stomachs and full employment are not necessarily the only measure of a healthy society. A pamphlet in 1943 by the left-leaning Workers' Educational Association, entitled 'The Permanent War or Homo the Sap', tried to warn its readers by satire that once the war was over, wartime prosperity and social benefits could easily disappear. In peace there would be 'no strangling government interference, no bossy political bureaucrats, no confiscating and ruinous taxation, no shortage of necessary materials, no ham-stringing priorities', and the consequence was likely to be a return to the bad old Depression days when impoverished rugged individualism replaced government control. The pamphleteer was fortunately proved wrong, partly because, as the opinion polls revealed, so many Canadians thought as he did and influenced King's reconstruction policy, partly because the satirist's picture was overdrawn—life may have been trying but it was not totally constricting.

But the controls were there and for the first time since the Great War the government managed the flow of information. To co-ordinate the dissemination of propaganda and to measure the state of opinion in the country the government established the Wartime Information Board, headed (as of 1942) by John Grierson. Through its offices the government was able to influence the interpretation of the war in the press, distribute and co-ordinate the dissemination of war propaganda, and conduct public-opinion polls. Propaganda went hand in glove with censorship. Directives in the handbook called *Radio Broadcasting Censorship*, issued in October 1941, stated that the object of censorship was

> to prevent the enemy, so far as may be possible, from obtaining naval, military, air, economic or other information of a nature inimical to the national interest.
>
> It is also the business of censorship to prevent the dissemination of news or talks which might cause dissatisfaction amongst the civil

1940   *Toronto Telegram*

143   PREMIER KING — "We can't have any criticism of my war effort."

population injuriously affect the morale of the armed forces, or prejudice His Majesty's relations with foreign powers.[22]

There was to be no indication or speculation on such things as the movement of troops, the progress of the BCATP from month to month, or the establishment and activities of prisoner-of-war and internment camps.

At a Round Table Conference of the Canadian Institute of International Affairs in May 1941, the elements of propaganda were summarized. It was supposed 'to have the groundwork of truth' and should 'evoke wherever possible an emotional response'. Stress was to be laid on developing:

    1.   A pride in Canada and in her achievements of the past and present. ...

2. Confidence in Canadian institutions. ...
3. A burning conviction that freedom is essential. ...
4. A realization, both emotionally and intellectually, of the consequences of defeat. ...
5. The identification of every individual with a nation at war in the common cause. ...
6. A sense of personal responsibility on the part of every individual to do his share to ensure that democracy works as the best policy.
7. Equality of sacrifice.
8. A sanguine confidence in our victory. This demands staying power (as a long war seems inevitable) and a cheery, serene, buoyant spirit.[23]

The popularity of films made the cinema a powerful focus of propaganda. Newsreels confronted viewers with many events of the war as they actually happened, and feature films, produced by studios in Hollywood and England, not only entertained but affected people's emotions and bolstered their feelings of patriotism, as they were intended to do. They dealt with loyal families suffering bravely under war conditions, families living without their men, war-service experiences, and successful military operations. *Dangerous Moonlight* (1940), unashamedly sentimental, presented the heroic but futile Polish stand against German armed might to the strains of the *Warsaw Concerto*, which became extremely popular, and left audiences with a message of inevitable victory. Noël Coward was both the writer and star of *In Which We Serve* (1942). In a thinly disguised portait of Lord Louis Mountbatten he embodied the British naval tradition—and the English class system—in which nobility, decency, and bravery were bound to prevail in spite of the enemy's apparent material superiority. *One of Our Aircraft Is Missing* (1942) did for British airmen what the Coward film did for British sailors. In the romantic *Mrs. Miniver* (1942) noble behaviour in a family context survived bombings, the evacuation of Dunkirk, and personal tragedy. This Hollywood depiction of wartime England had enormous popularity in North America, less in Britain. The titles of two other popular Hollywood films—*Since You Went Away* (1944) and *The Story of G.I. Joe* (1945)—are self-explanatory. *Desert Victory* (1943), about the British campaign against Rommel, and *Tunisian Victory* (1943), both made by the British Army Kinematography Unit, and *Target for Tonight* (1943), a British government film, used a documentary approach to give apparently realistic portrayals of the growing armed might of the Allies. In such quality films the enemy was for the most part a faceless entity, but a host of second-rate Hollywood productions made German and Japanese characters either unredeemably villainous or figures of fun—somewhat unsophisticated animations of the ideas expressed in political cartoons of the day.

144 One of the first security posters, issued about 1940 by the Directorate of Public Information, Ottawa.

In Canada, to counteract the prevailing dominance of Hollywood and to co-ordinate all government film activity, the National Film Board was set up under John Grierson in 1939. The talented film-makers he acquired were to make the NFB internationally known in the field of propaganda during the war. The immensely popular American newsreel *The March of Time* had its Canadian counter-parts in the *Canada Carries On* series, released once a month from 1940 (until 1960), and *World in Action* (1942-5).

Film was a relatively new propaganda weapon, but posters had been used at least since the French Revolution and various Canadian propaganda agencies—the Wartime Information Board, the informa-tion services of the army, navy, and air force, the Red Cross—seized upon this cheap and effective means of communicating with the pub-lic. About 500 posters (of which over 300 are in the National War Museum) vary in subject from rather conventional invitations to buy war bonds, through dramatic appeals to patriotism by means of arresting imagery, to sober warnings ('Careless Talk Brings Tragedy in Wartime').

Radio, which probably had an even more devoted audience than television today, was mainly escapist, with predominantly American programming. Newscasts, however, provided the most immediate and vivid contact with the realities of war and were listened to avidly. Among the Canadian correspondents, Matthew Halton and Marcel Ouimet gave on-the-spot reports of fighting at the front and of air raids over England, often including the sounds of the events them-selves. The written reports of war correspondents such as Peter Stursberg and Charles Lynch, illustrated with the photographs of Ken Bell and others, brought the war (with a strong Canadian slant) to readers of newspapers. Indeed, newspapers devoted almost all their space to some aspect of war activities. One woman recalled how they bombarded the public with war propaganda to a point of near saturation:

> The newspapers, they were just propaganda sheets. My goodness, on the front pages, war, war, war, and in the insides, how to cook cheaper, how to do Victory Gardens, why we should have car pools, buy Victory Bonds and tell our friends they were traitors if they didn't load up on them too ...
>
> You remember those Sunday supplements, they were jammed with war stuff. How to cook cabbage, make cabbage rolls, and then drink the cabbage juice. Or carrots. Swiss chard. Spinach. Did they think we didn't know that stuff, like how to make a dollar do the price of ten? You'd think the idiots in their big offices in Toronto and Ottawa didn't know about the Depression we just went through —ten years of nothing.[24]

One Home Front episode at the end of the war dramatized the consequences of a misguided application of controls on a frustrated,

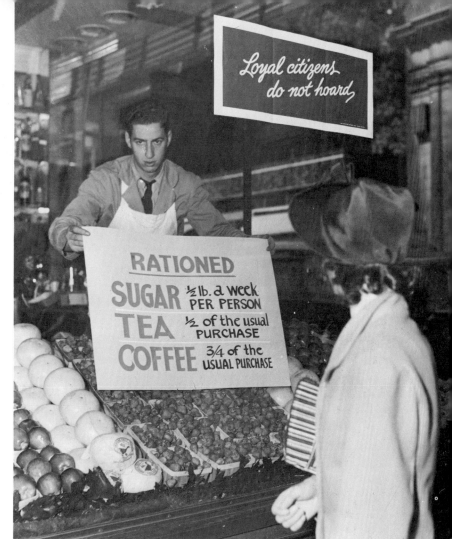

145 Food rationing was never severe. Montreal, May 27, 1942.

pent-up community. On VE-Day, May 8, 1945, Halifax was closed down—nothing was done to handle the spontaneous outburst of joy that was certain to mark the German surrender. There were some 7,000 soldiers and 17,000 naval ratings in the area, most of whom felt they had been victimized and abused by local establishments and had grown to hate the city. When the servicemen mingled with civilians on the streets, a jovial street party turned into a destructive rampage that spilled over into Dartmouth on the other side of the harbour. Liquor stores were broken open and 65,000 bottles of spirits and over 100,000 quarts of beer were soon exacerbating the situation. An orgy of vandalism followed, with 564 business firms suffering damage to their premises (mostly broken windows, but some arson) and 207 shops actually looted. Some of the latter were virtually destroyed before order was restored.

Other riots, though less severe ones, occurred elsewhere in Cana-

146 (ABOVE) Looters swarming in and out of the Holles Street liquor store, Halifax, May 8, 1945.

147-8 (OPPOSITE) More looting in Halifax on VE-Day, and the results of looting.

da: there *was* bitterness just below the surface of life on the Home Front—about the system that had given Canada ten years of nagging concern for sons, brothers, and fathers overseas, for the wounded, maimed, and prisoners of war. And there were blacker emotions evoked by loss through death, by horror at the atrocities revealed in Hitler's concentration camps, by a fear lurking in the minds of some that peace might bring depression upon the land again. But it would be wrong to suggest that negative feelings were uppermost when the war ended. It was on the whole a moment of high optimism, for belief in a future where in spite of all dangers individual freedom could flourish and the relative prosperity at home would continue unabated. There was pride in the nation's accomplishments and in the sense that Canada had a new and important place in the world.

The more than a million men and women in the armed forces had come from a profoundly innocent generation that had been confined to a world of sharply limited horizons. Only the rich, who could afford to travel, or the unemployed, who were often obliged to look for jobs far from home, had seen much beyond their own provincial surroundings. Now for more than five years they had been crossing from one end of the country to the other; many had gone overseas and some to the ends of the earth. Most had tested themselves successfully in unfamiliar and trying circumstances. Away from homes and families for years at a time, rubbing shoulders with strangers, and subjected to varying degrees of stress, they discovered that they had unique regional qualities—not only French and English but also maritimers, central Canadians, westerners, and British Columbians. The war brought self-confidence and a new awareness of national

identity. It also brought some political radicalization as contacts were made between different social classes and with people from other allied nations.

The general election of June 1945—with the CCF vote probably mainly responsible for cutting down government seats to 125 compared to 181 in 1940—reflected the new national mood. Though the overseas service vote was apathetic, it went strongly in favour of the CCF. The Prime Minister, who did not enjoy universal popularity, was cordially disliked in the armed forces overseas because of his manpower policy. (The service vote defeated King in his own riding of Prince Albert.) The total military vote, however, resulted in a narrow government plurality of 118,070 to 109,670 over the CCF, leaving the Conservatives far behind. Canadians supported the government because it had prevented inflation and satisfied widespread desires for social security. The Tories accused King of bribing the voters with the baby bonus, but he could claim that his majority proved the success of his wartime policies.

The Second World War had changed Canadians and altered their consciousness of themselves, their society, and their role in the world—perhaps even more than in 1918. King recognized this. His government's constant attention to reconstruction after 1944 allowed Canada to make a successful transition to post-war conditions. When peace finally came in August, the ominous implications of Nagasaki and Hiroshima did not pass unnoticed. But in Canada prosperity seemed assured, confidence reigned supreme, and hope for individual happiness was unlimited.

149   Sailors celebrating in Ottawa on VJ-Day.

EPILOGUE

Canada was very far from being ready for a large-scale war in 1939 and its efforts often fell short of requirements. One does not build an efficient war machine in only a few years without a great deal of experience, or failing that an enormous industrial and economic base like that of the United States. (Indeed, France, Britain, and the United States and Russia, because they too were inadequately prepared, suffered from extensive mismanagement.) Intitially Canadian industry was unable to cope with the unprecedented amounts and standards of production that would be required and was slow in getting into high gear—though it ultimately did to great effect. The army went through agonies of command problems and performed less well than the public realized or some historians have admitted. The navy also experienced terrible growing pains when large-scale expansions began in 1940, and until 1943 it was unable to hold its own in the war at sea. It was also not until 1943 that the air force was able to provide overseas units of greater than squadron strength.

It has to be admitted that in the final analysis Canada's effort was not essential to winning the war. Nonetheless the country did its utmost and that was more than enough to win the respect of other nations and to earn for Canada a place in world affairs of a totally unprecedented kind. Its provision of raw materials and munitions was an important contribution to Britain's survival. (Canadian raw materials were vital in the first three months of the war.) The extremely generous financial assistance to Britain, especially in the form of mutual aid, was crucial in relieving her dollar shortage. To convoy some 43,120 ships, amounting to 235,104,856 deadweight tons, across the Atlantic was a great strategic triumph of the war—one in which Canadian ships and aircraft played a major part, especially after 1943. The training of 153,000 aircrew out of a total of 239,761 used in British and Commonwealth flying operations was quite simply a decisive contribution to obtaining command of the air—an essential prerequisite to victory. The more than 815,000 motor vehicles produced in Canada, including most of those used by the British Eighth Army, was an industrial *coup*. The impressive growth of the aircraft industry made Canada important in this field. And the building of about a thousand ships was an enormous achievement for an industry that had been moribund at the beginning of the war, even though the number was a drop in the bucket beside British and American figures. The war effort can also be measured in terms of sacrifice. Casualties were not so appalling as in the Great War, but the Canadian men and women who lost their lives represented the supreme gesture a nation can make in support of its ideals and its allies: 22,917 in the army, 17,101 in the air force, and 2,024 in the navy.

At the war's end Canadians felt their part in the war effort had been beyond compare. Men and women returned from overseas to joyful receptions, even to cheering crowds and cascading tickertape.

> Back to Ottawa on a train crowded with returning soldiers. Train after train travels across Canada from east to west laden with them, dropping them off by threes and fours at small towns and in their hundreds at the big cities. The train windows are crowded with their sunburned, excited faces. They lean out in their shirt-sleeves, whistling at the girls at the station platforms, making unflattering jokes about Mackenzie King. We passed through one little station where there were a few mugwumps standing about on the platform staring bemusedly at the train and a group of soldiers on the train began themselves to cheer. 'Hurray! Give the boys a welcome.' The stations are crowded with them striding about self-consciously—men of the world—having proved something about themselves that is plainly to be seen in their sun-paled divisional patches and the ribbons on their chests—the 1939-43 Star, the Africa Star, the France and Germany award, the Voluntary Service Ribbon.[1]

For many of those who travelled across the country to their homes, Canada was

> ... still only half-real, familiar, and yet, because so unchanged, curiously foreign and a little frightening. The endless flow again of evergreens, log-flecked lakes, violently rushing rivers and little wooden stations knotted with people in strange variegated clothes, civilians looking bored, even a little resentful, or filled with childish noisiness.[2]

The government made generous preparations for returning soldiers, sailors, and airmen. There would be the best of medical care for the wounded and maimed, grants for education, land grants for farmers, clothing allowances for all, hefty cash settlements. Only a rich country could have provided such largesse and Canada was rich in 1945. The wealth the land had produced in the war years, the hard work on the home front and overseas, made all determined not to permit the blight of depression to settle on the country once again. The government's planning for the peace and its economic and social policies had been geared to this end.

The war made Canadians nationalistic and gave them confidence in themselves and their country. There was still loyalty to the British tie among English Canadians, but it was now somewhat different in cast. In 1939 England had been a great power, but in 1945 it was a debtor state, owing billions to Canada and ravaged by the war's efforts. The loyalty now was more nostalgic in tone than it had been

150 Two Canadian soldiers outside Nijmegen read a farewell message from their commander before starting for home.

PERSONAL MESSAGE
FROM
THE ARMY COMMANDER

Here is wishing you a satisfactory and speedy journey home, and that you find happiness at the end of it.

You go back with your share of the magnificent reputation earned by the Canadians in every operation in which they have participated in this war. A fine reputation is a possession beyond price. Maintain it — for the sake of all of us, past and present — in the days ahead.

I know that you will get a great welcome on your return. See to it that those Canadian units and drafts, which follow after you, get just as good a "welcome home" when they, also, get back.

Good luck to each one of you — and thanks for everything.

(H.D.G. Crerar) General.

151 Prime Minister Mackenzie King at the San Francisco Conference, 1945. Norman Robertson, Under-Secretary of State for External Affairs, is seated behind him with his hand to his head.

before the war. Attitudes also changed towards the United States. The Americans had stationed troops in the Canadian Northwest, building the Alaska Highway; the GIs were sometimes referred to as the 'army of occupation' only half-jokingly. But the Roosevelt government had helped Canada mightily during the war, co-operating in North American defence as a result of the Ogdensburg Agreement and accepting Canadian economic aspirations with the Hyde Park Declaration. Gratitude, therefore, was perhaps dominant over suspicion. That too was different from 1939.

In 1939 Canada was wracked by the Depression, dispirited, out of work. But in 1945 it was booming, its factories working at top speed. And, incredibly, the nation had become a power in the world, with the third largest navy, the fourth largest air force, and an army of six divisions, five of which had gone overseas, earning the respect of both enemy and Allied observers for its fighting qualities in the European war. For a country of 11 million people this was an astonishing achievement.

This new power was reflected in the way other nations regarded Canada. 'Canada' and 'Canadians' became household words in liberated countries where Canadians had fought, especially Holland. As one of the few countries that had emerged with its territory unscathed by war, as an industrial and agricultural producer and as a rich land, Canada was sought after by the less fortunate. Canadian aid, money, know-how, and technology were in demand, and the government and people were generous in providing what was required. Canadian diplomats and officials abroad received more respect than they had ever known. Their confidence was reflected in the way they argued for Canadian positions and approaches to world problems.

As early as 1943 Lester Pearson, as a member of the Canadian legation in Washington, had made the point that Canada was now irretrievably committed to international collective security: 'a bomb dropped on a Chinese village', he said, 'echoes across the St Lawrence'.[3] Mackenzie King in August 1944 argued in the House of Commons that the directing bodies of future international organizations, and particularly the United Nations, should consist of 'Those countries which have the most to contribute to the maintenance of the peace of the world.'[4] King and his advisors believed Canada had played a sufficiently prominent role in the war to earn a recognized place in the United Nations as a near-great power. This was an application of the so-called functional principle as defined by the Prime Minister in the House of Commons in July 1943, according to which 'representation on international bodies should not be restricted to the largest nor extended to all states, but should be on the basis of the contribution the state has to make.'[5] By the functional principle Canada could claim a major role in civil air transport, for example, or in questions concerning food and raw-material production, and possibly even in security matters.

There would be difficulties in establishing ready acceptance of this principle by the giants during the war and at the creation of the United Nations in 1945. Nevertheless at the war's end, instead of being the rather insignificant state the world had known in 1939, Canada had established its right to the status of 'middle power'. It had come out of the shadows.

NOTES

1. CANADA WILL RESPOND: THE NATION ON THE EVE OF WAR

1. Public Record Office [PRO] London, Cabinet Records, Cab 23/88, Cabinet Conclusion 34(37)5, June 16, 1937. Quoted in J.L. Granatstein, *Canada's War: The Politics of the Mackenzie King Government 1939-1945* (Toronto, 1975), p. 2.
2. C.P. Stacey, *The Arts of War and Peace 1914-1945* (Historical Documents of Canada, Vol. V, Toronto, 1972), Doc. 187, pp. 492-3.
3. Sir Maurice Hankey to Sir George Pearce, January 2, 1935. PRO, Cab 63/81.
4. Hankey, Memorandum to the Cabinet, 'Impressions of Canadian Defence Policy'. Ibid.
5. Prime Minister's remarks at caucus, January 20, 1937. Mackenzie Papers, File X-4. Quoted in C.P. Stacey, *Six Years of War* (Ottawa, 1955), p. 14.
6. King Diary, June 15, 1939.
7. J.W. Wheeler-Bennett, *King George VI* (London, 1959), p. 379.
8. 'Mackenzie King's Statement on Foreign Policy, 8 October 1923' in Stacey, *The Arts of War and Peace 1914-1945*, Doc. 173, p. 437.

2. AN UNMILITARY PEOPLE

1. Secretary of State for Dominion Affairs to Secretary of State for External Affairs, September 6, 1939. Quoted in C.P. Stacey, *Arms, Men and Governments: The War Policies of Canada, 1939-1945* (Ottawa, 1970), Appendix 'C'.
2. Canada, House of Commons Debates, Sept. 9, 1939, pp. 66-7.
3. We are grateful to Professor J.L. Granatstein for the substance of this passage, which depends upon his interpretation in *Canada's War* (Toronto, 1975).
4. Philip Stratford (ed.), *André Laurendeau: Witness for Quebec* (Toronto, 1973), pp. 23-4.
5. L.B. Pearson, *Mike: The Memoirs of the Rt. Hon. Lester B. Pearson, Vol. I: 1897-1948* (Toronto, 1972), pp. 138-9.
6. King Diary, September 12, 1939. Quoted in Granatstein, *Canada's War*, p. 20.
7. G.R. Stevens, *A City Goes to War* (Brampton, Ont., 1964), pp. 177-8; D.J. Goodspeed, *Battle Royal* (Toronto, 1962), pp. 355-6; T.H. Raddall, *West Novas: A History of the West Nova Scotia Regiment* (Toronto, 1947), pp. 24-5.
8. C.P. Stacey, *Six Years of War* (Ottawa, 1955), p. 63.
9. Memorandum by Loring Christie, June 19, 1939. John A. Munro (ed.), *Documents on Canadian External Relations* Vol. VI: *1936-1939* (Ottawa, 1972), Doc. 153, pp. 209-10.
10. Stacey, *Arms, Men and Governments*, p. 20.
11. Barry Broadfoot, *Ten Lost Years 1929-1939: Memories of Canadians Who Survived the Depression* (Toronto, 1973), p. 373.
12. Subtitle of *Canada's Soldiers* (Toronto, 1954; rev. 1960) by G.F.G. Stanley.
13. Humphrey Carver, *Compassionate Landscape* (Toronto, 1975), pp. 63-4.

3. THE SINEWS OF WAR

1. C.P. Stacey, *Arms, Men and Governments* (Ottawa, 1970), Appendix 'C'.
2. C.B.A. Behrens, *Merchant Shipping and the Demands of War* (History

of the Second World War, United Kingdom Civil Series, London, 1955), pp. 7-9, 35, 45, 55, 188.

3. J.L. Granatstein, *Canada's War* (Toronto, 1975), p. 49.

4. BCATP Agreement, December 17, 1939, especially paragraph 18. Stacey, *Arms, Men and Governments*, Appendix 'D'.

5. Stacey, *Arms, Men and Governments*, p. 25.

6. BCATP Agreement, December 17, 1939. *Ibid.*, Appendix 'D'.

7. Granatstein, *Canada's War*, pp. 48, 57; Harold Balfour, *Wings Over Westminster*, (London, 1973), p. 117.

8. R.J. Hammond, *Food* (U.K. Civil Series, London, 1951), Vol. I, p. 69; W.N. Medlicott, *The Economic Blockade* (U.K. Civil Series, London, 1952), Vol. I, pp. 315, 372-3, 541.

9. Lt Gen. Maurice A. Pope, *Soldiers and Politicians* (Toronto, 1962), p. 165.

10. J.L. Granatstein and R.D. Cuff, *Canadian American Relations in Wartime: From the Great War to the Cold War* (Toronto, 1975), pp. 69-92.

11. Howe Papers, File S-5(1), Howe to Ilsley, July 21, 1941. Quoted in Granatstein, *Canada's War*, p. 188.

12. F.M. Smith (ed.), 'History of the British Admiralty Technical Mission in Canada', p. 48. Directorate of History, Department of National Defence.

4. THE ATLANTIC BRIDGE

1. W.S. Churchill, *Their Finest Hour* (Boston, 1949), p. 598.

2. Gilbert Tucker, *The Naval Service of Canada*, Vol. II (Ottawa, 1952), pp. 31-2.

3. Barry Broadfoot, *Six War Years 1939-1945: Memories of Canadians at Home and Abroad* (Toronto, 1974) p. 174.

4. Alan Easton, *50 North: An Atlantic Battleground* (Toronto, 1963), p. 15.

5. Directorate of History files, Department of National Defence [DND], NHS 8000-HMCS *Chambly*.

6. Murray to Capt. R.E. Reid, October 15, 1941. Public Archives of Canada, RG 24, Vol. 11979/51-15.

7. Wolfgang Frank, *Die Wölfe und der Admiral: Triumph und Tragik der U-Boote (Hamburg, 1954), p. 303; S.W. Roskill, The War at Sea 1939-1945* Vol. I. (London, 1956), p. 96.

8. Memorandum dated January 5, 1943, Admiralty file M.015473/42. Quoted in Historical Records Office, Canadian Naval Mission Overseas, 'Canadian Participation in North Atlantic Convoy Operations June 1941 to December 1943'. November 27, 1945, Directorate of History files, DND, Kardex 122.013 (D2).

9. Easton, *50 North*, p. 99.

10. *Ibid.*, p. 166.

11. *Royal Canadian Navy Monthly Report*, No. 31, August 1944.

12. Air Marshal Sholto Douglas to Air Marshal L.S. Breadner, June 25, 1944. Directorate of History files, DND, R/57/162.

13. Roskill, *The War at Sea 1939-1945*, Vol. III, Pt II (London, 1961), p. 286.

5. THE ARMY OVERSEAS 1940-1941

1. G.W.L. Nicholson, *The Gunners of Canada*, Vol. II, *1919-1967* (Toronto, 1972), p. 55.

2. Farley Mowat, *The Regiment* (Toronto, 1955), p. 26.

3. L.B. Pearson, *Mike*, Vol. I, *1897-1948* (Toronto, 1972), p. 168.

4. First Brigade War Diary, Public Archives of Canada.

5. John Swettenham, *McNaughton*, Vol. 2, *1939-1943* (Toronto, 1969), p. 110.

6. R. Macleod and D. Kelly (eds), *Time Unguarded: The Ironside Diaries 1937-1940* (New York, 1962) p. 242.

7. C.P. Stacey, *Six Years of War* (Ottawa, 1955), pp. 440-3, 448.

8. *Ibid.*, p. 486.

9. Private information.

10. Directorate of History files, Department of National Defence [DND], Kardex 593(D3).

11. *Ibid.*
12. Private information.
13. 'Miscellaneous Reports on Dieppe Raid', Directorate of History files, DND, Kardex 594.013 (D17).
14. Lucien Dumais, *Un Canadien français à Dieppe*, (Paris, 1963), pp. 143-4. Author's translation.
15. Wallace Reyburn, *Glorious Chapter: The Canadians at Dieppe* (Toronto, 1943), p. 113.

6. SICILY AND SOUTHERN ITALY

1. Arthur Bryant, *The Turn of the Tide, 1939-1943* (London, 1957), p. 596.
2. C.M. Johnson, *Action with the Seaforths* (New York, 1954), p. 145.
3. G.W.L. Nicholson, *The Canadians in Italy, 1943-1945* (Ottawa, 1956), p. 178.
4. Viscount Montgomery of Alamein, *Memoirs* (London, 1958), p. 184.
5. Arthur Bryant, *Triumph in the West, 1943-1946* (London, 1959), p. 278.
6. Charles Comfort, *Artist at War* (Toronto, 1956), p. 38.
7. C.P. Stacey, *Arms, Men and Governments* (Ottawa, 1970), p. 232.
8. Waldo Smith, *What Time the Tempest* (Toronto, 1953), p. 181.
9. A.E. Powley, *Broadcast from the Front* (Toronto, 1975), p. 62.
10. Thomas H. Raddall, *West Novas: A History of the West Nova Scotia Regiment* (Toronto, 1947), p. 169.
11. R.H. Roy, *The Seaforth Highlanders of Canada, 1919-1965* (Vancouver, 1969), p. 292.
12. Johnson, *Action with the Seaforths*, p. 305.
13. John Windsor, *Blind Date* (Sidney, B.C., 1962), pp. 47-8.

7. OPERATION 'OVERLORD'

1. A.V. Sellwood, *Dynamite For Hire* (London, 1956), p. 129.
2. Quoted in John Winton (ed.), *The War at Sea 1939-1945* (London, 1967), p. 336.

3. Eric Luxton, *1st Battalion, The Regina Rifle Regiment, 1939-1946* (Regina, 1946), p. 34.
4. R.M. Hickey, *The Scarlet Dawn* (Campellton, N.B., 1949), pp. 194-5.
5. Warren Tute, *D Day* (London, 1974), p. 209.
6. C.P. Stacey, *The Victory Campaign* (Ottawa, 1960), p. 133.
7. Cornelius Ryan, *The Longest Day* (New York, 1959), p. 246.
8. Quoted in H. Essame and E. Belfield, *The Battle for Normandy* (London, 1965), p. 85.
9. *Ibid.*, p. 89.
10. 404 Squadron Operational Record Book, Directorate of History, Department of National Defence [DND].
11. D.E. Harker, *The British Columbia Regiment 1939-1945* (Vancouver, 1950), p. 17.
12. W.R. Bird, *The North Shore (New Brunswick) Regiment, 1939-1945* (Fredericton, N.B., 1963), p. 263.
13. Quoted in Alexander McKee, *Caen: Anvil of Victory* (London, 1964), pp. 336-7.
14. R.L. Rogers, *History of the Lincoln and Welland Regiment* (Montreal, 1954), p. 153.
15. 439 Squadron Operational Record Book. Directorate of History, DND.
16. A.F. Duguid, *History of the Canadian Grenadier Guards, 1760-1964* (Montreal, 1965), p. 281.

8. THE WAR IN THE AIR

1. Quoted in N. Macmillan, *The Royal Air Force in the World War, 1940-1941* (London, 1944), p. 215.
2. J.A. Kent, 'The Battle of Britain: Extracts from a Personal Diary', *The Polish Airman's Week Review*, June 1957.
3. J.E. Johnson, *Wing Leader* (New York, 1957), p. 166.
4. Directorate of History Biographical files, Department of National Defence [DND].
5. Quoted in *The RCAF Overseas: The First Four Years* (Toronto, 1944), pp. 164-5.

6. Jerrold Morris, *Canadian Artists and Airmen, 1940-45* (Toronto, n.d.), p. 89.
7. Quoted in *The RCAF Overseas: The First Four Years*, p. 172.
8. Directorate of History Biographical files, DND.
9. Quoted in Hans Rumpf, *The Bombing of Germany* (London, 1963), p. 94.
10. Six Group Monthly Engineering Reports. Directorate of History, DND, Kardex 181.005 (D2001).
11. Six Group Monthly Photographic Summaries, Directorate of History, DND, Kardex 181.009 (D4253).
12. Six Group Monthly Operational Summaries. Directorate of History, DND, Kardex 181.005 (D2002).
13. C. Webster and N. Frankland, *The Strategic Air Offensive Against Germany 1939-45*, (London, 1961), Vol. IV, p. 482.

9. NORTHERN ITALY AND NORTH-WEST EUROPE, 1944-1945

1. Martha Gellhorn, *The Face of War* (London), 1967), p. 125.
2. J-G. Poulin, *969 Heures d'Enfer* (Québec, 1946), p. 40.
3. 417 Squadron Operational Record Book. Directorate of History, Department of National Defence [DND].
4. E.L.M. Burns, *General Mud* (Toronto, 1970), p. 220.
5. Quoted in G.W.L. Nicholson, *The Canadians in Italy, 1943-1945* (Ottawa, 1956), p. 564.
6. Quoted in C.P. Stacey, *The Victory Campaign* (Ottawa, 1960), p. 337.
7. W. Boss, *The Stormont, Dundas and Glengarry Highlanders 1783-1951* (Ottawa, 1952), p. 217.
8. Private information.
9. D.W. Grant, *'Carry On': The History of the Toronto Scottish Regiment (MG) 1939-1945* (1949), p. 106.
10. W.R. Bird, *North Shore (New Brunswick) Regiment* (Fredericton, N.B., 1963), p. 447.
11. W.R. Bird, *No Retreating Footsteps: The Story of the North Nova Scotia Highlanders* (Kentville, N.S., n.d.), p. 257.
12. Roy Farran, *The History of the Calgary Highlanders, 1921-1945* (Calgary, 1955), p. 191.
13. Donald Pearce, *Journal of a War* (Toronto, 1965), pp. 102, 113.
14. J.E. Johnson, *Wing Leader* (New York, 1957), p. 271.
15. R.W. Thompson, *The Battle for the Rhineland* (London, 1955), p. 209.
16. Bird, *North Shore (New Brunswick) Regiment*, p. 523.
17. A. Fortescue Duguid, *History of the Canadian Grenadier Guards* (Montreal, 1965), p. 322.
18. J.F. Bartlett, 1st Battalion, *The Highland Light Infantry of Canada* (Galt, Ont., 1951), p. 107.
19. Pearce, *Journal of a War*, p. 164.
20. Battalion War Diary, May 5, 1945. Directorate of History, DND.
21. Pope interview, July 7, 1977, Directorate of History biographical files, DND.

10. THE WAR AGAINST JAPAN

1. Quoted in T.W. Melnyk, *Canadian Flying Operations in South East Asia, 1941-1945* (Ottawa, 1976), p. 29.
2. GS Historical Report No. 28, p. 8. Directorate of History, Department of National Defence.
3. C.P. Stacey, *Arms, Men and Governments* (Ottawa, 1970), p. 58.
4. J.B. Conant [Scientific Adviser to President Roosevelt], to C.J. Mackenzie [President National Research Council of Canada]. Quoted in Wilfred Eggleston, *Canada's Nuclear Story* (Toronto, 1965), p. 65.
5. Robert Jungk, *Brighter Than a Thousand Suns* (London, 1958), p. 198.

11. THE HOME FRONT

1. S.F. Wise and R.A. Preston, *Men in Arms* (New York, 1971), p. 304.
2. Philip Stratford (ed.), *André Laurendeau: Witness for Quebec* (Toronto, 1973), pp. 23-4.

3. Gabrielle Roy, *The Tin Flute* translated by Hannah Josephson (1947; New Canadian Library ed., 1958), pp. 33-4.
4. Richard Gentil, *Trained to Intrude* (London, 1974), p. 44.
5. Croil to Power, July 28, 1943, in Record Group 24, Vol. 3262, HQ 232-3-11, Public Archives of Canada [PAC].
6. C.P. Stacey, *Arms, Men and Governments* (Ottawa, 1970), p. 433.
7. *Ibid.*, p. 440.
8. King Diary, Oct. 31, 1944. Quoted in Stacey, *Arms, Men and Governments*, p. 455.
9. Directorate of History files, Department of National Defence [DND], Kardex 322.009 (D217).
10. *Ibid.*
11. The following discussion has been based in part on information contained in Ken Adachi, *The Enemy That Never Was: A History of the Japanese Canadians* (Toronto, 1976).
12. *Ibid.*, p. 182.
13. Maurice Pope, *Soldiers and Politicians* (Toronto, 1962), p. 177.
14. *Ibid.*
15. Daphne Marlatt, *Stevenston Recollected* (Victoria, 1975), p. 66.
16. *Ibid.*
17. Ian Mackenzie to Mackenzie King, December 27, 1939, PAC, Mackenzie Papers, Vol. 47, C.N.S. File 57. We are indebted to Professor John English for this reference.
18. J.W. Pickersgill, *The Mackenzie King Record*, Vol. I: *1939-44* (Toronto, 1960), p. 61.
19. *Ibid.*, p. 580.
20. 'Memorandum on Post-War Policies', November 18, 1943, PAC, King Papers, J 4, File 39-06, C 257111-18.
21. Directorate of History files, DND, Kardex 142.81A 22009 (D14).
22. *Radio Broadcasting Censorship: Handbook Consolidation of Directives* (Ottawa, 1941), p. 5.
23. G.C. Andrews, *Canada at War: A Report of a Roundtable held by the Canadian Institute of International Affairs, at its 8th Annual Conference, Kingston, Ont., May 1941* (Toronto, 1941), pp. 11-14.
24. Barry Broadfoot, *Six War Years 1939-45* (Toronto, 1974), pp. 31, 32.

EPILOGUE

1. Charles Ritchie, *The Siren Years: A Canadian Diplomat Abroad 1937-1945* (Toronto, 1974), p. 207.
2. Earle Birney, *Turvey* (Toronto, 1949; New Canadian Library ed., 1963), p. 277.
3. Quoted in James Eayrs, *In Defence of Canada*, Vol. 3: *Peacemaking and Deterrence* (Toronto, 1972), p. 35.
4. Canada, House of Commons Debates, August 4, 1944. Quoted in R.A. Mackay (ed.), *Canadian Foreign Policy, 1945-1954: Selected Speeches and Documents* (Toronto, 1971), p. 4.
5. Canada, House of Commons Debates, July 9, 1943. *Ibid*, p. 3.

BIBLIOGRAPHY

Readers interested in learning more about Canada's part in the war might examine any or all of the published works cited in the preceding Notes. Such studies may be rounded out with selections from the following list.

Canada's strategic assets—the relative security of its geographic position in a European and, later, a Pacific war; the economic significance of its proximity to the United States and of its natural resources and industrial capacity; the political implications of membership in the British Commonwealth—are the subject of discussion in various volumes in the British *Official History of the Second World War*, especially *North American Supply* (London, 1955) by H. Duncan Hall and *Studies of Overseas Supply* (London, 1956) by Hall and C.C. Wrigley. One official American study, *Military Relations between the United States and Canada, 1939-1945* (Washington, 1959) by Stanley W. Dziuban, examines sympathetically the 'triangle *versus* partnership' question.

Robert Rumilly propounds the widely accepted view that the war emphasised the basic division between French and English Canadians in his *Histoire de la Province de Québec*, tomes XXXVIII-XLI (Montreal, 1968-9), and in his colourful two-volume biography, *Maurice Duplessis et son temps* (Montreal, 1973). Pro-conscription forces found their chief spokesman in the Conservative leader, Arthur Meighen, whose biographer, Roger Graham, devotes considerable attention to conscription in his *Arthur Meighen*: Vol. III, *No Surrender* (Toronto, 1965). The most comprehensive and balanced work now available on this subject, however, is *Broken Promises: A History of Conscription in Canada* (Toronto, 1977) by J.L. Granatstein and the late J.M. Hitsman. General E.L.M. Burns, in a rather technical but still readable study, *Manpower and the Canadian Army* (Toronto, 1966), demonstrates that administrative weaknesses were at the root of the army's manpower shortage.

The impact of war on the economy has so far received less attention than the manpower issue. *History of the Department of Munitions and Supply: Canada in the Second World War* (Ottawa, 1950) by J. de N. Kennedy contains data that have not been published elsewhere, but it is not a full treatment of the subject and is a difficult book to use.

On the military side well over a hundred histories of army units, dealing either entirely or in large part with their experiences in the Second World War, have now been published. The total grows each year, and although the quality varies widely, anyone interested in tracing the adventures of a local regiment should be able to obtain an account of its war services through the public library system. Those concerned with examining the ethos of a typical fighting unit cannot do better than look at Farley Mowat's entertaining story of the Hastings and Prince Edward Regiment, entitled simply *The Regiment* (Toronto, 1955).

Two attempts at campaign studies from a Canadian standpoint are of doubtful value. *Gauntlet to Overlord* (Toronto, 1945) by Ross Munro is more propaganda than history, while *Maple Leaf Up, Maple Leaf Down* (New York, 1947) by Peter Symonds lacks critical and analytic insights. *Not in Vain* (Toronto, 1973) by Ken Bell and C.P. Stacey offers a reflective, essentially pictorial retrospect of the Canadian experience in Northwest Europe. The literature on Dieppe is voluminous; the best accounts in English, none of which is as good as one might hope, are *The Shame and the Glory* (Toronto, 1962) by Terence Robertson and *Dieppe at Dawn* (London, 1956) by R.W. Thompson.

First-person accounts worth reading, in addition to those cited in the references, include *Missing from the Record* (Toronto, 1946) by R.S. Malone, *Eleven Men and a Scalpel* (Winnipeg, 1948) by J.B. Hillsman, and the first part of *Dual Allegiance* (Toronto, 1976) by Ben Dunkelman. Malone was Field Marshal Montgomery's Canadian liaison officer, Hillsman commanded a Field Surgical Unit in Northwest Europe, and Dunkelman was a mortar officer and then company commander with the Queen's Own Rifles.

The navy and air force have been less well served in every respect. Joseph Schull's excellent popular account, *The Far Distant Ships*, discreetly passes over the less successful phases of Canadian naval operations. Naval and air force unit histories are much fewer in number and less well written than the army's regimental histories. William Sclater's *Haida* (Toronto, 1946) competently tells the story of a Canadian destroyer and gives some colour to the wartime navy. The flavour of the lower deck is preserved in William H. Pugsley's *Saints, Devils and Ordinary Seamen* (Toronto, 1945) and Harry Catley's *Gate and Gaiters: A Book of Naval Humour and Anecdotes* (Toronto, 1949).

The R.C.A.F. Overseas (Ottawa, 1944-9), a three-volume work compiled by the Air Historian, the first two volumes of which were published while the war was still on, offers nothing more than a simple narrative of events, liberally studded with names and numbers which, in the case of damage alleged to have been done to the enemy, are most unreliable. *There Shall Be Wings: A History of the Royal Canadian Air Force* (Toronto, 1959) by Leslie Roberts, which includes seven chapters on the Second World War, is a work of narrative strength somewhat lacking in interpretation or critical analysis. Monotonous though this refrain is becoming, essentially the same criticism must be made of *The Dangerous Sky: Canadian Airmen in World War II* (Toronto, 1968) by Tom Coughlin, an anecdotal survey of Canadian airmen and their more spectacular achievements.

INDEX

213